The
Elton John
Scrapbook

by
Mary Anne Cassata

CITADEL PRESS
Kensington Publishing Corp.
www.kensingtonbooks.com

CITADEL PRESS books are published by

Kensington Publishing Corp.
850 Third Avenue
New York, NY 10022

All Kensington titles, imprints, and distribution lines are available at special quantity discounts for bulk purchases for sales promotions, premiums, fund-raising, educational, or institutional use. Special book excerpts or customized printings can also be created to fit specific needs. For details, write or phone the office of the Kensington special sales manager: Kensington Publishing Corp., 850 Third Avenue, New York, NY 10022, attn: Special Sales Department, phone 1-800-221-2647.

Citadel Press and the Citidel Logo are trademarks of the Kensington Publishing Corp.

First Printing: June 2002

10 9 8 7 6 5 4 3 2 1

Printed in the United States of America

Library of Congress Control Number: 2001099133

ISBN 0-8065-2322-0

For Vincent and Grayson.

This is dedicated to all the Elton (and Bernie) fans
who have waited for such a book to truly call their own.
This one's for you!

FOREWORD

For more than thirty years, Elton John has endeared himself to millions of American fans by charting, touring, recording and entertaining with unparalled enthusiasm. The England-born star has confounded the oddmakers with his staying power. While many of his peers from the time of his 1970 U.S. debut have since disappeared from the public eye, Elton remains vital, vibrant and highly visible. Along the way, he has created a virtual soundtrack to life for generations of music lovers.

If you've ever seen him in concert, if you've ever admired his manic piano playing on albums like *Madman Across the Water,* if you've ever bopped to "Crocodile Rock" or hummed the chorus to "Sad Songs" or taken a child to see *The Lion King,* if you've ever been amazed by the blending of his music with the lyrics of Bernie Taupin—you know what it's all about.

You know why he's a legend. You know why he's one of the few people on a first-name basis with the world. And you will have fun with this book.

The Elton John Scrapbook offers a rollicking journey through decades of memories—a celebration of the life and career of one man. Whether you are a new fan or an old one, these pages will connect you with one of our premier entertainers and give you a greater appreciation for his genius.

—Tom Stanton, publisher of *East End Lights* (The Magazine for Elton John Fans)—1990-2001.

Preface

The year was 1971. The turbulent sixties were over. However, the turbulence was not over in my life; it was just beginning. My life obviously is not the subject of this book, but I must state that when I first heard the remarkable voice of Elton John and charismatic words of Bernie Taupin that poured out of the radio, I knew that my small, upstate life would never be the same.

To say that Elton (or Bernie) was an inspiration is an understatement. I was thirteen years old, and I knew then, as I know now, that I was destined to be an entertainment journalist. The brilliance of Bernie Taupin's words coupled with Elton John's magnificent piano playing and resonating voice would inspire me to write a million words over the years about one of the most celebrated songwriting partnerships in pop-music history.

Flash forward about ten years to 1980. I was already freelance writing for many popular national music and entertainment publications when I was assigned to cover the historic Elton John concert in Central Park. I was fortunate to be invited to view the concert from backstage, where I met and spoke with Elton, Bernie, and a couple of the members of the band for the first time. Later that night, I attended an after-concert party held at the South Street Seaport on a ship known as the *Peking*. Many of Manhattans' elite residents including John and Yoko attended the private bash. Of course, Elton, Bernie, Nigel Olsson, and Dee Murray were there as well, mingling with guests (though Elton didn't stay long). I talked with all of them—amazingly, even Lennon—throughout the night. It was a glittering moment, one that firmly cemented my childhood dream of being an entertainment writer.

That night would also be the first night of many over the next two decades that I would cover Elton and Bernie collectively and separately. Whether I am doing an interview, covering a press conference, reviewing an album or concert, or attending an industry gathering or EJAF charity benefit, I have always felt—and still do—that it is a supreme privilege to be asked to cover any Elton John event.

The purpose of this book is to celebrate the life and career of a man who inspires millions of people and instills a sense of hope through his music. The power of music has saved many an aching heart, and the songs of Elton John and Bernie Taupin seem to mystically pull us through hard times.

I wrote the final segments of this book as our soldiers were shipping off to Afghanistan. After the horrors of September 11 and the beginning of the current war, I think I can speak for most Americans by saying that we will never feel the same again. As I began writing I heard "Rocket Man" play on the radio. A strange feeling swept over me. I thought of all the brave men and women fighting over in the Middle East. It must be so lonely and terrifying, I thought. I'm sure more than one of them must be feeling like he is "burning out his fuse" out there alone or whispering "I miss my wife" to the evening sky. But a voice somewhere inside him probably tells him he's fighting for the all-important reasons and single-most-treasured thing we have: the freedom to live our lives as we see fit, which includes listening to any music we so desire. All these thoughts blew through my mind and it occurred to me: "What would the world be like if we didn't have our freedom and if we couldn't listen to Elton John?"

I wanted this book to be a scrapbook of unforgettable memories, achievements, projects, people, and special moments in time. As long-time fans already know, Elton John's astounding talent is bigger than life. His humanity, humility and cheeky English sense of humor are three of the qualities that make him so easily amicable. Perhaps Elton's uniqueness lies in such a delightful combination of supreme talent and personality. The world is a better place because he chooses to entertain us.

—Mary Anne Cassata

CONTENTS

Elton John, a *Man for All Seasons*, as depicted on the cover of this 1997 tribute from the U.K.-based *Hercules* International Fan Club.

CHAPTER ONE

ELTON JOHN
A (Piano) Man For All Seasons

Fans' love for Elton will never die; his fan base has grown continuously for more than three decades now. What makes him so beloved to so many people from so many different walks of life?

Well, whether you are two or 92, most likely Elton John has probably touched your life on some emotional or spiritual level. Not many entertainers of Elton's stature have across-the-board appeal— kids and their grandmas (maybe even some of their great-grandmas) praise him equally as much. What makes him get so much love from so many different people? Well, there are a variety of factors, and they include everything from his ability to tickle the ivories to his deep connections with

dozens of charities to that adorable gap between his front teeth.

Oh, and it can't be helped, but to love those crazy ensembles that make Little Richard look as conservative as President Bush. Fans have high expectations about what Elton is going to wear next, and rightfully so. He certainly knows the secret of blending classy and zany ever so gracefully!

"Have piano, will travel" could have been Elton's motto in the days when he was just the "piano man" for British blues band, Bluesology. It took time for Elton to go from being simply a "side man" quietly sitting at the Farfisa organ to being the most flamboyant of solo artists, but what a transition it truly was! It was a clear case of a cocoon evolving into a butterfly and probably had a lot to do with Elton's growing confidence as his talents became more defined. The more Elton's vocal and instrumental talents were praised by fans and press, the more he opened like a rose in the sun.

But talent alone does not make the music world love you…even incredible showmanship does not give an artist the legend that Elton John has established. He obviously has something intangible that make's him so loved by the masses, and his ability to laugh at himself obviously helps make him even more endearing. That twinkle in his eye and smirk on his face when he is asked a prying question on a late night talk show is surely priceless—and you just know he's about to unleash a zinger on that late-night host! These are very common and alluring Elton traits that make him such a sought-after TV guest.

The fact that Elton has one of the biggest hearts in rock 'n' roll is one of the major reasons he's a genuine "man for all seasons." While involved in a tremendous amount of charity work, and often donating proceeds from his songs to charities (including the "Candle In the Wind 1997" remake that benefited Princess Di's children's charity), he never gets preachy in his public statements. He and longtime collaborator, Bernie Taupin have always figured they would leave the political lyrics and complaints about what's going wrong in the world to the likes of U2 or Bruce Springsteen. Elton just quietly raises money for causes or opens up his own wallet and gives instead of singing about it.

Perhaps, another part of Elton's "every-man" appeal is the fact that he has dueted with

Elton on stage in Paris, France. He's checking out a banner a fan was waving from the front row.

all types of artists from every facet of the music industry. The short list of duets Elton has participated in is as follows: "Through the Storm" (with Aretha Franklin), "Perfect Day" (with Collective Soul), "The Show Must Go On" (with Queen), "Don't Let the Sun Go Down on Me" with George Michael, "I Know the Truth" (with Janet Jackson), "Written in the Stars" (with Leann Rimes) and "Deep Inside" (with Mary J. Blige). Now if that isn't a list of superstars from all forms of popular music, nothing is. Doing these duets have let Elton be exposed to fans from every walk of life, needless to say.

Elton is also not afraid to step on turf others fear to tread. It seems he judges others not by their public reputation but by his personal dealings with them. A great example of this is his casting Robert Downey Jr. in the video for "I Want Love." Elton's friendship with Downey started when they met on the *Ally McBeal* set (Downey played Ally's boyfriend in the 2001 season before having a relapse and heading back into rehab,) and Elton has been there as a shoulder to cry on ever since.

In fact Elton told *Rollingstone.com* at the time that he realized that the lyrics of "I Want Love" quietly echoed what was going on in Downey's personal life at the time: "I wanted to do a video that was mature. And [director] Sam Taylor-Wood said, 'I've got an idea of just doing it very simply, one person, not you, lip-syncing to the song. An actor, maybe.' I came up with the idea of Robert. I thought, 'God, the lyrics are very close to home. I wonder if he'll do it?' He was very interested. It all came together in five or six days. We sent him the album, and he said, 'Yes.' I'm thrilled with it.'"

Elton is also a great fan of the USA. He's had a lavish condo in Atlanta for nearly ten years now and lives there part time. He has sang "The Star Spangled Banner" at every concert on his *Songs From The West Coast* Tour and donated some of the proceeds from shows to the New York City September 11th Fund. He also participated in the televised Concert For New York organized by Paul McCartney.

Over the years, Elton has done an incredible amount of work for the charity set up in the name of AIDS victim Ryan White, participated in the annual Prince's Trust Fund show in London, and participated in the annual Save The Rainforest all-star benefit concerts organized by Sting. Elton has also lent his talents to numerous breast cancer research charity shows, and one of his best shows of 2001 was at a breast cancer benefit party at New York's Cipriani in August 2000—he treated the well-heeled audience to nearly all of his hits in chronological order (and the high vaulted ceilings provided awesome acoustics).

He also has his own charity founded in 1992, the Elton John AIDS Foundation (which is profiled in another chapter), and gives plenty of concerts to benefit that each year. The EJAF even has its own website that allows fans to leave comments on a bulletin board about their main man (both good and bad), make donations, apply for educational grants and buy fund-raising merchandise. Fragrance-minded fans can even buy candles in Elton's favorite scents, including hyacinth, freesia, jasmine and rose. They are quite collectable because each has his monogram on the lid. Fans love to attend the events for EJAF because Elton himself often hosts or attends these—his 2001 Oscar party out in Los Angeles raised $250,000 for the charity and by all accounts, a good time was had by all that attended.

Elton's "Disney factor" is what gives him appeal to the youngest of fans. Yes, even two-year-olds have been known to boogie down to Elton tracks a lá his contributions to *The Lion King* and *The Road To El Dorado*. In the last quarter of 2001, it was rumored that Disney considered giving Elton a speaking role in one of their "in-the-making" animated features. So don't be surprised if Elton turns up as a piano-playing crocodile or something similar in a Disney feature any time in the near future.

Elton's even got royalty appeal, and that's thanks to his well-publicized friendship with the late Princess Diana (who was supposedly a fan from age 14 onward) and getting the title of Sir in 1998 thanks to HRH Queen Elizabeth herself.

Obviously, it was Elton's charity work that helped propel him into the heart and mind of Queen Elizabeth, who stood up and took notice of all the help he was so selflessly giving the good people of the United Kingdom. Elton has always said he felt it was important to give back to the people of his homeland who have supported him in both his up and down phases.

Elton also has an appeal to the gay community thanks to admitting he was bisexual, and then finally gay, in the late '80s. He was happy that the pop music industry had opened up enough at that point in time to accept the fact that he wasn't straight. Although he got some outrageous tabloid press at the time that hurt his feelings tremendously, the music legend was glad to see that his admission did not hurt his career.

The gaining and losing of fortunes have also made Elton John seem more human than other rock stars. In 2001 he took in $2.75 million at a Christie's auction of 20 of his luxury cars (including the famed red Bentley we've seen Elton photographed in). So, it may be hard to exactly feel sorry for Elton, who was freaked out by the fact he supposedly spent $60 million in twenty months on flowers alone but many understand all the financial hassles he has endured, including the firing of his accountant and his longtime manager, John Reid. This resulted in a big lawsuit he had against them which seemed to go on forever. (It actually took forty-three days in a London court to reach a verdict.) Sadly, as many expected, Elton had lost the suit.

Elton, along with Bernie Taupin, wrote the entire soundtrack to the 1971 Paramount movie *Friends*.

It will undoubtedly be interesting to look into a crystal ball and see what the future brings for the legendary music superstar. It isn't hard to picture him with even more fans, still sounding flawless live, still making creative records and still shooting off those crazy answers in television interviews.

If ever there was a "classic rock" artist, it is without a doubt, Elton John. Who knows, maybe someday he'll even have his own network. One thing is for certain, his charisma will continue to charm young and old alike. Someday he might not be strong enough to climb on top of a grand piano, but sitting still he will still run rings around all the other piano men out there.❖

ROAD

ELTON JOHN

Elton, all mixe

Just the Stats 'N' Facts

Birth Given Name: Reginald Kenneth Dwight

Official Legal Name: Elton Hercules John. Elton legally changed his name from Reginald Kenneth Dwight in the early seventies.

Nicknames: "Sharon," "O'le Money Bags"

Date of Birth: March 25, 1947

Birthplace: Pinner, Middlesex England

Parents Names: Stanley and Shelia. Stepfather, Fred Fairebrother

Siblings: Four half-brothers from father, Stanley's second marriage

Eyes: Hazel
Height: 5 feet, 8 inches
Weight: Anywhere between 185 to 200 pounds

Hair: Currently a light golden brown, but has known to be "light ginger brown" at times as of late. In the recent past, Elton has sported both medium-blond and platinum locks, but in his initial heyday back in the seventies has had his hair streaked with pink, purple and, blue "crazy color" dye.

Astrological Sign: Aries

Occupation: Musician, songwriter, performer, humanitarian

Educational Background: Pinner Grammar School and the Royal Academy of Music

Childhood Musical Influences: Guy Mitchell, Johnny Ray, Frankie Laine, and later Elvis Presley

Sixties Musical Influences: The Beatles, the Beach Boys, the Rolling Stones, Aretha Franklin, and Dusty Springfield

Piano Influences: Winifred Atwell, Ray Charles, Fats Domino, Jerry Lee Lewis, Ramsey Lewis, Little Richard, Leon Russell, and George Shearing

Instruments: Piano, organ, keyboard, harmonium, and guitar (briefly)

Martial Status: Married once to Renate Blauel, a recording engineer on Valentine's Day 1984. Divorced November 1988. Currently involved in an eight-year relationship with boyfriend, David Furnish. They exchanged rings.

Children: None

Pets: Currently owns twenty-one dogs including Border Terriers, an Irish Wolfhound, a Labrador, German Shepherds, and Spaniels. In 1990, Elton adopted a mixed breed named Thomas from a London dog home. In the seventies, he also owned several dogs, a parrot, a pet rabbit and some horses.

Cars: Since the 'seventies Elton has owned dozens of cars, including: Bentleys, Jaguars,

Porsches, Rolls Royces, and Ferraris. Many have since been sold off in a British auction. It's a fact that Elton enjoys giving very expensive cars as gifts.

Personal Motto: "You can do anything in this life, if you actually set your mind to it."

Favorite Pastime: Enjoys shopping and giving expensive gifts

Hobbies: Collecting art and photographs

Favorite Stores To Shop: Cartier, Tiffany & Co. and Neiman Marcus

Favorite Restaurants: Buckhead Diner in Atlanta, and Mr. Chow's in New York and London

Sports: Tennis and soccer. In 1971 Elton was the vice-president of the Watford Hornets. From 1976 to 1990 he owned the team and his cousin Roy Dwight was a national star. In 1971 Elton became vice president of the Watford Hornets. He owned the team from 1976-90, and then bought back a share. He has since become the Chairman. He is also a big Atlanta Braves baseball fan.

Tantrums: It's a fact that Elton is known to have tantrums, screaming at people, kicking over keyboards, and often storming offstage

Charity: EJAF (Elton John AIDS Foundation founded in 1992

Hobbies: Collecting art and photographs

Early Jobs: First, a pub pianist at the Northwood Hills Hotel and later working as a "tea boy" (golfer) for Mills Music in London

First Amateur Band: Reg Dwight at age thirteen with friend Stuart Brown started the Corvettes, a neighborhood band

First Professional Band: Bluesology. Joined in 1962, when he was 15 years old

Film Credits: Born To Boogie (1972) *Tommy,* (1975) *Spice World* (1997)

Soundtrack Music By Elton: Elton (and Bernie) wrote the entire soundtrack to the Paramount movie *Friends* (1971); contributed several songs to Disney's *The Lion King* (with Tim Rice) in 1994; *The Muse* (1998) composed the entire soundtrack (Bernie wrote lyrics to title song); the animated *The Road to El Dorado* in 2000 (with Tim Rice) and Rocket Pictures' *Talking Dirty.*

Major Awards: Literally hundreds from all around the world. Some include: Five Grammys, particularly the 1995 Best Male Pop Performance for "Can You Feel The Love Tonight?," an Oscar for "Can You Feel the Love Tonight?" in 1994; and being inducted into the Rock and Roll Hall of Fame in 1995. A Tony Award for *Aida* Best Original Score in 2000. In addition, he's received a Golden Globe, The Polar Music Prize, a Brit, and the Ivor Novello.

Breaking World Records: In 1992 Elton broke Elvis Presley's record of 23 consecutive years of at least one Top 40 hit with "Simple Life"

Most Successful Album: Goodbye Yellow Brick Road

Most Successful Single: "Candle in the Wind, 1997." (sold over 450,000 copies.)

Least Successful Single: "Act of War" (duet with Millie Jackson)

Least Successful Album: Victim of Love

Favorite Concert Venue To Play: New York City's Madison Square Garden

Least Favorite Concert Venue: Anywhere that wouldn't sell out in two minutes!

Share Sir Elton's vision: The Elton John limited edition spectacles from *Oliver Peoples.* Sales of these trendy specs help benefit the *Elton John Aids Foundation.*

SHARE OUR VISION FOR A BETTER FUTURE

Concert Credits: Unlike some major rock music performers who tour less frequently, Elton has toured consistently since the release of his self-titled debut album in 1970. Since his first US performance at the Troubadour which literally turned him into an overnight sensation in America, Elton has toured the United States and overseas for every album for the very least, thirty years, not including his first professional band, Bluesology from 1962 to 1967.❖

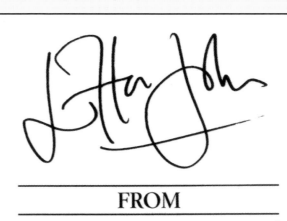

FROM

OLIVER PEOPLES®

"Reg is stuck with Elton and Elton is stuck with Reg."

CHAPTER TWO

Made in England 1947 - 1969

As an only child, Elton John was born Reginald Kenneth Dwight on March 25, 1947 just a half hour past midnight in Pinner, Middlesex England. His parents, Shelia, a loving mother always encouraged her son's love for pop music, though his father, Stanley, a squadron leader in the Royal Air Force did not. Elton remembers his childhood as "bad." mainly because he was "terrified" of his father. "He was very snobbish and sort of stiff," Elton has remarked over the years. "He never let me do anything I wanted to do. I couldn't even play in the garden because I might damage his rosebuds. I used to pray that my father wouldn't come home on the weekends."

Another contributing factor to his unhappy childhood was his weight: "I was short, I was fat and I was miserable." This helped him to develop a terrible inferiority complex, which years later would explain why Elton John was outrageous onstage in the seventies. "I missed a lot as a child. That's why I wear ridiculous clothes. I'm making up for all the things I couldn't do as a child."

His father (a trumpeter in the RAF) and Aunt Win both played piano, and three-year old Reginald was soon to follow. One day he surprised his parents by playing "The Skater's Waltz" by ear. In a 1991 television interview with David Frost, Elton explained how as a child he could hear a song once and then play it on the piano: "I found out early on that I had a gift for picking up tunes and being able to transpose them and play them on the piano immediately."

As Reg had a hard time making friends at school due to being shy and overweight, he grew more lonely and often turned to food for comfort. As a result he became angry with himself and sometimes the rest of the world. The hardships he endured at home weren't getting any better, either. His parents often fought which disrupted any chance of a peaceful family life. His passion for popular music and London Watford Football Club helped to soothe his most troubled childhood years.

Though Reg was forced to learn classical pieces on the piano, he often slipped into pop songs when his piano teacher or parents weren't supervising him. It was evident even back then Reginald Dwight was definitely destined to be involved with rock music one way or another.

Even after his divorce and remarriage, Stanley still tried to discourage his son's determination to become a rock musician, dismissing pop music as pure rubbish. One could easily wonder why a father would dismiss the blatantly obvious talents of his young son. What a terrible injustice it was to not even acknowledge his son's musical abilities. Those in Elton's closest circle know how deeply this affected him throughout his life. Sometimes it takes a lifetime to drown out the voice of a disapproving father. Thankfully, his mother Shelia, who by then, was remarried to Fred Fairebrother, a decorator, encouraged Reg to pursue his interest in popular music. She even eventually found a piano teacher who allowed him to play pop music songs of the day.

In fact, it was Shelia who introduced her young son to American rock 'n' roll in the first place, as Elton John recalled early in his career: "One day my mother came home with two discs, She said she never heard anything like it before and thought they were fantastic. When I heard them, I agreed too. It was Elvis Presely's "Heartbreak Hotel" and Bill Haley's "ABC Boogie." I will never forget it. I was really freaked out when I heard these two songs and I went on from there."

Before long Shelia was bringing home all kinds of American records that Reg would eagerly play over and over again. Because American rock sounded different from the British rock he was originally accustomed too, this new exciting sound began to intrigue him even more. Reg started saving what little pocket money he made every week so he could buy the newest American import rock

music. "I really couldn't believe how great some of these records were. For me, rock 'n' roll took over. I used to play artists like Jerry Lee Lewis and Little Richard on the piano and just thump those songs out. I mean I was really star stuck. Pop music was my whole life."

At thirteen he formed a neighborhood band with Stuart Brown (a friend of his cousin) called the Corvettes (which later evolved in Bluesology) and performed mostly at youth groups and churches in the Pinner area. From the ages of eleven to sixteen, he studied music formally at the Royal Academy of Music in London on Saturdays while still attending Pinner Grammar School during the week. A music teacher at the academy once remarked that young Reginald possessed quite a "remarkable ear" and could play a musical piece even after hearing it only once.

But playing classical music was not what Reginald Dwight had intended to do with his life. He had only one dream and that was to become a rock star. But, how would anyone have ever guessed that even back then the shy and lonely young man would someday become one of the world's biggest pop music legends? Perhaps some of the patrons from Northwood Hills Hotel in 1962, where Reg took his first job as a pub pianist could see this adolescent boy possessed a natural talent. Some of the tunes 15 year-old Reggie played included current hits of the day like Ray Charles' "I Can't Stop Loving You" and Bruce Channel's "Hey Baby" as well as old-fashioned traditional sing-along songs like "Bye Bye Blackbird" and "Roll Out The Barrel."

He was also asked to entertain requests, which Reg always welcomed with a smile. At the end of each long night performance, Fred Fairebrother would pass the tip box around for his stepson, where patrons often gave generously. Elton recalled: "I was paid a pound a night. When I first started, nobody came into a public bar, but after a while it was packed every weekend. At one point I was making about thirty-five pounds a week. I was making a fortune compared to what other kids were

"I'm still the same person as Reg Dwight, but Elton John gave me a feeling of confidence."

making at the time."

At seventeen, Reg dropped out of school just three weeks before his finals to pursue a full-time career in the music business. For several years he played a mix of rock and blues numbers and worked part-time as "tea boy" (a golfer) for Mills Music—a publishing firm located in London's Tin Pan Alley area. Later he joined Bluesology, the group that backed Long John Baldry. It was from Baldry and saxophonist Elton Dean that Reg Dwight linked the two first names of these musicians to rename himself, Elton John. He has explained that he had to change his name because "Reg Dwight sounded like a cement mixer and had a deep association with a part of his psyche of "something" that he evidently was missing in is childhood. 'When I changed my name, it really helped me a lot," he has said. "I'm still the same person as Reg Dwight, but Elton John gave me a feeling of confidence."

At which point, he was growing restless with Bluesology and it's musical changes and sought a new job. "We were always playing the wrong stuff," Elton stated in 1973. But "Bluesology was always two months too late or three months too early. Never playing the right thing at the right time." Despite the group's oft timing, Bluesology eventually was hired to back American visiting singers on tour in Britain like Patti LaBelle, The Drifters, Doris Troy, the Ink Spots and Billy Stewart. Before departing Bluesology, the group recorded two singles for the Fontana label, "Come Back Baby in 1965 and "Mr. Frantic" in 1966 featuring Reg Dwight on lead vocals.

In 1967, Reg Dwight aspired to be more than a sideman answered an advertisement in the *New Musical Express* from the new Liberty Music publishing company looking for "talent." However, he failed the audition, but that was the the end of it. But a seventeen-year-old lad from Lincolnshire named Bernie Taupin answered the same advertisement: "I had been writing poetry at the time," he recalled in 1971 to a Los Angeles music journalist. "It was all psychedelic, canyons of your mind stuff. I couldn't play any instruments, but I can hear melodies in my head when I write. I needed someone to do the music for my words." Since the ambitious young musician could only write melodies, he would need someone to write lyrics. Thus, the Elton John–Bernie Taupin songwriting partnership was born thanks in part to a young talent scout named Ray Williams, who placed the now famous ad and brought the world celebrated team together.

The two young men collaborated on several songs before even meeting each other in person. Seemingly in tune with the sounds and trends of the times, Reg and Bernie took their shot at writing contemporary pop songs. This effort included some early signs of the duo' potential. But mostly their copy cat imitations of the flower power movement. Bernie's non-sesnsical lyrics were about mimicking the more proven writers of the day, namely the Beatles and Bob Dylan. And Reg copied most of the psychedelic music and arrangements that he had heard and enjoyed.

Furthermore, Bernie's lyrics were not about personal experiences or observations. It wasn't until an employee at Dick James (Steve Brown) encouraged them to write from a more human and personal level. In short, they knew they had a knack writing songs but needed to not try so hard. In between their short-term short-term publishing, Reg Dwight made a small living recording sound-a-like pop records.

It was around this time that Reg had changed his name and recorded his last

Bluesology single on Polydor, ("I Found You Baby") in 1967. Like the previous two, the song was a flop and Dwight left the group.

As the story goes, Ray Williams took one of the Dwight-Taupin compositions titled "Scarecrow" to Dick James, a music publisher who had helped the Beatles rise to superstardom. He heard it and signed the fledging songwriting duo to a contract. For over a year they turned out commercial jingles and what Elton has described as "crude, pretentious" and dreadful" songs that were aimed at popular performers of the day such as Englebert Humperdinck, Tom Jones and Lulu (though none were never actually recorded).

One of the very first songs recorded in 1968 as the artist, Elton John was "I've Been Loving You." Later that same year, the first minor hit single in the U.K. "Lady Samantha" was followed in July 1969 by the album *Empty Sky*. One London music critic assessed the album as: "solemn, lavishly orchestrated, brilliant pastiche of everybody else." Though the album was practically unheard of (available only as an import) in America at the time it wasn't until 1975 that MCA Records released it (following the Number One *Captain Fantastic and the Brown Dirt Cowboy*), FM deejays started playing a couple tracks including "Lady Samantha."

"Making the *Empty Sky* album still holds the nicest memories for me," Elton had recalled in an interview, "I suppose it's because it was my first album. It's difficult to explain the enthusiasm we felt as the album began to take shape."

A year later Elton didn't know it, but his career was not only about to take shape, but would forever change his life, as well as and the lives of millions of people in the process.❖

Elton's Childhood Homes

55 Pinner Hill (his grandmother's house in Pinner)

111 Potter Street (Northwood Hills)

30 A Frome Court in Northwood Hills (where he and Bernie slept in bunk beds at his mother and stepfather's apartment)

The Early Demo Recordings Regimental Sgt. Zippo

Below is a "selected" list of songs recorded between 1967 and mid-1968 that never were "officially" released on any Elton John album.

"Angel Tree"
"Annabella"
"A Dandelion Dies in the Wind"
"I Can't Go on Living Without You"
"Regimental Sergeant Zippo"
"Scarecrow"
"Tartan Colored Lady"
"The Tide Will Turn for Rebecca"
"Velvet Fountain"
"And the Clock Goes Round"
"Reminds Me of You"
"Sing Me No Sad Songs"
"Taking the Sun from My Eyes"
"Turn to Me"
"When I Was Tealby Abbey"
"Year of the Teddy Bear"
"Color Slide City"
"Not the Man I Used to Be"
"There's Still Time for Me"

CHAPTER THREE

Superstar of the Seventies

One thing will never be said in the rock press, and that's that Elton John is not full of surprises. Just when you think he is going to put on his glitziest show ever, he takes an 180 degree turn. The perfect example of this is when Elton ended the Seventies the same way he started them—playing many of his early songs (including "Sixty Years On" and "The Greatest Discovery") with just his piano to accompany him on the concert stage. Gone were the flashy threads that were the hallmark of his reign over the glitter rock era—Elton had achieved such great fame by the end of the decade that all he needed was his talent and a set of eighty-eights.

The story of Captain Fantastic's conquering the U.S. shores for the first time is legendary. In 1970, Elton was a relatively unknown artist arriving in Los Angeles to perform at a small but famous club, The Troubador. He cut a somber, solitary figure that hardly hinted of the stardom and admiration that would be thrust upon him just a few

Breaking new ground: Elton with percussionist Ray Cooper at a 1979 performance in Moscow.

hours later. In this single night when L.A.'s rock elite took in his show, the music business was literally transformed into Elton Central. And no wonder he made rock history that night. The young musician brought heartfelt words and music that touched the souls of America looking for a new musical direction. Soon enough, "Your Song" was at number one on the charts and everyone wanted to know about that boyish-looking Englishman with the sweet disposition.

A little later on when his confidence had built up thanks to all the accolades, Elton brought humor and theatrics into his act through a wide array of outrageous stage costumes and a creative collection of "trademark" eye glasses. But everyone knew that the glitz was backed up by talent, unlike a lot of other here-today-gone-tomorrow sequined-jumpsuit-sporting acts that cropped up around the same time.

In the seventies (often referred to by critics as Elton's "golden decade"), he recorded his most groundbreaking and record-setting albums including *Madman Across The Water* (1971), *Honky Chateau* (1972), *Don't Shoot Me I'm Only The Piano Player* (1973), *Goodbye Yellow Brick Road* (1973), *Captain Fantastic And the Brown Dirt Cowboy* (1975). He released his first (greatest hits) album in 1974, following up with *Greatest Hits, Vol. II* in 1977 (most artists need twenty years' worth of material to fill up even one volume of greatest hits, but not Elton John).

Elton played several celebrated and historic shows throughout the era as well, including headlining gigs at the Hollywood Bowl, Madison Square Garden, Dodger Stadium and Wembley Stadium. His songs literally dominated radio playlists and record charts and his music soon became the soundtrack for those who grew up in the sensational seventies decade. Teens sported Elton tee-shirts and felt disappointed that his outrageous specs were not available for purchase at the local mall.

His duet on "Whatever Gets You Through the Night" with John Lennon not only topped the charts both here and overseas, but led to a close relationship with the late Beatle that resulted in Elton's becoming Sean Lennon's godfather. The "two Johns" even performed together at a Madison Square Garden concert that benefited the much neglected Willowbrook mental health facility in suburban New York in 1974. They also supposedly hung out in the Big Apple and did a lot of barhopping.

And in 1979, nine years after quickly ascending to superstar status and equaling the popularity and success previous rock icons like Elvis Presley and The Beatles, Elton was breaking new musical ground. Devoid of all the pomp, flamboyance and campy revelry that came to define the Elton John persona, here was Elton, a solitary man alone with his favored Steinway grand. On his solo concert tour (included percussionist Ray Cooper) of 1979, one that would ultimately be viewed as his most entertaining and poignant, he was rediscovering and enjoying those early songs that helped transform him from "the pudgy piano man from Pinner" to rock's undisputed Captain Fantastic. 1978's *A Single Man* album showed a more introspective Elton, as he was going through both personal and professional changes at the time. He

Elton at the Hollywood Bowl on September 7, 1973, his biggest extravaganza of the decade.

Song sheet to "Sorry Seems to be the Hardest Word."

In the '70s, Elton recorded some of the most groundbreaking and record-setting albums ever. His songs literally dominated radio playlists and record charts, and his music became the soundtrack for those who grew up in the decade.

"The '70s will mostly be remembered...for my albums," Elton once joked on the American Music Awards, where he sported some of his most outrageous specs and platforms ever.

eventually emerged with a more sophisticated sound that brought adults into his huge ring of fans.

Between 1970 to 1979, Elton reached a height of fame, quality, success and spectacle that few entertainers in history ever achieved. He sold out 25,000 seat concert arenas in two hours of less, made movies (like *Tommy*, where he wowed audiences as the campy but egotistical Pinball Wizard) and achieved first name only recognition (and that's an honor, as you know, bestowed upon very few performers).

From his first appearance on U.S. shores, playing with just a bassist (Dee Murray) and a drummer (Nigel Olsson), Elton turned audiences' heads and ears with both the flamboy-

ant aspects of his piano pounding and melodic and lyrical appeal of his songs. Together with his teen-idol looking behind-the-scenes lyricist, Bernie Taupin, Elton exploded onto a transitional music scene (still reeling from the surprise break-up of The Beatles) and helped lead a decade of decadence. He was a one-man party that everyone came to.

The Seventies belonged to Elton John on many different levels—not just as a musical genius, but as a fashionista and philanthropist as well. Elton's also has rock 'n' roll's biggest heart—but more on that in other chapters. ❖

An early '70s Christmas greeting from Elton to the legions of fans in his official fan club.

To all of my friends in the Fan Club... May I wish you and your families the very finest of Holiday Seasons.

A song sheet to "The Bitch is Back" signed by Bernie Taupin.

BILL GRAHAM PRESENTS IN NEW YORK

LEON RUSSELL

ELTON JOHN

McKENDREE SPRING

FILLMORE EAST
November 20-21, 1970

A rare 1970 Filmore East concert program.

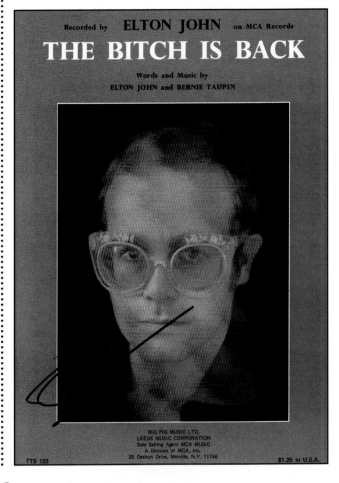

Duets "For One"

In the Seventies, Elton John not only topped the charts on his own, but held the coveted top spot with some of his musical friends as well. The following songs that Elton sang on (either credited or not) hit number one:

1. "Whatever Gets You Through the Night" with John Lennon

Though Elton is not credited as singing back-up on the single, this song from Lennon's Walls and Bridges album hit number one on November 16, 1974 and stayed there for one week. Based on this chart performance, Lennon agreed to appear with Elton in concert, which he did on November 28, 1974, which would be Lennon's last concert appearance.

2. "Bad Blood" with Neil Sedaka

Elton revived and re-energized Sedaka's career in the '70s by signing him to his Rocket Records label. Though uncredited, he shares much of the lead vocal on this song, which became a Number One hit on October 11, 1975 and stayed there for three weeks. Elton reportedly recorded his vocal parts in only seven takes. "Bad Blood" was immediately succeed at the Number One spot by Elton's "Island Girl," which also was the U.S.'s top song for three weeks.

3. "Don't Go Breaking My Heart" with Kiki Dee

In the spirit of the classic Marvin Gaye duets with Tammi Terrell and Kim Weston, Elton

Elton's duet with Kiki Dee made the coveted number one spot on July 17, 1976, and stayed there for four weeks. "Don't Go Breaking My Heart" became one of the year's biggest hit singles.

teamed up with his 1970s pal and protegé Kiki on this sugary but infectious piece of pure pop. Written under the pen names Ann Orson and Carte Blanche, Elton and Taupin composed this via the telephone, with Elton providing the song's title and humming the melody. It was recorded in Canada with Dee adding her vocals after Elton laid down his vocals. It hit number one on July 17, 1976, and stayed there for four weeks, making it one of the year's biggest songs.

The Risky Business of Goodbye Yellow Brick Road

In the early seventies, it was considered a risky business move to release a double album, even for heavy hitters like Elton John and Bernie Taupin, who in fewer than two years had cranked out five smash hit albums. There was also the stark possibility that the music-buying public had it's fill of Elton John.

Apparently, neither concerns were the case according to *Billboard* that over a staggering 75 million Elton John albums were sold between 1970-1975. *Goodbye Yellow Brick Road*, produced by Gus Dudgeon was no Elton's eighth album and

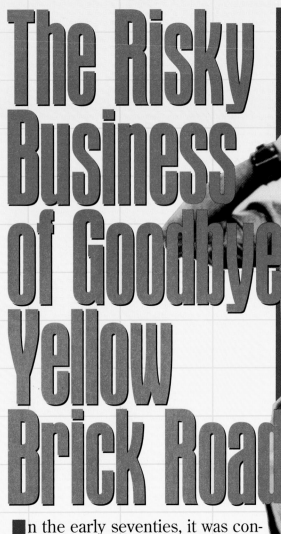

like many of the others was recorded outside of England. Some of the more popular tracks: "Saturday Night's Alright (for Fighting)," "Goodbye Yellow Brick Road," Bennie and the Jets," and "Harmony" were recorded at the famed Strawberry Studios in France.

"*Goodbye Yellow Brick Road*," the album really encompassed some many things, and could be looked at in many different ways," explained Bernie Taupin years later to a Los Angeles disc jockey. "Part of it can be part of the old *Wizard of Oz* situation and part of it came from coming up from the north of England and going down to London. It could also be Elton leaving certain things in his life behind, or it could be discovering new goals. It just seemed that *Goodbye Yellow Brick Road* worked well as an album title. There's a nice cinematic feel to it."

Regarding the lyrics to the popular single/title track which can be interpretated as either a lament or celebration Taupin added, "I think you have to find the disillusionment in order to appreciate the past. Here I was this country boy who packed his bags and went down to the big city (London) to see the bright lights. Because of what I wanted to achieve in my life at that time, that was the only way to do it. But I still had that yearning for the good ole ways like the country comforts. In a sense I was being pulled in both directions—being, the big city and a need to get back to the country with all the greenery and animals."❖

Together with lyricist, Bernie Taupin, Elton exploded onto a transitional music scene that helped lead a decade of decadence.

Elton John's Top 10 Songs of the Seventies

1. "Don't Go Breaking My Heart" (with Kiki Dee)
2. "Crocodile Rock"
3. "Island Girl"
4. "Philadelphia Freedom"
5. "Lucy in the Sky with Diamonds"
6. "Bennie and the Jets"
7. "Goodbye Yellow Brick Road"
8. "Don't Let The Sun Go Down on Me"
9. "Daniel"
10. "Someone Saved My Life Tonight"

Between 1972 and 1975, Elton John racked up an amazing seven consecutive Number One albums, including two albums, *Captain Fantastic and The Brown Dirt Cowboy* and *Rock of the Westies* that were released in 1975 and entered the *Billboard* charts at number one. This was the first time in history that an album had topped the charts in its first week—and Elton did it twice in a row!

The Top 10 Elton John Albums of the Seventies

1. *Greatest Hits*
2. *Goodbye Yellow Brick Road*
3. *Captain Fantastic and the Brown Dirt Cowboy*
4. *Caribou*
5. *Rock of the Westies*
6. *Don't Shoot Me, I'm Only the Piano Player*
7. *Honky Chateau*
8. *Blue Moves*
9. *Here and There* (recorded live)
10. *Elton John*

The 1991 *Two Rooms* album celebrated the John-Taupin hit songwriting team.

CHAPTER FOUR

Songwriting Partnership
Captain Fantastic and the Brown Dirt Cowboy

Beginning in the most ordinary of circumstances, thanks to an ad in London's *New Musical Express* in 1967, the songwriting partnership of Elton John and Bernie Taupin has been nothing short of extraordinary. For nearly thirty-five years, Elton has transformed Bernie's often brilliant lyrics to accompany his most memorable music. Though they never actually collaborated in the same room like traditional songwriters often do, the achievements of the John/Taupin musical team are some of the most famous songs ever written and recorded: "Your Song," "Daniel," "Candle in the Wind," "Bennie and the Jets" and "Don't Let The Sun Go Down on Me," "Someone Saved My Life Tonight," and "The One" among the many. The acclaimed 1991 album, *Two Rooms*, was a befitting tribute to the hit songwriting team by their musical colleagues—including George Michael, Sting, Phil Collins, Eric Clapton and Tina Turner.

In the conventional songwriting method, a single artist usually crafts songs note for note. Or a collaboration of two people, lyricist and musician, begin honing in on their composition just as a painter skillfully fills in his canvas. The two artists gently fill in the gaps with subtle nuances that gradually start to form the structure of a song. Some songs come quickly. Others may take a little longer.

But in the case of Elton John, things are a little bit different. Since he began to develop his craft, Elton always had a knack for a knocking out a melody quickly. During his first attempt at writing with his first band, Bluesology, when he wrote the lyrics and music to his first single, "Come Back, Baby" it was evident that his strength lies within the melody not the lyrics. He realized this early on and when he decided to go out on his own as a solo artist, he knew writing melodies and singing the songs were his true forte.

Enter Bernie Taupin, only two years younger than Elton and a ferocious reader. His ability to write intelligent, insightful and often compelling lyrics—but not melodies—proved to be the perfect fit for Elton. Never have two people so completely different in personality bonded before as Elton and Bernie did. As the old adage goes, opposites really do attract. A new record company (Britain's Liberty Records) was seeking talent in 1967 via an ad in the local music papers in London. Both Elton and Bernie answered the ad. Elton wrote in and indicated he could write melodies but not lyrics. Subsequently, Bernie said he could write lyrics (and included rough samples) but not melodies. Thus, this incredible songwriting partnership was born. A record executive provided Elton with the hand written lyrics and he began putting his melody and vocal to the lyrics. Bernie would actually meet

Elton later to hear the finished product and their "written" song.

Not much has changed since 1967. Bernie simply provides Elton the lyrics (first, handwritten, then typewritten, then faxed and now sometimes e-mailed). Elton takes the lyric, composes the melody around the lyrics and usually twenty minutes later, a song has been created. This process happens while neither of them are in the same room.

"I get a lyric, or I get a few lyrics," Elton has said. 'I think the melody should go with the lyric, having scanned the lyric first. For example for a song like "When a Woman Doesn't Want You"—it's not a cha-cha and it's not a raving song. It's going to be a ballad. I get the drum track going and I just start writing the chords and it's over and done within fifteen or twenty minutes. If it doesn't work, I just leave it and then come back to it."

During the recording of most songs, Bernie, in a separate room would be writing lyrics about any subject matter that interested him. Usually inspired by a title first, he builds a story around the title and would take the lyric to Elton.

Next, Elton, who had been eagerly awaiting, would read the the lyric and slowly develop chord structures. In the early days, Bernie didn't supply the lyrics in verse-and-chorus form. He would write the lyrics without any form or structure and Elton would break the lyrics into stanzas. In some cases, whole passages of lyrics would be omitted (as in the case of the hit "Daniel" to which further explains the story line of a Vietnam Vet returning home from the war. The third verse of "Daniel" till this day is still missing, leaving behind the

Captain Fantastic and the Brown Dirt Cowboy: For more than three decades Elton has transformed Bernie's lyrics to create some of the most memorable music of our time since the Beatles.

mystery of the song's true meaning.

"Many people write in many different ways," Bernie said in 1997 in an for *American Songwriter*. "As most people know the way Elton and I write is very different from the way anybody else does. We don't sit down side by side. We work very quickly because we both enjoy writing. Our best work comes when it's straight out—fast."

Elton has full liberty to make the lyric fit the melody and very rarely has Bernie ever complained. Upon completion of the song "Border Song" for instance, once the melody was complete, Elton found that he needs a few extra lines to finish out the song. Upon his own accord, he finished the lyric for Bernie. A rare occasion indeed!

And while the pair always over write for their albums, Elton has the choice of picking which lyrics work the best and has discarded lyrics that he can't find or fit a melody to. With no sense of rejection, Bernie moves on to the next lyric and the process starts all over again. If there are twelve songs slated for a future release, Bernie will write twenty lyrics. The duo will compose fifteen or so, and the rest will either be recorded and or even completely rejected if Elton cannot get a melody to fit the lyric.

"Don't let anyone ever tell you it takes a long time to write a song, because it doesn't," Bernie noted. "I don't think you'll find anybody more diverse than Elton and myself. We've written everything—country, blues, reggae—not just these pure pop songs. We've done it all."

Of course, with this type of arrangement, there are bound to be some surprises for example. For instance, on Elton's *Reg Strikes Back* album, the song "Since God Invented Girls" was initially thought to be a very Beach Boys-type up-tempo song by Bernie since the lyric even references Brian Wilson (founder and creative mind behind the Beach Boys). But Elton saw the lyric completely as a ballad and continued to purse that impulse and creat-

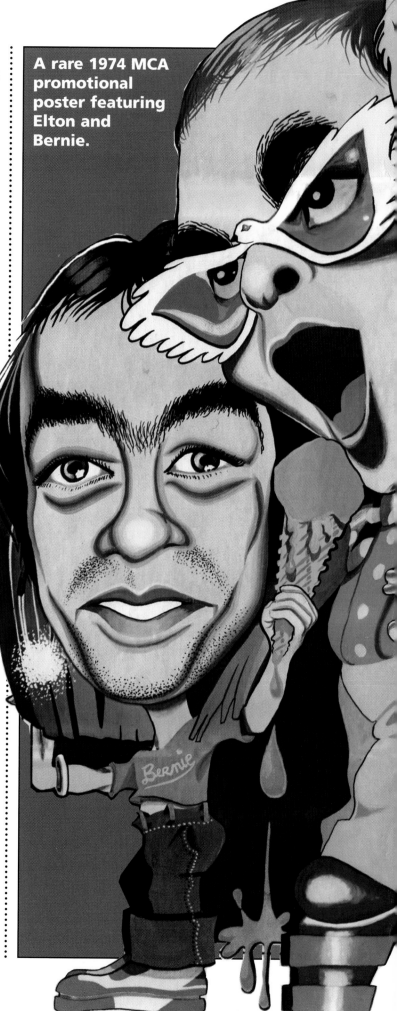

A rare 1974 MCA promotional poster featuring Elton and Bernie.

ed a very delicate ballad in the spirit of the Beach Boys sound.

Naturally, as the songwriting team continues to develop their craft, the rare difference on the songs tempo and mood has become as less and less. The synergy between Elton and Bernie allows each to know what the other is thinking. This is obviously a natural occurrence after more than thirty years of writing together. While they still write separately, the two have sat down in recent years to at least conjure up the feeling the lyric may have and the direction it may take.

When the pair began writing for their 1989 *Sleeping with the Past* album, they did exactly just that. The album was a tribute to the great 1960s rhythm and blues sounds they both grew up with and cherished. Each of Bernie's lyrics were steeped in part to a song or artist from the past. For example, the first single released, "Healing Hands" was reminiscent of The Four Tops' hit "Reach Out (I'll Be There)." Bernie wrote under the lyric for "Healing Hands," how he saw this song and a reference to the Four Tops hit. Elton, of course still had full control over the melody but for the first time heeded some advice from his longtime lyricist and friend.

Elton, during his lengthy career, has also written melodies first, then added the lyrics later. Such is the case regarding his 1978 album, *A Single Man*. Here, taking a short sabbatical from Bernie, Elton teamed up with lyricist Gary Osborne, who had the daunting task of making lyrics fit around a melody that Elton had. This was quite a reversal for Elton and one that would not be duplicated.

And as the 1990s focused on animated movies, movie scores and a Broadway play (*Aida*) for Disney, Elton worked with lyricist Tim Rice in the tradition of lyrics first and melodies second. "It is such a please to work with Elton," Tim Rice told *American Songwriter in a* 1999 interview. "For me, working with Elton on *Aida* was very much the same experience we had for writing The Lion King. We lived with it for a long time. We didn't have any major problems working together. If you are happy and relaxed with the people you are working with, then it's going to be a good experience. Elton and I respect each other's work. We certainly work well together."

Considering how Elton's writing experience with Bernie differs from working with other lyricists, is there a secret behind the successful songwriting partnership?

"We have the kind of a relationship that is between brothers," Elton remarked in a 1996 interview: "That's much more than being just friends. I don't ever remember a time in our lives that we had to question our writing partnership." But was there ever a time when the Pop Piano Man had seriously questioned his personal and professional relationship with Bernie? "No, I can't actually remember having a fight," he answered. "There might have been times where we were secretly tired of each other. But when you love and respect someone, you don't throw that kind of collaboration away."

Through it all, one thing remains. Elton John expressive piano playing and vocal phrases have played out many characters and story lines through song. And though he doesn't write the words, he sings them as convincingly as if he did. ❖

Never have two people so completely different in personality bonded before as Elton and Bernie.

Bernie grew up in rural England fascinated by the American Wild West and rock and roll music; two themes that are frequently reflected in his lyrics.

Bernie Taupin found his true "musician" voice in 1996, fronting his own band named Farm Dogs.

Bernie Taupin

From a Brown Dirt Cowboy to an L.A. Cowboy

"Without Bernie Taupin there would be no Elton John. We've been together for a very long time. Without him the journey would not have been possible. I love him dearly," stated Elton John in 1994 when he was inducted into the Rock and Roll Hall of Fame.

Following his acceptance speech, he called his longtime lyricist (who was not an inductee) and dear friend to the stage and handed him the trophy. Though there has been much reflected and written about Bernie Taupin and his songwriting collaboration with Elton John, the facts still certainly speak for themselves. For starters, together, they have sold over a staggering 150 million records world-wide which earned them rightful place along side some of the world's most celebrated songwriters including George and Ira Gershwin, Rogers & Hammerstein and more notably, Lennon and McCartney.

Considering the amazing amount of Bernie Taupin written lyrics sung by Elton John, it comes as no surprise that more than two hundred artists have recorded their songs. The most widely covered hits include "Your Song," "Daniel," "Don't Let the Sun Go Down on Me," "Tiny Dancer," "Country Comfort," "Candle In The Wind" (original version) and "Rocket Man."

A product of rural England, Bernie grew up in the post-World War II era fascinated with the American Wild West and the great legends of rock and roll, interests that are frequently reflected in his lyrics. "I love stories. I love to write a story and put it to music," he lamented. "I thought that was wonderful. Then I got obsessed with Americana. With everything I wrote up to and including *Tumbleweed Connection*, people were always talking about my cinematic vision and experience in the states, as if the songs were like a diary of us on tour. But in actuality they were all written before I got there."

In an excerpt from 1988 autobiography, *Cradle Of Halos*, Bernie described his idyllic English upbringing as a kind of special world, "one filled with adventure and romance." His literary heroes existed and secret places made themselves known to an imaginative young boy, who believed in the power of magic. "This was not to say," he wrote that "I was a complete introvert that saw goblins and gremlins in every waking shadow, I was merely the product of a warm, compassionate family who introduced me at an early age to the wonder of books."

It was with this kind of encouragement, that not only sowed the seeds of a rich imagination, but laid a deep-rooted groundwork for his distant future. Today, Bernie Taupin in his early fifties, has certainly exceeded many of his wildest expectations since driving a tractor in the rural English fields of Lincolnshire. Between 1972 and 1975, Elton and Bernie scored seven consecutive Number One rock albums, in addition to numerous hit singles. *Captain Fantastic and the Brown Dirt Cowboy* was the first album in history ever to enter Billboard's album chart at the coveted number-one spot. Incredibly, by the mid-'70s, the hit making songwriting duo were responsible for two percent of all records sold worldwide.

In 1991, Bernie's and Elton's efforts were

The 45 single for "Citizen Jane."

once every two or three years," Bernie explained, "so I really get into the songwriting mode when the time comes to write an album. My workload on an Elton album stretches to maybe two or three weeks at the most. It's a real labor of love when you make a record."

It's not surprising that Bernie's lyrics are not only recognized by some of the world's most renowned music organizations, but he has also earned nearly every imaginable songwriter award in the world. A few of his more noted honors, collectively with Elton and individually, include induction into the Songwriters Hall of Fame, six Ivor Novello awards (Europe's premier songwriting honor), and the 1994 ASCAP Songwriter of the Year honor.

The revered rock lyricist is also the proud recipient of the coveted INA International Achievement of

exemplified again with the tribute, *Two Rooms* which included an album, book and video. Celebrating the songs that will remain a part of our lives for years to come were interpreted by such major music talent as Sting, George Michael, Eric Clapton, Phil Collins and Rod Stewart. The following year they managed to even break Elvis Presley's previous record of continuous Top 40 Hits on *Billboard's* singles chart. It's hard to imagine that with Elton's 40th and latest album to date, *Songs From the West Coast*, he and Bernie have probably written more than six-hundred songs together. "Elton and I basically make an album probably

In 1992 and 1995—Taupin, singer, author, humanitarian and entrepreneur—used his influence for "the greater good" and produced benefits, Commitment to Life VI and VIII. These events included performances by Barbara Streisand, Joni Mitchell, Elton John, Liza Minnelli, Garth Brooks, and Billy Joel, and combined raised over $8 million for AIDS Project Los Angeles.

COMMITMENT
TO LIFE
VIII

Excellence and was initiated into the American Academy of Achievement. Incomparably, Bernie Taupin is only the second lyricist ever in popular music history to obtain the elusive ASCAP Golden Word award (Sammy Cahn was the first).

For those already in the know, Bernie Taupin dons a plethora of career caps—singer, author, humanitarian and entrepreneur—and he has successfully learned how to use his influence for "the greater good" in the world. For example in 1992 and 1995 he produced *Commitment to Life VI* and *VIII*, events which raised over 8 million for AIDS Project Los Angeles. These major musical benefits featured performers from all phases of the entertainment world including Barbra Streisand, Joni Mitchell, Liza Minnelli, Garth Brooks,

Billy Joel and of course, Elton John among many A-List celebrities.

In 1997, Elton and Bernie created history once again with their revised version of "Candle in the Wind." The lyrics were rewritten in honor of the late Princess Diana and Elton sang the revised version at her funeral. Beyond his numerous lyrical achievements with Elton, Bernie has continually explored his own varied interests which includes recording three solo vocal albums, co-writing all ten songs on Alice Cooper's 1978 *From the Inside* album and penning number-one hits for Starship's 1985 "We Built This City" and Heart's 1986 "These Dreams." Then there's a string of song lyrics written for such popular music artists as Rod Stewart, John Waite, Melissa Manchester, the Motels and others.

Celebrating his words. The early '90s fanzine, simply titled "Taupin" published for three years and featured fascinating insights into his lyrics, rare interviews, and a Q&A column on the lyricist.

Bernie Taupin Discography

45 RPM Singles
"Friend of the Flag" (RCA,1987)
"Citizen Jane" (RCA, 1987)

Albums
Taupin (Elektra, 1971)
He Who Rides the Tiger (Elektra, 1980)
Tribe (RCA, 1987)

Compact Disc Singles
"Friend of the Flag" (RCA,1987)
"Citizen Jane" (RCA, 1987)

Compact Discs
Tribe (RCA, 1987)
He Who Rides the Tiger (Japanese import re-issue), 2001

Cassettes
He Who Rides the Tiger (Elektra, 1980)
Tribe (RCA, 1987)

Farm Dogs Compact Disc Singles
"Beautiful" (Discovery, 1996)
"Daria" (Sire, 1998)
"Foreign Window" (Sire, 1998)

Farm Dogs Compact Discs
Last Stand in Open Country (Discovery, 1996)
Immigrant Sons (Sire, 1998)

Aside from an endless string of hit singles with Elton, Bernie Taupin has also written number one songs for Starship "We Built This City" and Heart "These Dreams." In 1987 he released his second vocal solo album, titled *Tribe*.

Bernie as Pictured in 1987.

But it wasn't until the mid-nineties that Bernie Taupin found his most comfortable "musician" voice with his own band called Farm Dogs. The 1996 CD *Last Stand in Open Country* (Discovery Records) cast a very different light on the insightful songwriter. Now being the lead vocalist and band co-founder, he fancied a more roots-oriented, acoustic sound and the 1998 Farm Dogs follow up CD, titled *Immigrant Sons* (Sire Records) continued to enforce his musical passion.

In addition, as a solo artist, Bernie has recorded one spoken word album, *Taupin,*

(Elektra, 1971) and two critically solo vocal albums, *He Who Rides the Tiger*, (Elektra, 1981) and *Tribe* (RCA, 1987). As an author, he has written the books: *Bernie Taupin: The One Who Writes the Words For Elton John*: (Knopf, 1976), *Elton: It's a Little Bit Funny*, (Penguin Books, 1977), *Burning Cold* (Harmony Books, 1979), *A Cradle of Halos* (Aurum Press Limited, 1988), *The Devil at High Noon* (Advantage Graphics, 1991), *Marilyn Monroe: Candle in the Wind*, (Pavilion 1993) and *Elton John and Bernie Taupin: The Complete Lyrics* (Hyperion, 1994).

For more than twenty years, Bernie has been an American citizen. He lives in California's Santa Ynez Valley on a thirty acre ranch, where he owns several dogs, horses and a variety of farm animals. He has been married three times and is currently divorced.

Bernie Taupin Stats

Birthdate: May 22, 1950
Birthplace: Lincolnshire, England
Parents: Daphne and Robert
Siblings: Two brothers (older)Tony, (younger) Kit
Fast Fact: Bernie is an American citizen and lives in California.

Songs Written by Bernie Taupin and Recorded by Other Artists:

"Lonnie & Josie," Kiki Dee (1973)
"Supercool," Kiki Dee (1973)
"The Last Good Man in My Life," Kiki Dee (1974)
"Hard Luck Story," Kiki Dee (1974)
"Lover Come Back to Me," Hudson Brothers (1974)
"Lonely School Year," Hudson Brothers (1975)
"The Man Who Loved to Dance," Kiki Dee (1976)
"Snow Queen," Kiki Dee (1976)
"Broken Woman," China (1977)
"Savage," China (1977)
"If I Weren't So Romantic I'd Shoot You," Derringer (1978)
"Julie," Cher (1980)

"For the Working Girl," Melissa Manchester (1980)
"Never Give Up on a Dream," Rod Stewart (1981)
"Sonny," Rod Stewart (1981)
"Guess I'll Always Love You," Rod Stewart (1982)
"Johnny and Mary," Melissa Manchester (1982)
"Hey Ricky, (You're a Lowdown Heel)," Melissa Manchester (1983)
"White Rose," Melissa Manchester (1983)
"Satisfied," Rod Stewart (1983)
"Into the Heartland," The Motels (1984)
"We Built This City, (on Rock and Roll)," Starship (1985)
"Love Rusts," Starship 1985

"These Dreams," Heart (1985)
"Hard Lesson to Learn," Rod Stewart (1986)
"I Engineer,"Animotion (1986)
"When the Phone Stops Ringing," Boomerang (1986)
"The Burn," Starship (1989)
"Deal For Life," John Waite, (1990)
"Dip Your Wings," Peter Cetera (1992)
"The Rain," Carlene Carter (1993)
"Monkey in My Dreams," Martin Page (1994)
"For Wanting You," Marianne Faithful (1999)
"Red," The Young Dubliners (2000)
"Mendocino County Line," Willie Nelson (2002)

Out of the Closet: The cover of *Reg Strikes Back* features over 15 years of Elton's clothing and accessories.

46

thanks to his friendships with both Gianni Versace and Giorgio Armani that he always got custom designs from them—and first dibs at the new collections before they even got on the runways. Elton got more into regular suits and gave up the jumpsuits; he also developed a real love for natural fabrics like silk, fine wool and cashmere. He started to wear more pastel colors in the eighties, keeping with the *Miami Vice*-influenced times, but somehow always threw in his own flair with some unusual jewelry or eyewear. Elton was not ready to give up his rocker image entirely! "I've changed. I don't want to wear an ridiculous sequenced numbers anymore," he stated in 1989. "It was great fun while it lasted. But now I want people to pay more attention to the music, again and see me as a serious artist and not just this larger-than-life personality or entertainer."

The nineties brought us an even more fashion-forward Elton. He kept up with the latest Versace and Armani suit designs, but started experimenting with newer designers who put a little edge in their gear. Elton started showing up in Richard Tyler and Moschino gear at various events and shows.

Richard Tyler is not only famous for elegant but unique evening wear that the likes of Courtney Love and Winona Ryder often sport, but he single-handedly brought back the classic flashy country -and-western outfits that k.d. lang and Dwight Yoakam sport. Richard's designs for Elton were uniquely Elton: he would take the best retro designs such as Beatle suits, and cut them more for Elton's body type, adding a little shoulder padding and

In the mid-'80s Elton often donned several outrageous wigs in concert.

making the jackets longer than in the sixties. Tyler also did some striking silk Nehru jackets in both black and bright colors for Elton.

Franco Moschino is a flamboyant designer who died in 1994 of pancreatic cancer, but his company continues on at the forefront of the Italian high-end fashion market. Elton always got a charge about how the designer would take a pretty conservative man's suit and add a whimsical touch, such as yellow smiley-face buttons or a dove made out of white sequins on the lapel. Elton loved his way of taking the old and making it new again. He still buys suits from this trend-setting company that generally appeals to the young and rich rock 'n' roll crowd.

The new millennium has brought us a new Elton with a whole new head of hair and sporting his favorite designer suits but occasionally throwing in the odd poet's shirt or loud tie. One of Elton's favorite designers of the moment is Gene Meyer, a New York designer who seems polka dot obsessed. As a matter of fact, Gene first got noticed seven or eight years ago for his fabulous line of matching polka-dotted and geometric design silk ties (with matching pocket hankies and boxer shorts) at Bloomingdale's, Macy's and other large department stores. The owners of posh eaterie LeCirque in New York were so impressed with Meyer's ties that the entire wait staff wears them. The most classic example of Elton wearing Gene Meyer's gear is the suit he wore for his duet with Eminem at the 2001 MTV Awards. Naturally, Meyer's constant use of geometric shapes appeal to the "mod" side of Elton left over from his teenage days in suburban England and he truly enjoys Meyers use of fine silk and bright colors.

"I have a great respect for anybody that designs clothes and continues to be successful whether I particularly like their clothes or not," Elton told *Interview* magazine.

Over the years, Elton's hair has been a great focus of the media, not only because of his lack of follicles, but also because of the many shades he has dyed it. In the seventies, during his initial phase of popularity, Elton seemed to change his hair color bi-weekly, and photos /video clips show that he ran the gamut from dayglo green to hot pink locks and back again. All this coloring eventually made what little hair he had nearly completely fall out. Forever being the jokester, Elton made more jokes about his hair problems than the witty but sometimes cruel British press.

Elton's hair-loss problems led to his hat phase of the eighties and the trials and tribulations of hair transplants, supposedly done in London, New York, Paris and Beverly Hills. In one year alone, he reportedly spent $17,000 to $28,000 dollars on "plugs," and his initial results weren't successful—which led to his "fedora phase," as he calls it.

A conservative and dapper-looking Sir Elton.

In 1991, Elton finally found a hair-replacement method that worked, and these days sports a very full head of golden light brown hair (usually with long bangs). While it hasn't ever been published just which clinic or doctor gave Elton those lovely locks, rumor has it that Elton's hair success came via the Bosley Medical Method. (Dr. L. Lee Bosley of Beverly Hills, who has been in the hair restoration business for twenty-six years and now has dozens of satellite offices around the country, is credited with developing the three most current methods of giving men back their much-missed locks—Micrograft®, VarigraftingSM, and MicrotechnologiesSM.)

Elton now doesn't sport nearly as many hats (this comes as no surprise), and he really flaunts his ample locks. He has long since learned his lesson about visiting the colorist too often as well. There's no doubt that Elton's confidence has been boosted tenfold by the fact he is no longer has to worry about potential baldness.

What's next for Elton in terms of fashion trendsetting? Well, for starters, he can be spotted at conservative and outrageous fashion week shows around the world. Whether it's Commes des Garcons or a Savile Row traditional tailor, Elton is there snooping around, seeking out fresh looks. Looking in Elton's closet is like looking at a kaleidoscope: there are so many colors and designs, the combinations are infinite. On his mellow days, he could pull out a fine Burberry cashmere sweater and a pair of black pants and JP Tod's or Gucci loafers. When in a wilder mood, he may pull out a viscose Commes des Garcons jacket with a Union Jack emblem on it. "What am I going to wear today?" is a welcome question as Elton wakes up each morning. Of course, he's got a personal stylist to call if he wants some advice (he can even get on the phone with Giorgio Armani if he'd like).

Elton visited the Beverly Hills Versace boutique the end of September 2001 and dropped a cool one-hundred grand. This reportedly "made" the store's month, since the September 11th attacks had caused it to have one of its slowest sales periods ever. Elton would have dropped even more but he used his VIP card with its special thirty percent discount.

Elton thrusts himself into fashion like he does his music. What he wears shows his mood and where his "head is at" on a particular day. It might sound cliche, but Elton's fashions are as unique and legendary as the man himself.❖

Elton's Five Most Wild Stage Costumes of the Seventies

1. Statue Of Liberty, worn in New York during his U.S. Bicentennial Tour in 1976.

2. Sequined Los Angeles Dodgers baseball uniform, worn during shows at Dodger Stadium in 1975.

3. Pinball Wizard with eight-foot Doc Marten boots from the 1975 film *Tommy*.

4. White suit with silver balls throughout and matching top hat, on the 1975 *Cher* TV Show.

5. A plumed, multi-colored and feathered bird-like costume, circa 1973.

The famous over-sized Doc Marten's Elton wore as the Pinball Wizard in the film *Tommy*.

"I love humor in clothes. I like people who are not afraid to take a few risks."

Elton's wild, wacky and wonderful fashion sense has made headlines around the world, like the Bob Mackie original peacock-feather costume he wore on the hit television show, *The Muppets*.

In the early '70s,
superstar Elton
meets the press in a
snazzy red satin suit.

Elton Eyewear

A natural outgrowth of Elton's extravagant taste in clothing both on and off the stage was an equally outrageous collection of eyeglasses. Throughout the 1970s, Elton John's flamboyant frames were a focal point of his popularity. Several myths about Elton's glasses floated during his eye wear heyday of the '70s.

Contrary to many reports, Elton's glasses are *not* simply sunglasses, but are prescription glasses (with a strong prescription at that!), and though it may have seemed like he had thousands, in reality, the actual count at his peak was in the 250-to-400 range.

Nevertheless, in the seventies, Elton John was responsible for making eye wear a wild fashion statement rather than an embarrassing sight enhancer. And though he's built a reputation for crazy glasses, in reality, it was only during the early part of his career when he regularly dazzled the world with his specs. But during that time, dazzle he did.

Press reports from the 1970s and 1980s detailed his ever-expanding spectacles collection to exceed over 500 pairs. In reality, Elton stated the number was closer to 366. In 1988 he cleaned house and sold his stagewear and other personal items including 75 pairs of eyeglasses in a highly publicized Sotheby's auction.

Of course Elton continues to wear vivid spectacles, but the frames are more toned down and stylish looking. He even sells his own eye glass collection which is available through the Oliver Peoples boutique and authorized dealers nationwide. The line of eye wear is of course, appropriately titled, The Elton John Limited Edition Spectacles collection.❖

Fans' favorite: a pair of Elton's illuminated glasses constructed from the letters E-L-T-O-N made of colored plastic inset with small electric light bulbs.

Overall, in the fifties, Buddy Holly made it cool to wear thick, black nerdy frames. In the seventies, Elton John made it cool to wear glasses with tiny, working windshield wipers.

Elton John's Top Ten Outrageous Eyeglasses of the Seventies

1. Round frames with dark mink-lining, circa 1972-1973.

2. Black, grand-piano-shaped frames, circa 1975-1976.

3. Square frames with each of the four seasons painted in each corner, circa 1976.

4. Large, lighted frames that spelled "E-L-T-O-N," circa 1972—1973.

5. Round, clear frames with huge concentric circles protruding from the top and bottom of the frames with leaf-like decorations strung on each of the round "branches," circa 1972-73.

6. Two frames, one red and one yellow with palm trees decorating the edge of each lenses, circa 1974-1975.

7. Star-shaped lenses, multi-colored or tinted red, white and blue, circa 1974-75.

8. Oversized, white, Sir Winston frames with multi-colored tinted lenses worn extensively during 1976 world tour.

9. Round, white feather-fringed frames, circa 1973.

10. Thick, clear frames with flowers painted over the top of each of the pink lenses, worn on the cover of the *Caribou* album, circa 1974.

CHAPTER SIX

Into the Eighties and Still Standing

The dawning of the 1980s was an unsure time for Elton. He'd released the not-so-highly regarded disco album *Victim of Love* in late 1979, and no one was quite sure what lie ahead for the Rocket Man. But as the world would soon discover, Elton had been writing a collection of remarkable new songs, soon to be released.

His first studio album of the decade was *21 at 33,* for MCA Records. The title referred to the album being the twenty-first he released through his current age of 33. With *21 at 33,* Elton soon found renewed respect and recognition, thanks to the huge success of the album's first single, "Little Jeannie," which reached number three on the U.S. charts. Elton was soon on tour to promote *21 at 33.*

Shortly into the tour circuit, Elton and his band performed a mammoth free concert for over 450,000 people in New York's Central Park. During the concert, Elton made mention of his friend John Lennon, who lived just down the road and even

performed Lennon's "Imagine." Just three months later, Lennon was gunned down outside his apartment building, affecting and confounding fans to the core. Elton included.

Before and during the promotion of *21 at 33,* Elton was growing evermore disgruntled with his record label MCA, and by September 21 he had jumped ship and signed on to David Geffen's newly founded record label, Geffen. Elton's first album with Geffen was *The Fox,* an album not without controversy. In what would be the start of a win-win relationship, Elton and David Geffen had disagreed early and often over song selections. Geffen rejected many of songs Elton had recorded for The Fox and forced the musician back into the studio.

Making matters worse, Elton and Geffen were sued by MCA, who had claimed ownership rights to the songs on *The Fox,* since they had been recorded in the same studio sessions as *21 at 33.* But Elton and Geffen won the case.

Through the mid-eighties Elton released albums and supported them with demanding world concert tours. His trademark stage outfits started to become even more outlandish as he donned some of his most flashy costumes since 1974.

The Fox, released in 1981, marked Elton's first album with Geffen Records.

A 1982 re-release of a "Your Song" music sheet signed by Bernie Taupin.

The Fox was released in May 1981 and featured new producer Chris Thomas. Despite all efforts, the album did not chart very high. By September of 1981, Elton was at work recording songs for his next Geffen release, *Jump Up!* Chris Thomas again produced the album, which was released in April 1982. The first single, "Empty Garden (Hey Hey Johnny)," was a lyrical and musical masterpiece, a dedication to John Lennon, and seemed to encapsulate all that everyone had felt about the departed songwriter. The song reached number thirteen on the U.S. charts, and featured a music video on MTV also received high airplay.

In June of 1982, Elton was off on a North American tour with his original bandmates: Nigel Olsson, Dee Murray and Davey Johnstone. It was the first time they'd all played together since 1975. And by 1983, Elton had

brought that most celebrated band back into the studio, as well, and was collaborating with Bernie Taupin again, exclusively.

His next album, *Too Low for Zero*, spawned three successful singles. "I'm Still Standing," with its flashy music video, "Kiss the Bride" and "I Guess That's Why They Call it the Blues," a bluesy number featuring Stevie Wonder on harmonica, which saw smashing success and hit #4 on the US charts. Elton was now a regular on MTV.

On February 14, 1984, Elton shocked the world when he married German sound engineer Renate Blauel. After only a short courtship, the two wed at a church near Sydney, Australia. Bernie Taupin was Elton's Best Man. Of the union, Elton said he hoped it would bring him contentment and maybe even children. But unfortunately, it brought neither. The couple divorced in November, 1988.

Through the mid-1980s, Elton continued releasing albums and supporting them with rigorous world tours. On the flip side, his drug and alcohol problems were escalating as quickly as his hairline was receding. Thus, his appearance took on more hats, and his stage outfits grew more and more outlandish, with Elton donning some of his most garish costumes since 1974.

In July of 1985, Elton took part in the all-star charity benefit Live Aid at London's Wembley Stadium. At the concert, George Michael offered backing vocals on Elton's "Don't Let the Sun Go Down on Me," a precursor to the 1991 remake. Charity-wise, Elton was soon turning his efforts to the AIDS cause. In November, he joined forces with Dionne Warwick, Stevie Wonder and Gladys Knight to release the Number One smash single, "That's What Friends Are For." The song benefited AIDS research and treatment.

Elton's strained relationship with Geffen resulted in the lackluster final album of original material for the label, *Leather Jackets*, in 1986. By the end of that year Elton had embarked on a series of large-scale concerts in Australia along with the Melbourne Symphony Orchestra. Though plagued by persistent voice troubles, Elton's forged ahead. A live recording was made from several of the shows in Sydney, Australia. The result was the June 1987 release, *Live in Australia with the Melbourne Symphony Orchestra*.

However, just after the taping of the album, Elton's voice could take no more. He underwent minor throat surgery to remove benign lesions from his vocal cords in January of 1987. To further complicate matters, The Sun, a

Elton married Renate Blauel, a German sound engineer, on Valentine's Day, 1984. The couple divorced in late 1988.

The 1984 Breaking Hearts Tour featured Elton wearing several different boater-style hats.

British tabloid, had published hurtful and untrue reports of Elton in a sex scandal with "rent" boys. The reports were proven false in court and Elton won. *The Sun* paid Elton a considerably large sum money, plus made a public apology.

Despite all the negative press, the *Live in Australia* album, his first with label MCA (with whom he'd signed a new contract), was well-received and enjoyed success with the release of a live version of "Candle in the Wind," which featured the Melbourne Symphony Orchestra backing him. The redone 1973 song reached number six on the U.S. charts by late 1987.

By 1988, Elton was showing signs of getting his personal life in order. While he hadn't conquered all the demons he was battling, he found the strength to shed many of his material excesses and even some of his emotional baggage. His new album, *Reg Strikes Back*, more than exemplified that. Its title refer-

Elton John fanzine, *The Fox* (1988).

enced the rebellion he felt, not only toward the British press, but to his father and all the repression young Reg had endured as a child. The album was a cleansing of sorts. Not only did one of its songs ("I Don't Wanna Go on with You Like That") ignite on the charts, reaching number two and sparking a fire within him and excitement among the public, but it represented a rebirth in his personal life, as well.

Hot on the heels of that triumph, Elton organized an auction through Sotheby's, selling off hundreds upon hundreds of items from his two decades as a rock star. Included were his record collections, stage costumes, jewelry and art. The auction raised more than $8 million. Reg had indeed struck back.

By August of 1989, Elton's final album of the decade, *Sleeping With the Past,* was released. Now seriously struggling with drug and alcohol addictions, Elton exhibited radical mood swings and anger during the album's concert tour. And while the album's promotion suffered due to problems with MCA, the album managed to become Elton's best-selling album of the 1980s.

Musically in the 1980s, Elton had seen highs and lows, but he wrapped the decade up on a high note. Personally, he was still battling his addictions, but at least was finally recognizing them. He knew he needed to seek help. And a new decade would bring forth a new man.❖

—Lori Sears

By the late '80s Elton was beginning to get his personal life on track again. Though he hadn't conquered all his demons as of yet, he still managed to find the strength to rid himself of many material excesses as well as emotional baggage.

Elton's Top 40 Hits of the 1980s*

"Little Jeannie" (1980)
"Sartorial Eloquence" (1980)
"Nobody Wins" (1981)
"Chloe" (1981)
"Blue Eyes" (1982)
"Empty Garden (Hey, Hey Johnny)" (1982)
"I'm Still Standing" (1983)
"Kiss the Bride" (1983)
"I Guess That's Why They Call it the Blues" (1983)
"In Neon" (1984)
'Sad Songs (Say so Much)" (1984)
"Who Wears These Shoes" (1984)
"Wrap Her Up" (1985)
"Nikita" (1986)
"Candle in the Wind" (live version) (1987)
"I Don't Wanna Go on With You Like That" (1988)
"A Word in Spanish" (1988)
"Mona Lisas and Mad Hatters, Part 2" (1988)
"Healing Hands" (1989)
"Sacrifice" (1989)

Elton donned a Donald Duck outfit for the "Your Song" encore at the free Central Park concert in 1980.

*According to Billboard Publications

Lost Tracks

As the 1970s came to a close, Elton found himself in an unusual position. His songwriting process always starts with the lyrics first. Now, for the first time, Elton had melodies that needed words. As a result of Bernie Taupin's working with Alice Cooper for his 1978 release *From the Inside,* Elton teamed up briefly with lyricist and jingle writer, Gary Osborne. Osborne provided Elton with a stream of lyrics that fit nicely into the melodies that had been stowed in Elton's head. The creative flow started with most of the Elton John album *A Single Man,* which featured one minor American hit "Part-Time Love" and the Top Ten Britain hit "Song For Guy." Several songs from this newly born partnership that didn't make the album have subsequently surfaced on the recently remastered *A Single Man* CD.

The next batch of songs Elton and Osborne wrote were scheduled for Elton's next release, 1980's *21 at 33*. Originally set to be a double album, *21 at 33* was pared down to a single album. Elton write the album was written with a couple of lyricists including Bernie Taupin, in highly anticipated return. The songs that didn't make the release were held over for the 1981's release *The Fox*. This is a significant release because it marked Elton's debut with a new record label, Geffen, after ten years with MCA. The resulting effort that Elton delivered to Geffen was not highly received, how-ever. Geffen rejected more than half of the songs on the album. New songs were written and recorded. So, with the songs not used on *21 at 33* and now *The Fox,* an abundance of songs was left over. The songs range from pseudo-reggae and country, instrumentals and ballads include the following:

- "Flintstone Boy"
- "Lovesick"
- "Strangers"
- "I Cry at Night"
- "Conquer the Sun"*
- "White Man Danger"*
- "Tortured"*
- "I Can't Get Over Getting Over Losing You"*
- "Lonely Boy"*
- "Dreamboat"*
- "Tactics"*
- "The Man Who Never Died"
- "The Retreat"
- "Fools in Fashion"*
- "Love So Cold"*
- "Hey Papa Legba"*
- "Take Me Down to the Ocean"*
- "Simple Man"*
- "Earn While You Learn"

(Note): *To date, only available on vinyl.—David Sigler

Elton's final album of the decade was *Sleeping with the Past*. By then he was seriously struggling with drug and alcohol problems during the album's concert tour. Despite Elton's addictions and ongoing legal troubles with his former label, MCA, this offering became his best-selling album of the eighties.

CHAPTER SEVEN

Elton in the 1990s
The Simple Life

Elton's third decade as a major recording artist launched the 1990s on a somber note. After years of struggling with his addictions (alcohol and drugs), he found himself on the side of sobriety for the first time. After checking in a rehab hospital near Chicago, Elton found the inner strength to get his priorities back in order and began anew once more. A collection of hits and rarities packaged in the popular trend of the times, a box set called *To Be Continued*...greeted his fans in October of 1990. This would set the stage for the decade as Elton reflected on where he has been and more importantly, where he was going.

As the 1980s came to a close with Elton still fighting his addictions, it was time to put things in order and gain some solid ground once again. With this new philoso-

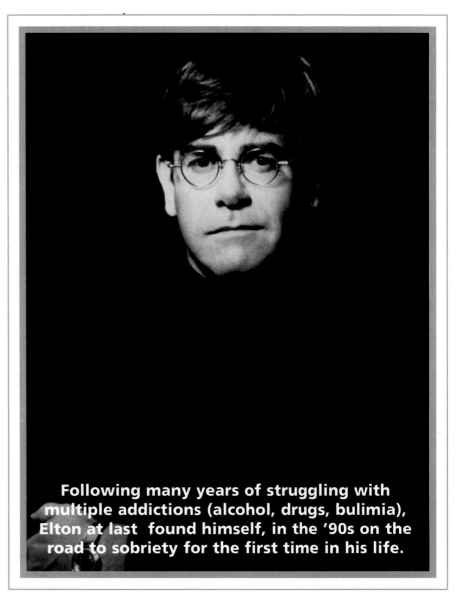

Following many years of struggling with multiple addictions (alcohol, drugs, bulimia), Elton at last found himself, in the '90s on the road to sobriety for the first time in his life.

Show Must Go On. Elton belts out Queen's hit "Show Must Go On" at the 1992 Concert for Life—a tribute to Freddie Mercury, who had succumbed to AIDS in 1991. Elton continued to perform this song throughout his 1992-93 concert tour and was said to offer prayers nightly to Freddie Mercury before taking the stage.

phy and outlook on life, he found new enthusiasm not only in just promoting his own albums and touring, but also causes that were near and dear to his heart. He read a story about a little boy named Ryan White who contracted the Aids virus from a blood transfusion. The courage Ryan and his family demonstrated made Elton realize how his priorities were out of order. This, in part, led to the creation of the Elton John AIDS Foundation. His organization had two main priorities: getting the medication in the hands of the HIV-positive people who needed it most and education efforts.

Plus, he began to donate royalties from his singles to the foundation. But AIDS wasn't the only cause Elton was fighting for. He became a regular at benefit concerts in general and on tribute albums often contributing specially written songs just for these releases.

But no other song raised more money than the tribute to Princess Diana after her sudden death in 1997. With new lyrics to one of her favorite songs, "Candle in the Wind," courtesy of Bernie Taupin once again, Elton sang at her funeral and released the song to raise money for her pet charities.

The 1997 *Billboard* tribute to Elton and Bernie.

$5.95 (U.S.), $6.95 (CAN.), £4.95 (U.K.), Y2,500 (JAPAN)

NEWSPAPER

Billboard

THE INTERNATIONAL NEWSWEEKLY OF MUSIC, VIDEO AND HOME ENTERTAINMENT • OCTOBER 4, 1997

A TRIBUTE
ELTON JOHN
30 YEARS OF MUSIC WITH BERNIE TAUPIN

THE BILLBOARD INTERVIEWS BY TIMOTHY WHITE AND CRAIG ROSEN

$5.95 US $6.95 CANADA

40 >

0 74808 02552 7

PHOTOGRAPH BY DAVID GAHR (1970)

(In loving memory of Diana, Princess of Wales), a "Candle in the Wind" 1997 song sheet.

The overwhelming success of "Candle in the Wind 1997" sent it right past the old chestnut "White Christmas" by Bing Crosby as the biggest selling single of all time. It is with such irony that Elton would lend his support to Diana since just weeks earlier before her death, she comforted Elton at the funeral of his friend, Gianni Versace. Versace, created a fashion image that Elton adored and Versace defined the image of Elton John in the fashion sense for the 1990s.

Elton and Bernie also released several albums in the nineties. They included *The One* (his first Top 10 album since 1976), the critically acclaimed *Made in England* and the reflective *The Big Picture*. But Elton most lucrative lyrical partnership of the decade came through the pen of Tim Rice, rather than of Bernie Taupin. Together, Elton and Tim wrote the massively popular Disney backed animated film *The Lion King* in 1994 and rewrote the Verdi's opera *Aida,* which became a hit on Broadway and won a Tony for "Best Original Musical Score" in 1999.

The 1990s concluded with Elton refreshed, energized, and heading into the new millennium with the optimism that he had in the early 1970s. His professional career was hitting new strides and his personal life was also intact. He and his partner, David Furnish, have been together for almost ten years and are still going strong. Elton's life had come full circle.❖

—David Sigler

Elton, who was inducted into the Rock and Roll Hall of Fame in 1994, promptly gave his trophy to Bernie Taupin. (At the time lyricists were not recognized by the organization, but they are now).

Piano men: Billy Joel and Elton John from the 1994 "Face-to-Face" Concert Tour. The concert opened with the two piano men facing each other with their grand pianos center stage. That year the stadium-only concert tour grossed over $47 million. Since then, Joel and John have paired up for more tours when time allows in their individual concert schedules.

Elton released the critically acclaimed *Made in England* album in 1995.

AIDA

The Musicals

The Lion King

Walt Disney was set to work on their new animated cartoon for release in summer of 1994. They selected Tim Rice as the lyricist (after he co-wrote the Disney smash Aladdin) and when he was asked whom would write melodies, Rice suggested Elton John. Much to Tim's delight, they accepted and a brand-new chapter in Elton's musical journey began. Elton and Tim had briefly worked together on an obscure track from Elton's 1982 album, *Jump Up!* The song, "Legal Boys" hinted at greater possibilities for them. The hit soundtrack for *The Lion King* was released in the summer of 1994 and spawned two Top 20 singles with the lead ballad from the film, "Can You Feel the Love Tonight?" peaking at number four and "Circle of Life" at number eighteen. The film became a huge hit for Disney and the soundtrack sold more than ten million copies making it the biggest-selling album of 1994. Elton's and Tim's work on *The Lion King* also earned two Grammy awards (one for Best Male Pop

Elaborate Lives: The Legend of Aida before the title was changed to simply *Aida*. (Pictured): Hank Stratton (Radames) and Heather Headley (Aida).

Performance for "Can You Feel the Love Tonight?" and one for Best Album for Children) and an Oscar for Best Song for "Can You Feel the Love Tonight?"

"Can You Feel the Love Tonight?" matched the style of many of Elton's best ballads. It had all of the enduring trademarks of an Elton John ballad. "Circle of Life," the other big hit, was also rich in the Elton sound, complete with African-style chanting that added to the aura of the song. Filling out the soundtrack was another song "I Just Can't Wait to Be King," sung by Elton. The rest was lifted from the movie with characters singing the songs and Hans Zimmer filling in the remainder with incidental instrumentals. The film was also adapted for Broadway as a musical in the fall of 1997 to even greater success as it became one of Broadway's biggest hits in years.

Aida

Elaborate Lives: The Legend of Aida was the original title of the Elton John and Tim Rice modern interpretation of the Verdi classic Aida. The story is about a woman named Aida, who is the daughter of the king of Nubia. Aida is taken as a slave by Radames, an Egyptian soldier. They fall in love despite Radames already being the chosen heir to the ailing Pharaoh because of his marrying the Pharaoh's daughter, Ammeris. This sets up the classic doomed love story rich in the Romeo and Juliet tradition. As is the struggle between the leaders of the countries and racial prejudice that ensues. *Aida* is a compelling and contemporary as today's newspapers.

It was this timelessness of the story that first drew Elton John and Tim Rice to the work on the project. "It is such a compelling tale," says Rice, who already collaborated with John on the huge hit *The Lion King*. "When you approach the creation of a new musical, the story is the most important thing, and we began with one of the great ones. If you can add a wonderful score, you have a really good chance of coming up with a great show."

Elton concurs: "It was appealingly dangerous. Verdi had already done it, so comparisons would be inevitable, and we could get critical bricks thrown at us. But I had never written anything directly for the stage, and I really wanted to give it a try."

The public actually never heard the first signs of the songwriter's attempt at producing a brand-new original musical. The unique plans included an all-star cast singing their interpretation of the songs. Some of these included duets with Elton as well. Janet Jackson, Sting, Lenny Kravitz, Heather Headley (who played Aida in the musical), and Tina Turner among many others contributed. What they heard was only a demo of the song they would sing. These were much sought after as Elton and band members Guy Babylon, Davey Johnstone, and Bob Birch arranged them.

Calling them "demos" is a bit of an understatement because these were songs the likes of Sting would have to listen to, to get a feel on the type of interpretation he would do. They were released on a promo Rocket Records CD and given to the participating stars.

However, the all-star album however, simply titled *Elton John and Tim Rice's Aida* was not a cast album in the tradition Broadway sense. The songs were not in running order of the show (as the show was still being rewritten at the time of the album's release) and music covered virtually all styles. The public seemed little interested in the project with the exception of the story's main love song, "Written in the Stars" a duet with LeAnn Rimes that became a minor hit. That shouldn't diminish the quality of the effort put forth. There are some stunning moments however. Sting's reggae "Another Pyramid," Shania Twain's earnest "Ammeris' Letter," Dru Hill's soul bearing "Enchantment Passing Through," and the expected rocker from none other than Lenny Kravitz on "Like Father, Like Son."

The opening night on Broadway was set for March 23, 2000 just two days prior to Elton's 52nd birthday. The reviews were generally good, considering Disney's backing which is not a favorite of the Broadway elite crowd. The *USA Today* touted "it's a highly entertaining, often moving diversion—and proof of the enduring power of a great story." And *The New York Times* praised Heather Headley as the lead in *Aida* yet cautioned "for those who live to follow the trajectories of rising stars, a trip to "Aida" may be worthwhile. Everyone else is advised to wait for the cartoon." Yet, another cynical swipe at Elton and Tim for *The Lion King*'s success. This wouldn't matter because *Aida* went on to become the Number Two attraction behind the still-successful *Lion King* on Broadway. Elton and Tim had conquered Broadway with a one, two punch! Much to their delight, *Aida* went on to win four Tony awards at the ceremonies held on June 4, 2000: Actress (Musical) Heather Headley; Original Musical Score; Scenic Designer and Lighting Designer.❖

The Elton John AIDS Foundation
Not "The Last Song"

In this the beginning of the 21st century there is still no cure for AIDS. Elton John, who has long been an active supporter of the fight against AIDS, established the Elton John AIDS Foundation in November of 1992. His single "The Last Song" (about a gay man who is dying of AIDS and makes peace with his estranged father) launched the organization, where Elton serves as its chairman. Many can relate to the horrific abandonment AIDS victims experience, and in particular Eltons sympathy for these oft-times neglected people.

"When I got sober and clean," Elton said, "I wanted to do something positive with my life. I'd been around a lot of people who had died, a lot of close friends who had died and I'd been around the Ryan White family in America. I'd been at Ryan's funeral and with him during the

Elton and pal Billie Jean King at the annual Smash Hits Tennis event. The big fundraiser for the EJAF made its debut in 1993, and witnessed Elton and King defeat Martina Navratilova and Bobby Riggs in a tennis match.

"Elton's Angel" crystal figurines by Lalique and a line of "Elton I" and "Elton II" Candles and home fragrances from Slatkin & Co. are some of the specially designed products made for the EJAF.

last week of his life. It was a point in my life that I was so unhappy."

The Elton John AIDS Foundation proved to be the perfect vehicle for the artist and former substance abuser, who now only wanted to find ways to heal and relieve the unbearable suffering. In 1990, he announced that the royalties from the single "Sacrifice" would be donated to four British AIDS charities.

Elton's inspiration to start his own charity organization came from Jeanne White, the mother of Ryan White, whose teenage life was shortened by AIDS. "Elton John was the first entertainer to step forward and fight against AIDS," Jeanne White once told a reporter. "I will always consider Elton my guardian angel."

It didn't take long for Elton to start auctioning off his personal art, jewelry, stage costumes and record collection, in an effort to help raise millions for his new foundation. In fact, at a national media event, he announced that all proceeds from his American and British singles from then on would go to the foundation—as they still do more than a decade later.

The Oscars, which are held in Hollywood are a prime fundraiser for the Elton John AIDS Foundation. Since 1993, Elton has hosted the annual Oscars viewing party where attendance is restricted to "A-list" type celebrities from film, music and sports. The celebrities' support often brings in a six-figure sum for the foundation.

Another big fundraiser is the annual *Smash Hits* tennis tournament with Elton and Billie Jean King playing in a match. The 1993 premiere event witnessed Elton and King defeat Martina Navratilova and Bobby Riggs in a doubles match. *Smash Hits* are held in Boston and Chicago and are usually accompanied with a special concert by Elton and an auction. Some memorable items auctioned over the years to raise money for the Foundation included the original lyrics sheet for "Skyline Pigeon" which sold for $22,000. Other successful drives have included sales of Elton's personal designer clothes, limited-edition Oliver Peoples fashion eye wear, Lalique crystal figurines, Slatkin & Co. Candles and home fragrances. Among other specially designed items for the Foundation include signature jewelry, limited logo watches, and a VISA Platinum Plus credit card.

Elton does not personally fund the organization that bears his name. However he did give it a financial nudge at its inception. Soon, thereafter EJAF has been supported solely by fund-raising efforts, public donations, and merchandise sold.

The Elton John AIDS Foundation has a very powerful but yet meaningful mission statement. Eliminating prejudice and educating society is no easy task. One's ideology towards people living with HIV/AIDS varies based on their education and sometimes on their religious conviction towards this epidemic.

With offices in Los Angeles and London, The Foundation is an international non-profit organization that provides funding for prevention education programs and direct patient-care services supporting men, women, young adults, children, infants, minorities and entire families living with HIV or AIDS. Since it's inception, The Foundation has incredibly distributed more than $22 million in grants worldwide. In North America over 80 percent of all money raised goes directly to patient care grants.

"I have lost so many of my friends to AIDS, and I know so many more living with HIV and AIDS," Elton has said. "It continues to be a personal battle for me." As chairman, it's Elton's job to oversee the funds and run a prudent operation to ensure that as much money as possible could go to AIDS victim care and prevention programs. Since the beginning, Elton has maintained low administration costs in an effort to ensure that a high percentage of funds raised reached the victims and AID related programs.

Over the years, the EJAF has also reached out internationally through its United Kingdom location and CARE. In 1993 CARE began its Living with AIDS Project. This project, partially funded by the EJAF, reached out to those living with HIV and AIDS in Asia, Africa and Latin America.

Most of Elton's charitable offerings are in support of his foundation, he does however, still participate in a few of his celebrity friends' causes, such as in 1997 he worked with Beatles producer George Martin to help aid victims in the Monseserrat volcano in the Caribbean. Environnmental causes are also a major concern for the musician. He has performed for Sting's Rainforest Foundation and Don Henley's Walden Project, not to mention that he often lends support to youth-oriented programs. Two of these special programs well worth noting are Andre Agassi's Boys & Girls Club of Las Vegas and Neil Young's Bridge School Benefit.

Today, the Elton John AIDS Foundation is one of the most successful charities in show business.❖

"I have lost so many of my friends to AIDS, and I know so many more living with HIV and AIDS. It continues to be a personal battle for me."

Elton meets the British press at one of his favorite fund-raisers for the EJAF—Out of the Closet. Fans travel from around the world for the chance to buy a piece of Elton— that is, his fabulous clothes at a reasonable price.

Elton's View on AIDS

In 1993 Elton John held a rare press conference in New York City at this hotel of choice, the St. Regis. There he spoke about what he was planning to do with the proceeds from the single "The Last Song." Elton's brief public announcement was to let the world know that profits from every single from thereafter would go to AIDS-related charities in America. Those charities included AIDS Project Los Angeles, Gay Men's Health Crisis, Pediatric AIDS Foundation, Project Open Hand in Atlanta and the Ryan White Foundation.

Previously, Elton's single "Sacrifice" had been released in Britain, plus with every United Kingdom release after that, proceeds went to various AIDS foundations. Now, Elton intended to do the same in America. This marked a profound time of deep introspection

Since 1993 Elton has donated proceeds from his singles to various AIDS charities worldwide.

for the entertainer. Few people outside his close circle realized just how deeply the death of Ryan White had affected him. He was also a witness to several friends tragically dying from AIDS as well, sometimes with no family or loved ones to comfort them in their painful dying moments. Elton—maybe for the first time in his life—felt comfortable telling the world he was gay. After all, who in the world would judge a man for his sexual preference, when wonderful human beings were suffering and dying of the terrible virus? Elton felt in his heart that devoting much of his time and money was what he needed to do to.

The following is an excerpt from the press conference, plus additional interview material obtained directly from Elton later that day.

What influenced you to include the United States in your fundraising efforts?

America means so much to me. I felt like I hadn't done enough in America. I thought it was time to get off my backside and do something in America. When my record company, MCA announced they wanted to do this, I was very pleased to go along within the idea. Every single I release in America will benefit AIDS research. While I am around this disease and thus fund-raising for AIDS, I find all kinds of people pulling through. We still have a long way to go.

What is the story behind single and video for "The Last Song"?

The song and video are about compassion.

76

The song and video speak for themselves. It is about understanding. I've seen so many situations like this myself, first hand. I've lost a lot of friends who were not able to make amends with people. This disease affects my life daily. The song is about the anger, the tragedy and the hope. I've seen a lot of people who have AIDS suffer greatly to their impending death. Yet, they face death with such courage and such dignity.

What was the inspiration behind the song?

I got the lyrics from Bernie. I was recording an album in Paris. The lyrics came shortly after Freddie Mercury died (Nov. 24th, 1991). I don't think it was specific. We both lost so many people in our lives. I thank Bernie for writing these words.

What was your primary incentive?

I just want to do everything humanly possible to help fight the disease. I have lost so many friends. I'm quite a compassionate man and I hate any fatal disease that takes people's lives, or a disease that causes people pain. I feel as passionately as anybody else about people's suffering. It's not just men dying, but women and children too.

Why did you choose Gus Van Sant to direct the video?

I wanted somebody gay to do the video. I approached a lot of people who were busy at the time. Gus was terrific and he did it very quickly. I like to work fast in a video, he did it in between other work and I finished it within two or three hours, he did the rest without me, which I thought was great.

What are your future personal goals?

I am keeping a balance between my personal and professional life. I just want to keep being as happy as I am now. I am very healthy, fit and trim, and now best of all, I am enjoying my life."❖

Elton John's Top 40 Hits of the 1990s*

"Sacrifice" (1990)
"Club at the End of the Street" (1990)
"Don't Let the Sun Go Down on Me" (1991)
"The One" (1992)
"The Last Song" (1992)
"Can You Feel the Love Tonight?" (1994)
"Circle of Life" (1994)
"Believe" (1995)
"Blessed" (1995)
"Candle in the Wind 1997" (1997)
"Something About the Way You Look Tonight" (1997)

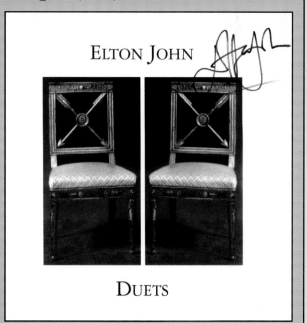

A *Duets* album slick signed by Elton John.

*According to Billboard Publications.

Early in Elton's career music critics were stunned by the musician's prolificacy. From 1970 to 1975, incredibly, Elton committed himself to writing, recording, and promoting no less than three albums of original songs every year.

CHAPTER EIGHT

The Big Picture
Reg Dwight's Piano Goes Pop: A Quick Guide to Elton the Musician

He's not just another pop stylist. Elton John has the great musicianship to back up his fame. He blows those three-cord rockers and one-hit-wonders out of the water. As a matter of fact, top-notch musicianship is probably to real key to Elton's longevity and long-term dedication of his fans.

"Some people aren't as driven as I am. Sitting around doing nothing doesn't appeal to me. The thing that saved my life was that I worked (in music). No matter what shape I was in, I still managed to perform and make records. I love to tour. The greatest thing in the world is to get onstage. Some nights you feel wonderful, and it just doesn't happen. Other nights you've got a headache, but it just goes away. It has always been an escape for me to be performing. I think most performers are seeking attention, seeking approval. The tragedy is when you don't know how to be off-stage." This is what Elton told *Vanity Fair* in the November 1997 issue, and undoubtedly it is a long way of saying something simple: Elton lives for his music even if sometimes, the other aspects of his life suffer.

Elton started tinkling the ivories at age three, and his parents were proud when at age eleven, he won a coveted slot at London's Royal Academy of Music—but when he dropped out of the school during finals week, his folks were less than happy. But at that point, Elton was on the road to becoming a pro, getting gigs playing with the well-known U.K. based group Bluesology from 1961 through 1967. He also sat in on countless sessions by top pop and rhythm and blues acts recording

In the studio recording tracks for *The Lion King* soundtrack.

in London in the mid-to-late-sixties. Those artists he did session work for were amazed at his ability to pick up a tune in minutes flat, and the way that the studio seemed like his second home. Elton had the patience to deal with indecisive artists, the countless retakes and the way he had to play a piano track as a producer or artist wanted it—with little room for creativity. But that last aspect of the studio led him to want his own solo career where he could decide how a song would be recorded and get to change the chart arrangements to his liking.

While in the studio, Elton picked up quite a bit of knowledge about what happens in the control booth, something that really impressed producer Gus Dudgeon down the road in his career. Elton always knew that music would be the love of his life. Even though his shopping sprees, money problems, romantic life and celebrity pals keep him in the news even more than his hits these days, music is still the top focus in his life and what he falls back on when he is feeling either emotionally or professionally blue. Elton recently said that his 2001 tour with Billy Joel was not based so much on the fact that it seemed like a good commercial match-up, but that both of them could yak for hours about collecting music, preferred piano makers and a mutual love for the process of writing music. EJ and BJ, as they jokingly referred to themselves, are also, interestingly enough, two of only a handful of pop musicians who can actually both read music and play by ear.

Elton's own music is often a tribute to those he has been influenced by. As a celebrity, he has gotten to duet with many of his idols and has custom-written songs that he thought would be right up their alley. One of his favorites is the now very rare Austrian single, "A Woman's Needs," performed with the late Tammy Wynette in 1994. As a musician, Elton loves everything from country to classical and back again, although his million-sellers have always been of the pop genre. His duets have been with the brightest stars from all aspects of music, including Aretha Franklin and even Eminem.

Pop artists who have influenced his song-writing include Leon Russell, the Beach Boys, the Beatles, Sting, Aretha Franklin, Dusty Springfield, Joni Mitchell, James Taylor, the Rolling Stones and the Band. His love of R&B from the earliest days of his career is still going strong, and his record collection (what he didn't sell at auctions) boosts Motown rarities that even Berry Gordy would like to get his hands on these days. Elton also loves to say he's got "stacks of Stax," the lesser known R&B label of the sixties that boasted the best of Southern soul. (Their most famous single and album were, respectively Otis Redding's "Dock of the Bay" and Isaac Hayes's *Hot Buttered Soul*, and are two of Elton's favorites, along the six-disc boxed set called *The Complete Stax Singles: 1959 To 1968.*)

Elton keeps his finger on the pulse of what is happening in the music world these days, and is never afraid to pay homage to his heroes. For instance, *Songs From The West Coast,* pays tribute to the California sounds popularized by The Beach Boys and Elton legend tells us that his earliest group, The Corvettes, was a tribute to the surf music movement back then. But his tributes are uniquely Elton—heavy on the keyboards and the camp. His piano pounding puts an indelible mark on any tribute or remake song he records (but hey, we didn't have to tell you that!), especially on songs that were originally guitar-heavy in their original versions.

As a musician, Elton is as proud of *Songs From the West Coast* as anything he has ever done. In fact he told MTV: "I don't think I could have made a better album at this stage in my life. When Bernie [Taupin] and I talked about doing it last year, we wanted do a much more simple album—piano, bass, drums, guitar, a little bit of organ and some orchestra. It's the same lineup as all the early albums. Because of technology, I've been diverted musically on the last few albums. There hasn't been a flow from track to track. On this album,

From 1968 to 1970 Elton was doing recording sessions for other well-known artists. He played backup, sang demo songs by other songwriters, and recorded sound-alike records of popular hits of the day. It was this type of work that gave him the experience he needed to decide how he would record his own songs in the studio and ultimately perform them live.

At 55, Elton John is still at the center of his profession. His record releases may not be as furiously paced as in his earlier career, but nonetheless, each new album is still an event.

there is. It starts with piano and finishes with piano. A lot of my vocals on this album don't have any echo on them. I'm used to having a lot. I was kind of shaky at first, like, 'Where's the echo?' They said, 'You don't need it.' I don't. I'm singing better than ever."

What new musicians does Elton hope to work with someday? Ones that he finds himself influenced by as a musician (as opposed to as just a fan). He recently admitted that he would love to work with Macy Gray because of her interesting vocal stylings that one journalist described last year as "Minnie Mouse through a cheese grater." He also has been influenced by the recent "ambient sound" that has been popularized by U.K. deejays and is supposedly thinking about a way to make it more palatable to mainstream audiences. He revealed to *MTV.com's* Rebecca Rankin, "I've been trying to do an ambient track, or a dance track, and that's not really what I do best. I'm a musician, I'm allowed to experiment. I'm not competing against myself, I'm competing against the influence of so many other people and trying to be like so many other people I can't be. You can only be like yourself." (If only Elton's piano's could talk—it knows him better than anyone else!)❖

Elton John the Performer

From the End of the World to Your Town...

If ever there was a consistent live performing musician, Elton John is it. He has given his fans every opportunity over the years to catch him on tour performing each and every one of the albums he has released, from his self-titled American debut album his latest, *Songs From the West Coast* and everything in between. Unlike other artists of his genre who only tour a few times a decade, thrives on performing live and has since his days with Bluesology. His exhaustive touring schedule (sometimes on the road for eighteen months straight) has made him an international music superstar, and having chart-topping albums in the Britain as well as other foreign countries like Japan, Germany, France, Italy, only adds to his performing appeal.

Elton's seemingly endless touring has produced many memorable moments in his thirty-plus year journey. A few choice events: In 1979 he became the first major Western artist to tour the Soviet Union; in 1984 performed in Sarajevo and 1986 saw the *Live In Australia* Tour co-starring the Melbourne Symphony Orchestra; in 1992, he toured with Eric Clapton and in 1994, he joined Billy Joel in the Face—to-Face Tour. Just ask a concert promoter from any country about the legendary performer's music and public appeal and you'll most likely hear: "People everywhere relate to Elton John's music and look forward to seeing him in concert."

Though Elton fills the stage with his presence alone, he is no stranger to musical collaborations. Through the years he has shared the stage with many key performers from Tina Turner to Billy Joel, Shania Twain, Sting, the Backstreet Boys and the controversial Eminem. Elton makes his musical preferences known through his collaborations with other artists, who gladly share the stage with him. He did receive some back-

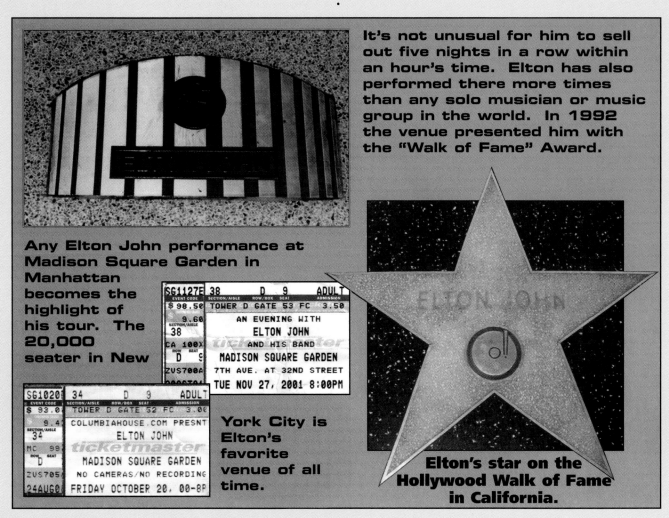

It's not unusual for him to sell out five nights in a row within an hour's time. Elton has also performed there more times than any solo musician or music group in the world. In 1992 the venue presented him with the "Walk of Fame" Award.

Any Elton John performance at Madison Square Garden in Manhattan becomes the highlight of his tour. The 20,000 seater in New York City is Elton's favorite venue of all time.

SG1127E 38 D 9 ADULT
EVENT CODE SECTION/AISLE ROW/BOX SEAT ADMISSION
$ 98.50 TOWER D GATE 53 FC 3.50
9.60
SECTION/AISLE
38
CA 100X
ROW SEAT
D 9
ZVS700A
AN EVENING WITH
ELTON JOHN
AND HIS BAND
MADISON SQUARE GARDEN
7TH AVE. AT 32ND STREET
TUE NOV 27, 2001 8:00PM

SG1020 34 D 9 ADULT
EVENT CODE SECTION/AISLE ROW/BOX SEAT ADMISSION
$ 93.0 TOWER D GATE 52 FC 3.00
9.4
SECTION/AISLE
34
MC 99
ROW SEAT
D
ZVS705
24AUG0
COLUMBIAHOUSE.COM PRESNT
ELTON JOHN
MADISON SQUARE GARDEN
NO CAMERAS/NO RECORDING
FRIDAY OCTOBER 20, 00-8P

Elton's star on the Hollywood Walk of Fame in California.

lash from the gay community for his Grammy collaboration with Eminem, but he quickly diffused the situation by making his case known to the *Los Angeles Times*: "As a gay artist, I'm asked by a lot of people, 'But what about the content of Eminem's music?' I think there is far more humor on the album than people think. It appeals to my English black sense of humor. When I put the album on the first time, I was in hysterics from laughing. We live in an age of political correctness where you can't say this or that. I honestly don't think people will go out and start beating and killing people because of this album."

In 1999, Elton John took to the stage with some of the biggest divas in showbiz on *VH1's Divas Live*. Elton accompanied the ladies—LeAnn Rimes, Faith Hill, Cher, and Tina Turner—for one night of pure musical bliss for the fans. It was raucous at times, but no different from any other night for Elton onstage. Those who have come to know Elton over the years as a live performer saw his true love for the art as well as his appreciation for the support of his many fans.

Elton John has been known for his "theatrical" performances onstage. His look of the 1970s was as flamboyant as ever with his wigs, feather boas, rhinestone-rimmed glasses and costumes bright enough to make you squint. He was larger than life up there onstage, performing all of the hits his fans wanted to hear, as well as some new tunes mixed in from whichever album he was touring for. He gained momentum in the 1970s as a live performer, as everyone was waiting for what he was going to wear next or what he would look like at each show. His theatrics were as anticipated as his singles.

The 1980s saw Elton changing with the times, while mixing up his styles a bit. His music became a bit more "pop" wearing the funkier prints, wild hats and accessorizing with the best of them. He was beginning to get away from the theatrics of his live performances, moving into a new era of pop culture that was dictated by MTV. Songs like "Sad Songs (Say so Much)" and "I Don't Wanna Go on with You Like That"

On stage in Las Vegas, 2000.

Lucy fan Caryl Simpson scored a front-row ticket for an Indianapolis concert, her first ever in 30 years, thanks to Elton's official website, which helps fans secure good seats.

An obliging Elton signs autographs for a lucky few in the front row during an encore.

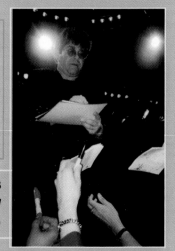

Elton performs in Central Park in 1976 as Kiki Dee's special guest. He joined her for what else but, "Don't Go Breaking My Heart."

Putting on the Hits: Since Elton has been performing live for more than three decades, music critics now cite his performances as "hit shows." Incredibly, since 1970 Elton John has had at least one song every year in the Top 40.

and "I'm Still Standing" were hitting the airwaves, and Elton was proving that he was an artist that could not only compete with the times, but transcend with the changes. He kept in mind his fans' developing musical interests and styles, and never shied away from anything new.

In the 1990s, Elton John evolved into his musical-icon status, dropping the stage theatrics and wild clothes (for the most part) and becoming more involved in social issues including the Rainforest Foundation with Sting and Trudie Styler. He has performed in many benefit concerts for the foundation with other artists that have traditionally been super shows.

The eighties saw Elton changing with the times. He was one music artist that proved he could face the changes without losing sight of his fans' growing musical interests.

He also took on a more traditional role when it came to fashion, donning more conservative Versace and Armani suits and putting the rhinestone-rimmed glasses back in their cases.

His styles and social focus may have changed over the years, as did his live performances. But his performances never suffered through the changes. Rather, they were enhanced. Elton still has the same raw energy onstage that he had twenty years ago and taking a look at his audience will confirm that. It is not unusual to see three generations of fans at a sold-out Elton show.

Elton has had so many hits over the years that his live

performances can only be classified as "hits shows." He pulls out all of fan favorites for the shows—not too a difficult task considering he's charted at least one song in the Top 40 every year since 1970. He, of course does mix in some new music, but for the most part, his set lists are similar as well as his encore performances. Concert-goers are treated to two of his all-time greatest hits, "Your Song," which he plays at each and every show and (the original) "Candle in the Wind." A set list (songs performed) from a 2001 show included "Your Song," "Skyline Pigeon," "The Greatest Discovery," "Border Song," "Daniel," "Harmony," "Honky Cat," "Rocket Man," "Tiny Dancer," "Someday Out of the Blue," "Philadelphia Freedom," "Blessed," "Sorry Seems to be the Hardest Word," "I Guess That's Why They Call it The Blues," "Ticking," "Carla/Etude," "Tonight," "Burn Down the Mission," "The One," "Blue Eyes," "Empty Garden," "Take Me to the Pilot," "Don't Let The Sun Go Down on Me," "Crocodile Rock." The first encore consisted of "Can You Feel the Love Tonight?" and the second encore featured "Bennie and the Jets," and "Candle in the Wind."

Elton's tribute song to Princess Diana was a long-standing chart-topper, one that touched millions of admires of both Elton and the late Princess Diana. Millions of people worldwide appreciated the sentiment and sincerity of the song, once again sealing that bond between Elton and his legion of admirers. Such acts have proven that Elton is a performer for the people, and that makes him seem more accessible to the fans, more "down to earth." Elton's concert reviews are filled with quotes like, "He had the audience in the palm of his hand," "His energy should be bottled and sold," and "The audience didn't know what to expect next."

Elton has a major online presence, too with an official site as well as scores of fan sites where fans keep running tallies of concerts they attended and trade notes on message boards about what they thought of the last show they saw. Many of the more popular music/entertainment sites keep a concert file on Elton where a list of every gig Elton John ever performed is kept along with a list of songs performed at the gig and first-hand accounts and reviews from fans. Because fan response to Elton's live performances is so overwhelming, the Web is really offering the best place to swap stories about past and upcoming shows.

There's no question that Elton John's music reaches all generations of people. His credibility as a live performer is one of his strongest assets—and without a doubt will be for years to come.❖

Taking flamboyance to a higher plateau, circa mid-'70s.

"Elton is a performer for the people, and that makes him seem more accessible to the fans, more down to earth."

CHAPTER NINE

For The Record

Stripped of all the wild eyeglasses, feather boas, Donald Duck outfits, Versace suits, powerful concert appearances, charitable work, headline-making scandals, record-breaking sales figures and everything else that has come to define the entire entertainment package known as "Elton John," it is his musical legacy that will ultimately carve his permanent place in history.

Though unquestionably popular with the public, Elton John's vast catalog of music has often withstood critical arrows, dismissal, or worse, complete neglect. Any artist with a career than spans more than four decades is bound to experience peaks and valleys in creative output, and positive and negative reactions to it throughout the years. And Elton John has certainly gone in and out, and in and out, and in and out of fashion since he burst on the music scene in a real way in 1970 with his self-titled, debut album.

Elton John began his career as a critics' darling, with a sound that was bold but pop-based, unashamedly putting the piano back into rock 'n' roll as a lead instrument for the first time since pioneers including Little Richard, Fats Domino and Jerry Lee Lewis did it in the 1950s. His early albums mixed orchestral arrangements, straight rock, moving ballads, and obvious influences of The Beatles, Bob Dylan, the Band, The Beach Boys and other rock visionaries that impressed critics and initially made him a hip, "must-hear" FM radio, alternative artist rather than an AM radio, Top 40 mainstream teenybopper.

After this supposed anointing, rock critics felt betrayed when, in 1972, he released his commercially-targeted album *Honky Chateau*. After a series of solid, but small-selling albums, this record included the huge hit singles "Rocket Man" and "Honky Cat," and suddenly Elton John became a glittery pop star that sold millions of records, rather than the underground rock artist they wanted him to be and remain. And when his live concerts got more theatrical and his onstage costumes and eyeglasses more outrageous, he was viewed as a sellout—rock 'n' roll's Liberace instead of its new Leon Russell.

His career has gone through many phases: acclaim in the seventies, indifference in the eighties, rediscovery in the nineties; and growing, overdue respect as the new century begins. Elton's music has received sustained adulation by the public and continued critical questioning; somewhere between these two divergent opinions is where Elton John's true musical legacy lies.

In this chapter, the attempt is to unearth that misunderstood middle ground, and help better define his legacy. This chapter will strive to explain Elton John's canon for each of his original studio albums (not the various greatest hits compilations, which simply repackage his hits in as many commercially-viable configurations as possible) in terms of their individual historical relevance, influence, importance and acceptance at the time and how well they each have battled against the test of time. Also included here are original live recordings.

Some diehard fans believe Elton John has never written a bad song. Some hardened, biased journalists believe he has never written a significant one. The truth is, he has written both, and countless songs that fall into several other extreme categories. The following pages examine these extremes and aim to shed a new light, understanding and appreciation of Elton John, his music, his influence and his legacy.

Elton John's music may not be as important as Dylan's, influential as the Beatles, defining as the Rolling Stones, loud and ambitious as the Who's, as groundbreaking and quiet as the Beach Boys', as desperate and blue collar as Bruce Springsteen's, as derivative and rude as the Sex Pistols', as spiritually inspiring as U2's, or as angst-ridden as Nirvana's. Instead, Elton John's music includes all those classic rock traits and perhaps the one that's most important and its defining aspect: Elton John's music is damn entertaining.

So, read on. Listen to the music and decide for yourself.

▲ ● ▲ ● ▲ ● ▲ ● ▲ ● ▲ ● ▲ ● ▲ ● ▲ ● ▲ ● ▲

ELTON JOHN

Originally released on MCA, April 1970
Defining—that is the best way to describe the self-titled *Elton John*, officially Elton's second album, but America's first real dose of the curious superstar-in-waiting. It was dubbed "the black album," and its unique series of enigmatic songs may have sounded different from the hit-single-driven days of the early seventies, but was still contemporary and fresh.

Released in April 1970 in Britain and a few months later in the states, *Elton John* was an intriguing series of contradictions worthy of

musical analysis. Dominated by dramatic orchestrations, stirring ballads, raw but finely-produced rockers and multi-layered homages to the past and present, *Elton John* sounds buoyantly rich 31 years later. More important, it stands as perhaps Elton's most purely enduring and influential work evidenced by how Elton continues to spice his concerts with many of this album's varied repertoire.

Elton John was far from a singular triumph. There are others were vital to the overall effect thrust on the listener. So who was the real star here? From the first strains of the evergreen "Your Song" to the dynamic coda "The King Must Die," the album's crisp production was unmistakable. Producer Gus Dudgeon captivatingly captured the breadth of Elton John's talent by supplying each song with agreeable accents that punctuated but never overshadowed. The influence of Brian Wilson and *Pet Sounds* played a large part in Elton's songwriting and Dudgeon's production during Elton's prolific period from 1970 to 1975, and the varying instruments and musical passages here certainly owe a debt to the eternal Beach Boy. To get a true appreciation for Dudgeon's immeasurable contribution in defining an Elton John sound, just compare *Elton John* to *Empty Sky,* released less than a year earlier. Its producer, Steve Brown, introduced Elton John in 1969; Gus Dudgeon presented Elton John in 1970.

Dudgeon took this somewhat naive, meandering monotone musician/singer and completely transformed him into a focused, confident artist capable of charismatic nuances. Dudgeon's refining would be hollow, though, without Paul Buckmaster's swirling, encompassing orchestral arrangements that are the album's most defining traits.

Dudgeon's masterstroke was the ease with which he consistently incorporated Buckmaster's bursts of lushly blended strings, succeeding in synergizing them with rock to give *Elton John* a distinct, rough edge. "Take Me to the Pilot" and its multiple personalities are proof of this accomplishment.

While a casual listen could deem songs like the longing "First Episode at Hienton" or "Sixty Years On," with is eerie *Dark Shadows/Twilight Zone* like arrangement, as simply classical intrusions, a closer ear hears how they feature strings with tasteful power. Then there was Taupin. He, too, took his talent to a higher level. *Empty Sky* drifted to almost supernatural destinations, but here Taupin's lyrics were more grounded and universal. He succinctly capsulized love in "Your Song" which is timeless; he addressed social ills without getting preachy on "Border Song," tapped into his rural roots on "No Shoestrings on Louise," tenderly evoked brotherly love in "The Greatest Discovery" and still got esoteric, but now with flair on "Take Me to the Pilot." And finally, there was Elton. Ultimately, this was his star turn. His melodies immediately emote and consume, effortlessly seducing the listener.

But the most magnetic factor in the album's success was his singing. His voice resonated whether caressing a ballad, attacking a rocker, evoking a message or even affectionately aping idols like Mick Jagger and the Band.

This album holds the DNA of Elton's musical individuality and continuing legacy. *Elton John* is Elton John.

▲ ● ▲ ● ▲ ● ▲ ● ▲ ● ▲ ● ▲ ● ▲ ● ▲ ● ▲ ● ▲

TUMBLEWEED CONNECTION

Originally released on MCA, October 1970

Tumbleweed Connection was the fulfillment of the hype. Though many heard the stories of Elton's wild and raucous live rock shows, on record up to this point, a more sedate performer was highlighted. But with the release of *Tumbleweed Connection* in October 1970, practically on the heels of his lush debut, that image was quickly dispelled.

Tumbleweed's aggressive mix of bashful ballads like "Love Song," folk/rock novellas including "Ballad of a Well-Known Gun" and

"Son of Your Father," Old South eulogies like "My Father's Gun," the stark and lonely "Talking Old Soldiers" and the unrepenting rustic rock of "Burn Down the Mission" were all corralled under Bernie Taupin's lyrical homage to America's history, old-time traditions and folklore. It was a quasi-concept album that allowed Elton's music to abruptly change forward.

This progression was possible mainly because of the focused lyrical content of Taupin's tales, which admittedly owed a great debt to the likes of Bob Dylan and the passionate, spiritual travels of the Band on its watershed album, *Music from the Big Pink*. Though Taupin based his fables on a passed American era and his own rural upbringing, the references, themes and environment he created are real and yet innocently legend affirming. Ironically, this vinyl valentine to America's rural history was written by Taupin before he ever stepped foot on U.S. soil. It may explain the glorified reverence the songs offer in tribute to the American West and Civil War days.

Taupin's words dictated the sound of this album, with descriptive lines. Elton advanced vocally, too, assuming varied roles of specific characters rather than signing as an undefined narrator. While the songs invited us into this rustic time machine, producer Gus Dudgeon was the real tour guide, giving the album instant charisma, personality and texture. He enabled the listener to be enveloped by each song, helping us feel the dry dust on our lips, the hot sun on our necks, the softness of the cool grass and the rage and uncertainty that ran through Taupin's vignettes. And without question, the spirit of Robbie Robertson reigned.

The appearance of the band Hookfoot, featuring old pals Caleb Quaye and Roger Pope, contributed heavily to the album's overall rock/folk sound and no doubt was also responsible for some of the confidence Elton displayed throughout.

Tumbleweed Connection had no hit singles, but contained some of Elton's best songs.

"Come Down in Time" with its expressive vocal is as good as any mystic love song; "Country Comfort" effortlessly rollicks and sways; "Where to Now, St. Peter?" with its dashes of pyschedelia and religious ambiguity is a testing ride; "Amoreena" Taupin's first outright horny makeout song; and "Burn Down the Mission," with its sweeping changes of mood and strength, accelerated by Paul Buckmaster's driving backing arrangements and Elton's excited piano pounding, gloriously ends the album, cementing Elton's reputation as rock's first legitimate piano man since Jerry Lee Lewis.

The greatness of most albums is often determined by a lack of wasted songs. *Tumbleweed Connection* doesn't waste any.

▲ ● ▲ ● ▲ ● ▲ ● ▲ ● ▲ ● ▲ ● ▲ ● ▲ ● ▲ ● ▲ ● ▲

11-17-70

Originally released on MCA, April 1971

After his stunning live American debut at Los Angeles's Troubadour club in August 1970, and his captivating self-titled album, Elton John was becoming Britain's next special import. In fact, by mid-1971 Elton John had officially released four albums. He was rock's "Next Big Thing."

The rough and live *11-17-70*, officially released in April 1971, was a strategic move by MCA Records to fight off bootleg recordings. There was no higher artistic cause at the time, however, more than thirty years later, this early performance is historic in a sense, offering an insightful, exciting glimpse into Elton's talents, passion and stage presence at the outset of his career (as evidenced by the vague silhouette of Elton standing and frantically attacking the piano on the album cover).

The album was taped at the WABC studios in New York on November 17, 1970, (thus the title), for a live radio broadcast. Ironically, the program was engineered by another future pop music legend, noted producer Phil Ramone, known best for his more than 10 years of hitmaking with Billy Joel, and who would later work on Elton's *Aida* "all-star" album in 1998 and the live album, *One Night Only* in 2000.

The hundred or so people lucky enough to be in the studio in 1970 and those listening (and taping at home) heard a new brand of rock star. And this version of Elton John was far removed from the semi somber sounding Brit on this then small body of recorded work. The album's most compelling jolts come from the genuine sense of enthusiasm in his singing and playing and it showcased the fine-tuned talents of drummer Nigel Olsson and bassist Dee Murray, who together with Elton formed a classic rock power trio—able to explode in a flurry of hard driving rock at one moment and tone it down and deliver an impassioned ballad the next.

This package, which includes wildly energetic performances of stirring John-Taupin originals such as "Take Me to the Pilot," "Sixty Years On," "Bad Side of the Moon" and "Burn Down the Mission" and a few well-chosen covers, including The Rolling Stones' "Honky Tonk Woman" and The Beatles' "Get Back," (Elton also did six other songs in the set not included on the original release) is the closest re-creation fans have a Elton's triumphant Troubadour stand.

In those days of guitar dominance, Elton showed the piano could be the center of the sound. The sixties put the piano on the back burner after the instrument helped launch rock 'n' roll in the fifties, but here, just as the seventies began, this new upstart was proving a thumping, piano pounding could rival any screeching guitar solo.

From the opening crashing chords of "Take Me to the Pilot" to the final burst of "Get Back," Elton proved he's not only a skilled, emotional performer, but has a special musical charisma that is able to please a crowed of any size. He would build on this innate gift to become one of the most popular and respected live performers in entertainment history. And on *11-17-70* we are offered a rare opportunity—hearing the raw potential of a future legend.

▲ ● ▲ ● ▲ ● ▲ ● ▲ ● ▲ ● ▲ ● ▲ ● ▲ ● ▲ ● ▲ ● ▲

FRIENDS

Originally released on Paramount, May 1971

In 1971, Hollywood looked to the newly anointed pop songwriting team of Elton John and Bernie Taupin to add some of their stylings to a low budget, *Love Story* knock-off titled *Friends*. And although the songs barely appear in this sappy Lewis Gilbert project and weren't really written "for" the film in any strict sense—Taupin has admitted not even reading the entire movie script—the misguided soundtrack to *Friends* is a difficult but occasionally worthwhile listening experience.

Released just a month after *11-17-70*, the "album" is a collection of John-Taupin originals, interspersed with some sugary orchestral arrangements and movie background filler by Paul Buckmaster. As a whole, it does not hold up as either a soundtrack or an official album release, but when selectively dissected, does reveal some faint foreshadowing of the diversity of lyric content, tempo, mood and melody that would establish Elton and Taupin among the most popular and successful songwriters of the twentieth century.

Most longtime fans probably bought *Friends* in the vinyl cut-out bin, despite its amateurish and gaudy pink cover, complete with a shamefully derivative illustration of two young lovers who bear a striking resemblance to Ryan O'Neal and Ali MacGraw during the *Love Story* days. It still managed to reach gold record status.

Packaging faux pas aside, *Friends* does have its share of genuinely worthy moments. The title cut is a catchy "Up with People" urging for worldwide companionship, a thin attempt at an anthem for the disillusioned and still-clinging flower children of the early seventies. The song "Friends" does manage to overcome its naivete with a grand chorus and impassioned vocal. "Honey Roll" is an inspired gospel/rock revival in which Taupin allows Elton to declare he is "Mr. Funky" and prove it with a rollicking piano and some soulful backing vocals. "Can I Put You On?" boasts tasty twangy guitar bits and effects, and bounces with the funk/rock that dominated the Band influenced *Tumbleweed Connection*, but still lacks the maturity to endure.

Buckmaster, who so masterfully injected powerful and passionate orchestral passages on the *Elton John* album, is relegated to writing syrupy New Age-like love scene filler, and the insipid recitation during "I Meant to Do My Work Today" is now just good high camp.

But *Friends* does redeem itself almost solely for the brief ode "Seasons Reprise." It is the sweetest and shortest love song in the John-Taupin canon, one that deserves a high rank. It contains some of Taupin's most touching lines, capturing young, blooming love at its first glance. In fact, this song was used in an episode of the coming-of-age television series, *The Wonder Years*, to signal the blossoming "love" between the show's two young characters, Kevin and Winnie. It proves how, perhaps, if given the correct source material, maybe these songs could have added to a story's development.

Friends is one just for the completists, however, "Seasons" is an overlooked classic that Elton should resurrect in concert so more people can become appreciate one of the best songs that got away.

▲ ● ▲ ● ▲ ● ▲ ● ▲ ● ▲ ● ▲ ● ▲ ● ▲ ● ▲ ● ▲ ● ▲

MADMAN ACROSS THE WATER

Originally released on MCA, November 1971

Madman Across the Water is not really Elton John's fourth album. It is Reg Dwight's last. His stage name may have been Elton John (legally changed soon after this album's release), but his music, outlook and life were still distinctly Reginald Kenneth Dwight. *Madman*'s commanding, even at times intimidating songs, signal the close of Reg Dwight's music, appearance, image, lifestyle and fame. The entire album—sound, lyrics and mood—is the introverted Reg Dwight's final, virgin-like effort before losing his innocence to the flamboyant Elton John and a level of stratospheric superstardom that would change his music and life forever.

The dreamy, frozen-in-time sincerity of "Tiny Dancer" kicks off the album, and a closer listen to its lyrics uncovers a restlessness that begins to grow deeper and more angry as the album's nine songs march ahead. Most of the stories Taupin tells are of beaten anti-heroes—a lonely, bitter miser ("Levon"); a down-trodden homeless man ("Razor Face"); a paranoid mental patient ("Madman Across the Water," a defeated Native American ("Indian Sunset"); a bored, complaining rock 'n' roller ("Holiday Inn"), a frustrated chain gang prisoner ("Rotten Peaches"); a revenge-filled public figure ("All the Nasties") and a melancholy spirit ("Goodbye"). Hardly the subject matter of most top-ten hits.

Still, the songs' lyrical tone and the melodies they inspire create a package that, after almost thirty years not only retains its strength, but feels more poignant. These songs are written from a realistic, crusted first-hand experience of life, love, pain and nomadic rock 'n' roll lifestyle. Heightened once again by Paul Buckmaster's graceful yet surging orchestral arrangements, dominating and driving many of the melodies, the music on *Madman* especially soars and gently rocks against a dark background.

The songs—even the ballads—and the production attack with directed aggression, forcing the listener to take immediate notice. Producer Gus Dudgeon scatters the sound with touches of unique sounds, instruments, chords or breaks that give each song a distinct personality and take it to thrilling unexplored rock territories. In addition to many of the musicians who appeared on previous Elton efforts, this is the first major contribution of

such later stalwarts as Davey Johnstone (whose mandolin and sitar playing on "Rotten Peaches" probably got his permanent gig) and percussionist Ray Cooper.

Elton reportedly viewed *Madman* as a make-or-break album for his career. A sense of restlessness is evident. In fact, if the album has one flaw, it's that it sounds like it's trying too hard to sound too big, too impressive or too perfect.

Songs like "Tiny Dancer," "Levon" and "Rotten Peaches," especially, though vocally exploding with patches of the unbound emotion in their lyrics and musical arrangements, to punctuated crescendos, still sound a bit forced. It's as if Elton's afraid to let loose, the Reg Dwight in him still holding him back from losing total control. In the ensuing years in concert, however, Elton loosened the reigns and has given new zest to many songs from *Madman*, which has helped propel this album to new appreciation.

Director Cameron Crowe's bittersweet placement of "Tiny Dancer" in his 2001 film *Almost Famous* crystallized its place in pop culture. *Madman* stands as an encompassing, charismatic chapter in Elton's songbook, filled with classic passages and a full, acoustic and orchestral sound Elton John didn't return to until Reg again struck back in 1995 with *Made in England*.

▲ ● ● ● ● ● ● ● ● ● ● ● ● ● ● ● ● ● ● ▲

HONKY CHATEAU

Originally released on MCA, May 1972

Between 1970 and 1972, the forces of Elton's professional competitiveness and a record company convinced it had a potential star in its hands resulted in a flurry of album releases. This saturation strategy succeeded in generating significant commercial commotion. However, the end goal of turning Elton John into a motivated, supersonic king of the scene still proved elusive.

On vinyl, Elton had distinguished himself

to listening audiences as an innovative, somewhat somber musician/singer/songwriter. Onstage, though, live audiences were treated to an entirely different performer. It was the "live" Elton John who needed to emerge to a larger record-buying, radio-listening public. A shift was in order.

Therefore, after *Madman Across the Water*'s commercial disappointment and its continuance of the orchestral sound first introduced on the *Elton John* album, Elton's braintrust correctly decided to transfer his flashy, exuberant stage persona and bank sound to vinyl. The album was written quickly (in about five days) in the assembly-line style of the early John-Taupin days. It was recorded within the inspirational, home-like feel of France's Chateau d'Hierouville. It was a number-one album masterstroke. It was *Honky Chateau*.

Released in May 1972, *Honky Chateau* brought an edgy, cogent, communal-band feel to Elton's recorded music. A band's chemistry and trust come from playing live without a safety net. That intangible musical charisma, along with Elton's rock-n-roll-loving—personality, emerged on the album's ten songs, which alternated between jumpy pop tunes ("Honky Cat," "I Think I'm Going to Kill Myself"), mid-tempo funk grooves ("mellow," Salvation," "Slave," "Susie (Dramas)"), stark ballads ("Rocket Man," "Mona Lisas and Mad Hatters") and all out rockers ("Amy," "Hercules"). Launched by the eerie, timeless suspension of "Rocket Man" and followed by the radio-ready pouncing of "Honky Cat," *Honky Chateau* was the fulfillment of the promise. Almost overnight, the uniqueness of the John-Taupin collaboration—music, voice, lyrics and production—captured a huge audience.

More than twenty-three years later, to their credit, these songs retain their initial freshness. *Honky Chateau* also challenges the listener almost three decades later. It's easy to take for granted the special moments of some of its often-heard hits. A closer listen to "Rocket Man" not only yields the obvious— Elton's drop-dead vocal and Johnstone's

galactic guitar riffs—but Johnstone's textured acoustic strums and, most notably, Dee Murray's expressive bass lines (which carry their weight throughout the entire album and are among its overall highlights).

In the album's first track, "Honky Cat," just a lightweight pop tune? Not a chance! Elton's piano playing is among his best. The well-placed bursts of horns explode. And Taupin's lyrics of discarding his country roots are deeper than the jaunty melody sometimes allows to explore. Other standouts help to further the album's loose feel: "Mellow" with its appropriate tempo; "I Think I'm Going to Kill Myself," the ode to teenage lust; "Amy," which was probably Elton's hardest rocker to date; and the fifties charge of "Hercules."

Perhaps what's most responsible for the album's overall success is the rhythm section of Murray and Olsson. They stand out on this album, which is filled with impressive musical contributions (including tasty violin strokes from the respected Jean-Luc Ponty). Bass players are easily overlooked by the average listener, but you owe it to yourselves to listen for Murray's other great moments on selections such as "Salvation" and "Slave." Olsson not only keeps the beat, but adds the needed muscle throughout. If you haven't visited *Honky Chateau* lately, make a reservation soon.

▲●▲●▲●▲●▲●▲●▲●▲●▲●▲●▲

DON'T SHOOT ME, I'M ONLY THE PIANO PLAYER

(Originally released on MCA, January 1973)

By 1973, on the heels (mostly the three-to four-inch variety) of two single smashes ("Rocket Man" and "Honky Cat"), Reg Dwight finally reached the professional pinnacle he had aspired to after days of playing piano for a few pounds in Pinner, banging away in the background of Bluesology, and toiling with Taupin in Northwood Hills hoping for that "I wanna be a teenage idol" break.

Don't Shoot Me, I'm Only the Piano Player pushed the Elton evolution along. Some may argue "de-evolution," in that the album's pop feel was an overt break from Elton's previously complex sound. *Don't Shoot Me* was indeed a musical shift, but a necessary one that reflected Elton's newfound pop star fame and mass acceptance. As negative as that may sound, *Don't Shoot Me* (named in homage to Groucho Marx, with whom Elton once traded this barb) was no throw-away release. Though less spectacular in scope and admittedly more musically derivative than previous efforts, this album was a step forward. Perhaps not a giant step for "Eltonkind," but a positive step, nonetheless. It found Elton's songwriting more crisp, his vocals more adventurous and Taupin's lyrics more suited to pop melodies rather than a textbook of existential free association or extended story telling. Most important, it marked producer Gus Dudgeon's initial sculpting of the masterful meshing of melody, lyric and soaring harmonic background vocals that would become "the Elton John sound."

Elton, an admitted Beach Boys disciple, had to be pleased with the larger, diverse and transcending *Pet Sounds* influence that Dudgeon injected into *Don't Shoot Me*, a feel Dudgeon perfected one album later, on *Goodbye Yellow Brick Road*. An attentive ear will appreciate *Don't Shoot Me* for far more than just "the album that has 'Daniel' and 'Crocodile Rock' on it." Those two songs (pop at its purest) are among Elton's most populist favorites and still can convey their initial excitement almost thirty years later. But there are several overlooked gems on this collection.

For instance, there are the back-to-back retro rockers, "Teacher I Need You" and "Elderberry Wine." Taupin's lyrics on both are clever and carefree. And Elton evokes the devilish spirit of Jerry Lee Lewis with his keyboard bravado. But more impressive are several respected album tracks, including "Blues for Baby and Me," which travels on a folksy, California groove thanks to Johnstone's sitar

and Paul Buckmaster's inviting strings; "Have Mercy on the Criminal," a breakthrough "stunner" with Buckmaster's grippingly tense arrangement and Elton's desperate vocal rendering; and "Texan Love Song," which perfectly re-creates a redneck country yearn, complete with vintage Elton twang. The best, though, is the album's overlooked and relatively under-appreciated, bittersweet closer, "High-Flying Bird." The purest Brian Wilson-inspired song Elton and Taupin ever wrote— lyrically and melodically— it emotionally drips with words of melancholy and hope in true Taupin style. Elton creates a musical bed that enables the song to rest its wings and gradually glide to tingling heights. His vocal—aching and captivating—is among his best on record anywhere, and the backing vocals of Dee Murray, Nigel Olsson and Johnstone complete this enchanting tribute to Wilson's legacy of mixing haunting, painful images amid a joyful, redemptive melody.

Don't Shoot Me is the most commercial album Elton had recorded up to this point, but somewhere in the process commerce gave way to creativity, and Elton and the gang produced an album that never stops sneaking up on you.

GOODBYE YELLOW BRICK ROAD

Originally released on MCA, October 1973

Goodbye Yellow Brick Road. That's it, next subject. The simple mention of the title conveys more than anyone else can say about it. What more can be added to the twenty-eight years of previous descriptions and emotions tied, for instance, to the eerie majesty and unbridled energy that drives its kick-off epic song, "Funeral for a Friend/Love Lies Bleeding"? And is there any new reason to look for any undiscovered nuances in "Candle in the Wind"? Especially now that it has taken on an almost reverential mystique as the funeral eulogy to Princess Diana. Doesn't every Elton fan worth his or her salt already realize that the brief but ethereal "Harmony" still ranks among the best John-Taupin compositions? Do you really need someone to point out the sleepy, seaside charm of "Sweet Painted Lady"?

Goodbye Yellow Brick Road was an album of its time, as well as a signpost of the future. Its sprawling musical landscape indulged in a wide variety of genres and broke many rules of the day in terms of song length, subject matter and its inherent sense of pop importance. It began with an eleven minute, eight second sonic smorgasbord ("Funeral For a Friend/Love Lies Bleeding") and ended with a two-minute, forty-five second dirge of despair ("Harmony") that somehow soared with hope enough to make Brian Wilson proud. In between, Elton and Taupin squeezed in 15 additional songs that define their masterpiece.

From its substantial and elaborate packaging—two albums, tri-fold album sleeve, each song's lyrics personified by an accompanying color sketch inside and classic album cover art that connoted a futuristic nostalgia and melancholy that reflected the collection's reflective content—to its equally prodigious production, *Goodbye Yellow Brick Road* demanded to be noticed. It felt, looked and sounded important. And the music it contained lived up to this declaration.

At times, running order unwittingly doubled for a greatest hits compilation, but periodic blasts of eclectic pop/rock, which inspire even the most cynical ear, took it to a revered realm. Throughout, Elton's piano and keyboard work resonated with power, sadness, arrogance, anger, reflection and every other emotion Taupin's complex, eccentric, sexual, bitter, diversely charismatic and just plain brilliant words dictated.

This covalent made combination makes *Goodbye Yellow Brick Road* an accomplishment few songwriting teams could hope to achieve. This album is been credited as a major influence on many rock superstars who have followed in the last thirty years. Rather than a tired, indulgent burned-out double album

effort by a pop star with a few catchy singles under his belt, *Goodbye Yellow Brick Road* was instead a musical extravaganza that defied easy categorization and solidified Elton John as not simply some piano guy with goofy glasses but a musical thoroughbred who galloped to the head of the pack.

Is *Goodbye Yellow Brick Road* Elton John's masterpiece? Just listen. And listen. And listen.

▲ ● ▲ ● ▲ ● ▲ ● ▲ ● ▲ ● ▲ ● ▲ ● ▲ ● ▲ ● ▲ ● ▲ ● ▲

CARIBOU

Originally released on MCA June 1974

It was just three months after the release of his masterpiece, *Goodbye Yellow Brick Road*, that Elton John was faced with the daunting task of recording a worthy follow-up.

Burdened with a new dose of professional pressure and the minute-by-minute stress of stardom that can engulf an offstage life, Elton and his band tried to retreat from the rock lifestyle in the "back to nature," organic atmosphere of Colorado's famed Caribou Ranch studio.

Elton initially flirted with titling this album *Ol' Pink Eyes is Back*, a possible public wink about his still-hidden homosexuality. Perhaps Elton both satirically enjoyed his new stature among the entertainment world's upper crust.

Elton had to deal not only with industry expectations and fan anticipation but also with rigorous time constraints. The team had ten days to bang out a new album before embarking on a tour of Japan. At the outset of recording *Caribou*, Elton and producer Gus Dudgeon wisely abandoned any attempt to match the majesty of *Goodbye Yellow Brick Road*. Da Vinci didn't paint Mona Lisa's sister next, did he?

Instead, Dudgeon looked for a looser rock sound that would bite hard with the brass bravado of the Tower of Power horn section, float with harmonic backing vocals and attain new flavors, thanks to the tasteful timpani touches of percussionist and new band member Ray Cooper.

Caribou is defined for most by its two unmistakable and monstrously popular hit singles, "The Bitch is Back" (Elton's ironic de facto anthem) and "Don't Let the Sun Go Down on Me" (the soaring Roy Orbison-inspired ballad that has become almost a religious experience in concert). Failing to go deeper is a brash oversight.

There are small but special songs here such as the beautifully layered "Pinky," the bouncy ode to Taupin's homeland "Grimsby," the nonsensical, faux-Mediterranean feel of "Solar Prestige a Gammon," the toe-tapping country comfort of "Dixie Lily" and the horn-charging repudiation of the Big Apple, in "You're So Static."

"Pinky" is a good example of where *Caribou* attains its endearment for longtime fans. It makes its mark with punchy piano passages, romantic backing vocals and a great Taupin lyric.

"Ticking," though, is the album's stunner. An almost eight-minute long dramatic tome which Taupin tells a chillingly realistic story of an emotionally disturbed young man, who one day takes out his repressed anger and frustration with a gun and kills fourteen people in a local bar. The song's relevance remains sadly as strong today than when it was written more than twenty-five years ago, punctuated by the rash of student school shootings and the Oklahoma bombing.

Accompanied by Elton's captivating piano playing, which instinctively ebbs with the swirling emotion of Taupin's words, and Dave Hentschel's eerie A.R.P. synthesizer, the song's power is immediate and lasting, and its ultimate conclusion is accented with a droning silence reminiscent of the Beatles' "A Day in the Life."

While *Caribou* didn't top *Goodbye Yellow Brick Road*, it didn't make the sun go down on Elton's career. It still had enough moxie to send the message that the bitch never really went away.

CAPTAIN FANTASTIC AND THE BROWN DIRT COWBOY

Originally released on MCA May 1975

For most Elton John fans, their "once upon a time" came when they first heard a John-Taupin composition. That moment marked a small personal chapter of a much bigger fairy tale spun by the fates and executed through the uniquely meshed music and talents of messengers John and Taupin. The fanciful "once upon a time" quality of *Captain Fantastic and the Brown Dirt Cowboy* is "the essence." *Captain* stands as the most complete and charismatic of all Elton John albums. Its personality is the musical and lyrical embodiment of the composers themselves, and you can feel and hear the care, emotion and revealing reminiscence running throughout its forty-six minutes and forty-three seconds.

Despite its grandiose title, media hype and the expectation of another radio-ready commercial product, *Captain Fantastic* was an overtly non-commercial, personal and sentimental musical storybook—not to be blared from speakers as disposable pop/rock background noise. It demanded a closer and more serious listen. And look.

Captain Fantastic boasted the most elaborate album cover and packaging of any of his albums. The bi-fold cover art (which lost its jolting effectiveness in the CD format) was a satirical and sexy sensation for the eyes and imagination. Drawn with the dark pen of Alan Aldridge, the cover depicted the two diverging personalities: Elton as the self-proclaimed "city-slick Captain" breaking out of his inner shell to ride confidently into the world on a piano and dream-weaver Taupin as the bucolic "Brown Dirt Cowboy," still green and growing and secluded tightly in his own glass ball by the simplicity of a country-like setting.

Written in original running order, *Captain*

Fantastic had a cohesiveness unlike any other album. The lyrics led the listener from page to page of this enlightening tome, en route to a grand climax. Taupin's lyrics were central to the album's overall imprint and style. He unfolded the duo's storybook-like beginnings—both individually and as a team—by deftly sprinkling these ten tightly-written musical remembrances with numerous references to actual people, places and occurrences. And while grounding the album in reality, he also allowed his words to meander into some of the best turned and deliciously descriptive phrases he had ever put to paper.

Producer Gus Dudgeon also offered his finest production performance. Elton's piano, often times the dominant sound, here was simply a component of the mix. This decision was also responsible for showcasing just how interlocking the Elton John Band had become. Dudgeon pushed the musical talent of each band member to its limit—and in the process got incredible moments from all of them on a song-for-song basis. Ironically, after laying down the best sound of their tenure, Elton broke up his band, leaving *Captain Fantastic* as it lasting legacy.

Like a book, this album plays chapter by chapter, with each song building on the previous one momentum of the previous one and moving the story to its next destination. *Captain Fantastic and the Brown Dirt Cowboy* is fittingly rustic and rocking and introduces the protagonists with a vulnerable but determined swagger. It continues with denouncing diatribes on he music business ("Tower of Babel" and "Bitter Fingers"); defining life decisions ("Tell Me When the Whistle Blows" and "Someone Saved My Life Tonight"); the struggle for cool, acceptance and fame ("Gotta Get a Meal Ticket" and "Better Off Dead"); the discovering and excitement of combined talents ("Writing") and the emotional recognition of a special loving bond of friendship and eternal connection ("We All Fall in Love Sometimes" and "Curtains").

The only thing this album lacks is a sequel.

Captain Fantastic and the Brown Dirt Cowboy are two characters whose continued lives and career deserve to be explored in greater musical detail. This first installment offers an inviting once upon a time. And the album proves, no one can tell the Elton John and Bernie Taupin story like Elton John and Bernie Taupin.

▲ ● ▲ ● ▲ ● ▲ ● ▲ ● ▲ ● ▲ ● ▲ ● ▲ ● ▲ ● ▲ ● ▲

ROCK OF THE WESTIES

Originally released on MCA, October 1975

How does a Captain Fantastic follow up an album that made history by entering the American music charts at number one? If you're Elton John, you do something worthy of Superman. Using your super-powers, you amaze all the other mere mortals and simply do it again. The nine-song *Rock of the Westies* was written and recorded in only two weeks during the summer of 1975 at Captain Fantastic's own Fortress of Solitude at the time—Caribou Studios in the Colorado Rockies (which contributed to the parodied title).

Released in October, just five months after *Captain Fantastic, Rock of the Westies* was an impromptu, surprise attack designed to give Elton's career a rock 'n' roll overhaul and give his fans a jolt. Forming a new band of honored holdovers Davey Johnstone (guitar) and Ray Cooper (percussion), former friends from the early days Caleb Quaye (guitar) and Roger Pope (drums), and newcomers Kenny Passarelli (bass) and James Newton-Howard (keyboards), this incarnation of the EJB rocked like no other lineup.

Although *Rock of the Westies* doesn't rank among Elton's classic albums, it is Elton's best rock 'n' roll album. It wants to kick your butt, but not caress your cheek. The bombastic opening of "Medley: Yell Help; Wednesday Night; Ugly" (one of the stranger Taupin titles) is Elton's way of announcing, "Gentleman, start your engines!"

Elton and producer Gus Dudgeon create an urgent, live sound that establishes this new band's gutsy, guitar-guided force. And in the ultimate compliment to the production, Dudgeon is able to give each musician his own place within this larger, louder sound.

While loud guitars, drums and keyboards dominate the album, a close and careful listen will reveal, ironically, for all the hard rocking here, Cooper's unobtrusive percussion touches on obvious heavy hitters like "Grow Some Funk of Your Own," "Hard Luck Story" and "Billy Bones and the White Bird," as well as on "Island Girl" and "I Feel Like a Bullet (in the Gun of Robert Ford) almost steal the show from the guys with the picks and sticks.

Rock of the Westies stands out on the strength of the unselfish guitar tandem of Johnstone and Quaye. This double-barreled attack gives Elton's music a hard-hitting one-two punch combination that it previously lacked.

Taupin also obliged Elton's need to get gritty. The songs cover the ever-reoccurring prostitute dalliance ("Medley," "Island Girl"), bar room brawls ("Grow Some Funk") and urban toughs ("Street Kids"), drug additions ("Feed Me"), domestic strife ("Hard Luck Story") and troubadour crusty sea tales ("Billy Bones").

The album's lone love song, "I Feel Like a Bullet," even has its own bite, with Taupin's words painfully comparing the regret of harshly ending a relationship to the cowardice and stone-like emotions of Jesse James's assassin.

In the end, as on every album, it's Elton who best flexes his muscles. He attacks the piano keys with the kind of furious finger play. His trills at the top of "Grow Some Funk" and his banging at the end of it are classic Elton. And in "Hard Luck Story," which teasingly emerges with a masterful slide of mixing board button, his performance is everything Elton John piano solo should be.

On its musical merits, *Rock of the Westies* shouldn't have matched *Captain Fantastic*'s record-breaking feat of instant number-one status. But after more than twenty-five years, it's

a tribute to all those involved that these *Westies* still rock.

● ▲ ● ▲ ● ▲ ● ▲ ● ▲ ● ▲ ● ▲ ● ▲ ● ▲ ● ▲

EMPTY SKY

Originally released on MCA, 1975

Even the most loyal Elton John fans never came as close to wearing out the vinyl copies of *Empty Sky* (originally released in the U.K. only in 1969 and re-released in America in 1975) as they did those *Goodbye Yellow Brick Road*. But when taking a new look back at this aging debut effort, which is more than thirty-two years old, one finds his most overlooked piece of work—and perhaps his most revealing.

Despite its raw quality and overt dollops of pretentiousness, *Empty Sky* is a true reflection of not only the talent of the twenty-two-year-old wanna-be rock star, but of the almost birthright melding of his well-crafted melodies and the wandering but magnetic lyrics of the then-still green-and-growing Bernie Taupin.

Make no mistake, *Empty Sky* is far from perfect and definitely an album of its time-filled with low-rent psychedelia, patches of production gimmicks and a good amount of forced attitude. It's a cry saying, "Notice me! I'm worth it!"

However, while *Empty Sky*'s somewhat regal sound may have been outdated in the sugary, disco-fried seventies or out of place in the synthesizer-consumed eighties, Steve Brown's daring production—complete with classical interludes, flutes and other non-traditional rock instruments—can be better appreciated in these more experimental times.

From the outset, Elton sounds determined to make the most of his arrival. Backed by a young but solid nuts-and-bolts four-piece rock ensemble that includes recognizable names such as guitarist Caleb Quaye, drummers Roger Pope and Nigel Olsson and bassist Tony Murray, *Empty Sky* is an impressive showcase.

The listener hears Elton playing piano,

organ, electric piano and harpsichord, as well as the varying layers of his talents: the rocker ("Western Ford Gateway"), the classically talented student ("Skyline Pigeon"), the expressive vocalist ("Sails"), the loose hipster (on the bopping, impromptu jazz "Hay Chewed") and shadows of a properly raised Englishman. The vast-sounding bravado of the title track (all eight minutes and 26 seconds) sets the tone for this diversity.

Overall, the songs with the most impact are those that when stripped can easily be classified as forerunners to the now-famous John-Taupin style: the esoteric "Valhalla," the infectious hook of "The Scaffold" and the delicate reminiscing of "Lady What's Tomorrow." Though unpolished around the edges, they still manage to shine. And this can be traced to the lyrical framework Taupin creates for Elton.

Empty Sky isn't just Elton's debut, of course. It's also a coming-out for Taupin. The heart of the songs centers on Taupin's condition of the moment—adolescent angst and restlessness, disillusionment with the establishment, insecurity, unsure inner reflection and ultimate escapism. And, yet, this young romantic doesn't include a straight love song in the bunch. The timeless "Skyline Pigeon," the album's highlight and a John-Taupin classic, combines a longing Taupin lyric accompanied by a graceful, soaring John melody. Though the harpsichord tends to dominate, perhaps a subtle recognition of one of his idols, Brian Wilson—whose ground-breaking *Pet Sounds* was released just a few years earlier—will allow the adventurous listener to unearth a tasty treasure here. Because the vocal was recorded on one track and the music on another, by shifting all the sound to one speaker, you are chillingly entertained by just Elton's emotive, spiritual vocal. This early "unplugged version" is then heightened by a touch of organ that gives "Skyline Pigeon" a haunting, dirge-like feel, far removed from the original.

Though *Empty Sky* has its faults, you owe it to yourself to venture into it, It hints at the blindingly bright career that awaited Elton John.

HERE and THERE

Originally released on MCA, April 1976

The surprising success of Peter Frampton's double live album *Comes Alive* in 1976 started a live album trend that found most major rock stars at the time either going through their archives for notable performances or staging new shows to record and quickly release. Elton John's contribution to this craze *Here and There*, was released to fulfill Elton's contract with Dick James Music, his long-time record company in England.

Here and There definitely had the look and feel of an afterthought or obligation, with minimal packaging and a mere nine songs taken from two different shows. And it stands as an embarrassment that an artist of Elton John's stature would have such a slipshod release put out under his name. Ironically, the concept for *Here and There* was creative and inspired. The first side, the "Here," a documentary of an important live show from England, recorded in May 1974 at a benefit at the Royal Festival Hall, and the second, the "There," taken from a historic November 28, 1974 concert in New York's Madison Square Garden.

The intentions were noble, the execution poor. *Here and There* was an incomplete snippet of history and it sounds like it. On Side One, from the England show, during which Elton cleverly paced the show by playing early songs to the present, he began, like his career, alone at the piano playing one of the first songs he and Taupin felt proud of, "Skyline Pigeon." This was followed by "Border Song," accompanied by drummer Nigel Olsson and bassist Dee Murray. But after these moving performances, the remaining three songs failed to create much excitement. A main reason was the selection of songs. The version of "Honky Cat" here sounded flat and was probably better seen than heard. On "Love Song," a duet with its author Lesley Duncan, Elton gave a strong vocal, but the song was too slight to make an impact. And "Crocodile Rock," has a standard run-through.

On Side Two, the show during which John Lennon appeared with Elton to a raucous ovation and would turn out to be his final live performance ever, the three songs Lennon played weren't even included—either a tease or just a foolish mistake that pervaded this entire release. From this show, again, came just standard fare including "Rocket Man," "Bennie and The Jets" and "Take Me to the Pilot" and performances that were hardly memorable.

The disgrace of *Here and There* is that Elton John was one of the era's best live performers, but this album, there is just the slightest glimmer of his ability and showmanship. Thankfully, in 1995, an expanded and re-mastered version of *Here and There* was released, and it included more songs from both shows. The Royal Hall show now comes alive with the addition of choice cuts including "Country Comfort," "Bad Side of the Moon," "Burn Down the Mission." Similarly, the excitement and electricity of the Madison Square Garden show explode, as we hear rocking versions of "Grey Seal" "Your So Static" and, yes, finally, Lennon singing "I Saw Her Standing There," "Whatever Gets You Through the Night" and assisting Elton's rock-and-reggae version of "Lucy in the Sky with Diamonds."

The re-mastered collection of *Here and There* is the definitive version. It's still not a great live album, but a major improvement over the pale imitation that was originally passed on to the public.

▲ • ▲ • ▲ • ▲ • ● • ▲ • ● • ▲ • ● • ▲ • ● • ▲ • ● • ▲ • ● • ▲ • ▲

BLUE MOVES

Originally released on MCA /Rocket, October 1976

Reactions to Elton John's most enigmatic album, *Blue Moves*, wildly vary. It may not be Elton John's obvious best, but *Blue Moves* is Elton John's bravest. The reasons for the conflicting emotions surrounding *Blue Moves* is due to the conflicting emotions within it. Born from both Taupin's morose, mangled emotions of a mishandled marriage, and Elton's own losing battle with his isolating fame and a hidden personal life, there is real pain here. Its tone surprises many, and at the time of its release, October, 1976, disappointed most.

Elton proclaimed, in true Monty Python fashion, it was time for something completely different. Led by the authoritative, time-tested guitar leads of Caleb Quaye, a new band of talented multi-instrumentalists enabled Elton to explore a mixed bag of his favorite genres including rock, soul, gospel, blues, classical, folk, jazz and early techno. The band was disbanded after this release, but its performance here stands as a lasting tribute to one of the best versions of the Elton John Band.

Blue Moves is a challenging listen. Most of the tempos are slow, the lyrics brooding. It is a double-album retreat to sadness rather than a haven to search for optimism. No wonder its original title was *Black Moves*. Not surprisingly, if Elton and MCA Records heeded producer Gus Dudgeon's fruitless protests for a single album, a tighter, lighter, more satisfying eleven song version of *Blue Moves* would exist.

Blue Moves is a different Elton John album. Or is it? On first blush it may sound different, but when we consider that it includes instrumentals ("Your Starter For," "Out of the Blue" and "Theme From a Non-Existent TV Series"), mournful ballads ("Cage the Songbird," "Chameleon," "Sorry Seems to be the Hardest Word," "Someone's Final Song,"), demonstrative orchestral arrangements ("Tonight," "One

Horse Town," "Crazy Water"), and all-out rock ("Bite Your Lip (Get up and Dance!), we realize *Blue Moves* is not different at all. It is well within the Elton John tradition.

The difference lies in how it boldly abandons all caution and constraint. But if this is a fault, it is also the album's innate virtue. Producer Dudgeon again logs in a stellar performance behind the board. He broadens Elton's songs with a wide assortment of sounds and instruments and despite its dire tone, makes each mournful ballad a distinctive elegy.

Blue Moves boasts the best single side of any Elton John album to date. Side one, with "Your Starter For," "Tonight," "One Horse Town" and "Chameleon," crystallizes the heart of the Elton John sound. "Tonight" deserves special mention for its driving orchestral arrangement by James Newton-Howard, Taupin's anguished words of a love's lost glow

and Elton's piano playing, which conveys both anger and sorrow. Elton accompanies this with one of his greatest recorded vocal performances. "Chameleon," a curious, mournful ballad originally written for the Beach Boys has Elton's rolling piano, longing vocal, and hopeful harmonies. They all combine for a haunting, dreamy atmosphere echoing the best of Brian Wilson's writing on *Pet Sounds*.

Blue Moves includes several other classics that unfortunately aren't known by more than the Elton elite. "Cage the Songbird" which is a beautiful acoustic ode to French torch singer Edith Piaf; "Crazy Water" which wades in an infectious hook, and the album's lone hit, "Sorry Seems to be the Hardest Word," which codifies all the entire album's lamenting mood. *Blue Moves,* with its reflective cover painting, The Guardian Readers, by Patrick Procktor, is the most cathartic album Elton and Bernie ever created, with songs holding a power only genuine pain can convey. Guess that's why they called these moves blue.

Blue Moves Alternative Song Selection

This is a track listing of what many fans believe would have made a great eleven-song version of *Blue Moves*.

Side One
"Your Starter For"
"Tonight"
"One Horse Town"
"Chameleon"

Side Two
"Sorry Seems to be The Hardest Word"
"Cage the Songbird"
"Crazy Water"
"Between Seventeen and Twenty"
"Shoulder Holster"
"Idol"
"Someone's Final Song"

A SINGLE MAN

Originally released on MCA, October 1978

By 1978 Elton John's amazing rock 'n' roll run was over. One day he was rock's darling, the next day, he was just gone. His temporary disappearance from the upper tier of the music charts could be traced to at least three main occurrences: the public backlash—especially in the United States—to his frank admission of bisexuality; a seemingly non-stop glut of product that included fifteen official album releases since 1970; and changing musical tastes that found heavy metal and disco duking it out and punk rock causing anarchy in the United Kingdom.

In October of 1978, after lukewarm responses to a second greatest hits package and a one-off, under appreciated single, "Ego," Elton suddenly re-emerged from his amicable exile with *A Single Man*. The question was, did anyone

103

care Elton John was back?

Or better, was he really back? No Gus Dudgeon producing. No true version of The Elton John Band playing. No Bernie Taupin lyrics. Who was this impostor? In a brave show of independence, Elton formed a creative team that included a few selected remnants from his past including percussionist Ray Cooper, orchestral arranger Paul Buckmaster, sound engineer Clive Franks to help him co-produce, and a stable of studio musicians including noted guitarist Tim Renwick, to give the sound some punch. But it was the addition of longtime acquaintance Gary Osborne as lone lyricist that defined this as a major departure.

A Single Man is an imitation of an Elton John album. It re-creates his past rather than looking to the future. The results were acceptable, but not as revolutionary as one would think, considering he needed to prove his relevance to a music world looking for new sounds and new heroes.

Debates about Osborne's place in Elton's history abound. On this first outing as sole lyricist, Osborne delivers adequate words to match Elton's little better than adequate melodies. Songs like "I Don't Care," "Part-Time Love" and "Madness" are catchy but ones Elton can write and sing in his sleep. The biggest difference between the writing styles of Taupin and Osborne lie in their rhyming scheme and depth of subject matter. Taupin's lines don't always end in a true rhyme, which gives them an edge, as he willingly sacrifices meter for meaning. Osborne's words, on the other hand, tend to contain a singsong rhyming formula, and this rigid adherence to style often stifles the thoughts and messages he can explore or convey.

There are a few good things that make *A Single Man* more than listenable. For instance, the opening ballad, "Shine on Through" is one of Elton's best unknown songs. Here, the gentle melody and Osborne's simple, touching lyrics mix beautifully. "Big Dipper" is notable for its New Orleans jazz sound and campy, gay

overtones that only helped to fuel the lingering snickers concerning Elton's sexual preference. "It Ain't Gonna be Easy" grooves thanks to Renwick's guitar parts and Elton's pleading vocals, but is about four and a half minutes too long. "Georgia" soars due to Elton's sentimental vocal rendering; and last, the mid-tempo yet somber "Song For Guy," ends the album on an appropriately quiet note because, in all, *A Single Man* is an album of restraint rather than bravado.

A Single Man never established itself among Elton's albums because it left more like an elaborate demo session than a completely committed project. In retrospect, *A Single Man* stands alone as proof that Elton's truly great music needs more than a single man to make it.

▲ ● ▲ ● ▲ ● ▲ ● ▲ ● ▲ ● ▲ ● ▲ ● ▲ ● ▲ ● ▲ ● ▲ ● ▲

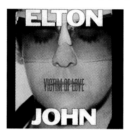

VICTIM OF LOVE

Originally released on MCA, October 1979

Victim of Love is *not* Elton John' s worst album. Unless, of course, it is indeed classified as an Elton John album. Then, no question, it's Elton's bluest recording move.

But considering that all he contributed to this misguided effort was a few hours of vocal duties, it's difficult to consider this an album by Elton John. A better description is "an album with Elton John." It's a stretch, but let's try to give Elton a break here, folks.

Victim of Love, with its flat, unimaginative production of six vapid, studio created songs confused most fans when it was first released in October, 1979. Even amid all the shallow disco nostalgia of the nineties, it's still difficult to justify its existence and significance within Elton's otherwise impressive, consistent and respected catalog.

The most obvious question is, "Elton, why disco?" Why not a "disco Elton"? Well, first, Elton made an unconvincing disco ambassador because, as much as he tried, Elton couldn't dance. Anyone who has seen him put on his boogie shoes in concert knows when he strays from the security of the piano, the rhythm that freely flows through his veins never quite makes it to his legs, hips and arms. The patented "Elton waddle" probably was best presented when he appropriately dressed as Donald Duck in Central Park. Also, if he really wanted to make a disco album, he should have participated more in its development, rather than allow a longtime "friend" and disco devotee Pete Bellotte (how does that phrase go about who needs enemies?) take complete control over it and just jet into Munich for an eight-hour vocal session.

The overriding fact is *Victim of Love* is not a very good album—even by disco standards. Bellotte supplies Elton with a mere six "originals" (plus a clueless, disco-ized version of Chuck Berry's guitar riff classic "Johnny B. Goode," which Elton, the rock 'n' roll fan that he his, should never have agreed to desecrate). This entire fiasco clocks in at a little more than thirty-five minutes. In true disco fashion, the songs don't end—one clumsily segues into another—leaving us with what seems like one, long monotonous song filled with every disco music cliché in the sound engineer's handbook.

Unfortunately, Bellotte's boring production never gives any of these songs a chance to even get your toes tapping or enticing you to extend your arm a finger into the air ala-John Travolta. Despite what some would characterize up to this point as harsh criticism, it must be noted that, for that is wrong with the concept and execution of *Victim of Love*, the only aspect that makes this collection semi-listenable is Elton's vocals. Though he fails to pull of the "Johnny B. Goode" massacre, his voice sounds vibrant and energetic on the cuts "Warm Love in a Cold World," "Spotlight" and "Thunder in the Night."

Elton's attempt to take on the persona of "E.J. & The Sunshine Band" must be considered a failure, best to be acknowledged but not paid too much attention. It's a shame that

Victim of Love closed out the seventies for Elton's recordings. The decade began with the fresh, innovative and timeless *Elton John* album, which showcased unlimited potential. And the decade ended with an uninspired musical product that left many Elton fans wondering if there was any future for him in the eighties.

Consider *Victim of Love* an unfortunate wrong turn on Elton's mostly well paved and sparkling yellow brick road. Elton's disco sucks.

▲ ● ▲ ● ▲ ● ▲ ● ▲ ● ▲ ● ▲ ● ▲ ● ▲ ● ▲ ● ▲

21 AT 33

Originally released on MCA, May 1980

After almost three years of soul-searching for a clearer personal and professional identity, in 1979 Elton John made what could be described as his greatest discovery: a genuine acknowledgement of his music, and most important, a deeper appreciation for Bernie Taupin's lyrics. He gained both from doing a stripped-down, semi-solo tour of the world, with just percussionist Ray Cooper, his piano and Taupin's words to carry the weight.

Through this cathartic exercise, Elton John again realized what it meant to be Elton John. The first recorded result of this epiphany was 1980's re-focused *21 at 33,* which was diversely written (four lyricists) and performed (a host of musicians). It also spanned many musical genres including rock ("Chasing The Crown"), country ("Take Me Back"), gospel ("Dear God") and pure pop ("White Lady White Powder").

Recorded in France in August 1979 and released in May 1980, *21 at 33* found Elton writing with recent collaborator Gary Osbourne, Tom Robinson, Judie Tzuke and the man in that "other" room at the end of the world, Bernie Taupin. The album, which Elton co-produced with sound engineer Clive Franks, had a an easy, inviting sound, and thanks to the Osborne-penned hit "Little

Jeannie," put Elton back at the top of the charts as the new decade began.

In his canon of hits, "Little Jeannie" is often forgotten, but is one of his best soothing silly love songs, anchored by a gentle melody and the great lyric lines. Robinson's contributions here, two impressive ballads, "Sartorial Eloquence" and "Never Gonna Fall in Love Again," are among the album's best because his writing style and mind-set matched Elton's better than any of the other "outside" word-smiths Elton used in addition to Taupin.

Ultimately, though, it is Taupin's first return to the fold since 1976's *Blue Moves,* that is *21 at 33*'s greatest attribute. Even on a part-time basis (he wrote three songs), a little John-Taupin is better than none at all. Taupin's ravenous love affair with cocaine in the eighties is evident on "White Lady White Powder," an insider's view of the California drug scene. Boosted by soaring backing harmonies from Eagles Don Henley, Glenn Frey and Timothy B. Schmidt, the song is as addictive as the substance it celebrates.

The album's centerpiece is "Two Rooms at the End of the World," which metaphorically describes the unique bond, friendship and writing arrangement between Elton and Taupin. He uses the "two worlds" to explain that while different in many ways, when they came together to pool their talents, the two of them are "mining gold." The song blares with a charged guitar riff offset by equally booming horns and a tight pop hook. It's a great way for the John/Taupin partnership to start a new history in a new decade.

For its musical merits, *21 at 33* can stand on its own. It's not one of Elton's classic albums, but one of his most enjoyable. Upon hearing the power chords of Taupin's "Chasing the Crown" that begins the album, weary fans were grateful Elton abandoned his soul, disco and single man experiments of the late seventies and returned to a sound closer to the innate strengths that made his a megastar. And with Taupin's renewed participation—limited as it was—*21 at 33* was a positive reassurance Elton would remain a relevant rocker rather than a subject for "What ever happened to?" questions.

▲ ● ▲ ● ▲ ● ▲ ● ▲ ● ▲ ● ▲ ● ▲ ● ▲ ● ▲ ● ▲ ● ▲ ● ▲

THE FOX

Originally released on Geffen, May 1981

The release of one of Elton's most misunderstood albums, *The Fox,* in 1981, signaled the beginning of an important chapter in his career—one that introduced two central characters—one who helped orchestrate his commercial re-emergence (record executive David Geffen) and another who had a major effect on his music and sound throughout the eighties and nineties (producer Chris Thomas). The album itself, though not a hit by any measure, remains a solid, diverse collection and one of his most mature and challenging.

Geffen signed Elton as one of the first major acts to his new fledgling label at the time, and to insure that this first release since Elton left MCA Records would be a dynamite hit, he strongly suggested, shall we say, that Elton abandon the initial work done for the new record and start from scratch. This meant writing and recording new songs, and dumping producer Clive Franks, who co-produced Elton's last album, *21 at 33,* a mild success.

Enter producer Chris Thomas, an accomplished musician and producer (The Pretenders, Pete Townshend) who also worked with The Beatles and Pink Floyd and had attended London's Royal Academy of Music with Elton when they were lads. He would produce Elton almost exclusively for more than sixteen years, through Elton's 1997 *The Big Picture* album.

Though Geffen's orders didn't produce the hit he wanted, his changes did help in Elton eventually finding his way back to the charts. On *The Fox,* Elton was still looking for a musical identity in the pre-New Wave movement of the early 1980s. The album failed to grab the public fancy, but did push Elton into varying his styles with rock ("Breaking Down Barriers"), pop ("Heels of the Wind," "Just Like Belgium"), blues ("Heart in the Right Place"), classical ("Carla/Etude"), and Europop ("Nobody Wins").

Sadly, this approach left record-buyers cold and radio programmers wondering where it could fit. Still working with a number of lyricists (Taupin, Gary Osborne and Tom Robinson) and musicians (including a refreshing cameo appearance by his original rhythm section, Nigel Olsson and Dee Murray), Elton gave *The Fox* a classic dose of his strongest suits, but the public was looking for something new. It's difficult not to appreciate the great energy and fantastic finger flourishes that drive the rocker "Breaking Down Barriers," or the catchy and organic sound of the high-spirited "Just Like Belgium." *The Fox* also got risky on several tracks, including the synthesizer-laden lament, "Nobody Wins," which probably was ahead of its time, because this was a New Wave sound that a year later was making stars of Human League.

Also, one of Elton's most beautiful instrumentals, the classically pleasing "Carla/Etude" (named for Clive Franks' then-wife) was a lush, flowingly-arranged, atmospheric piece that was both dainty and powerful. On the aching ballad "Chloe," again lead by swirling strings and a haunting guitar, some of Osborne's best lyrics were given their due.

The albums' last two songs end the affair with high drama and assuredness. Robinson's passionate pleading "Elton's Song," the tale of unrequited love from afar is one of Elton's best ballads of his career. Elton's vocal conveys the love, hope and dreams, and his simple piano accompaniment compliments the power of a hurting heart. And the country-wired title track, "The Fox" is a sly Taupin lyric accented by Willie Nelson harp player Mickey Raphael's harmonica and many sharp Olsson fills.

The Fox shows how well Elton John can master any mood or musical genres, and though it may not be familiar, it does beg repeated listens.

JUMP UP!

Originally released on Geffen, April 1982

The eighties brought us MTV, which meant a new music medium. New faces. New sounds. New Wave. And the old Elton John. But that was good. After searching where and how he could fit in the eighties, he wisely decided being himself was the best solution. So in April 1982, he released *Jump Up!,* his most "Elton John-sounding" album since 1973's *Don't Shoot Me, I'm Only the Piano Player.*

The album is important historically because it again expands Taupin's re-occurring role as main lyricist since 1980, as he contributes his words to half of the album's ten songs. It also marks the foreshadowing of a writing partnership that would blossom more than ten years later, as Elton puts music to Tim Rice's words for the first time here. This album also hinted at the eventual clean break with Gary Osbourne, whose lyrics do appear. But Osbourne would soon fade into a question for *Rock 'n' Roll Jeopardy.*

From a commercial standpoint, *Jump Up!* was known most for its hit singles, Taupin's compelling elegy to John Lennon, "Empty Garden (Hey Hey Johnny)" and the elegant Osborne heartwarmer "Blue Eyes." This song, onging and lonely, benefited more from Elton's sultry, breathy vocal performance than Osborne's words, but nonetheless was notable note for Osborne because it was one of Elton's best-selling singles of his career. Osborne's infectious "Princess," a veiled fan letter to Princess Diana pushed for the John-Osborne mating to continue, yet it was all but discarded.

"Empty Garden" may be one of his most emotionally-draining and sad moments on record. Elton is awash in anguish and grief in the vocal, elevating this from a simple tribute to a moving, unanswered love song to a dear friend. It's also one of Taupin's best lyrics, seamlessly comparing Lennon's love of life and humanity to that of a caring gardener. This is a powerful song in content and subject, and yet, it has oddly has never become the definitive tribute to Lennon one would expect. Former Beatles Paul McCartney and George Harrison both wrote songs honoring their former mate but neither approached the depth, sorrow and inspiration as "Empty Garden."

The album also includes patented rockers including "Dear John" and one of the worst songs Taupin has ever penned, the idiotic "I Am You Robot." But he also redeems himself with the venomous "Spiteful Child" that rolls thanks to Elton's rollicking piano and nasty vocal. "Ball & Chain," an instant toe-tapper that won't change your life but will brighten any stray three minutes and twenty-six seconds you have lying around. And kudos to Thomas for employing friend Pete Townshend to add his acoustic strummings.

The collaboration with Rice, who at this time found his fame writing stage musicals with Andrew Lloyd Webber, is "Legal Boys," an angry, dark narrative about divorce and the lawyers who preside over the disillusion of marriage. Rice offers a terse deposition of a once sacred union now mired in legal positioning, and Elton complements the song's bitterness with an expressive vocal filled with sarcasm, and a staccato melody that turbulently mixes blasting guitars and crashing drums.

Jump Up! isn't great, but is a good album. It's important, though, because it forced the music world to find a place for Elton rather than vice-versa, and was a healthy precursor to the fully realized "comeback" Elton mounted in year later with *Too Low for Zero*.

▲ ● ▲ ● ▲ ● ▲ ● ▲ ● ▲ ● ▲ ● ▲ ● ▲ ● ▲ ● ▲ ● ▲

TOO LOW FOR ZERO

Originally released on Geffen, June 1983

In 1983, in a New Wave flooded with the likes MTV, Michael Jackson, Prince and British mascara-and-lip-gloss bands like Duran Duran, Billy Idol and Culture Club, it was clear that genuine Elton John music could still stand among the crowded pop field. The release of *Too Low for Zero* marked the long-overdue reunion of the original nucleus of the "Elton John sound" (absent producer Gus Dudgeon) that most diehard fans were hoping would occur ever since he broke up the band in 1975.

With Nigel Olsson on drums, Dee Murray on bass, Davey Johnstone on guitars and the most important returning ingredient of them all, the lyrics of Bernie Taupin, Elton reached his previous level of excellence. The trial and the error of his master plan—dabbling with a series of seasoned and accomplished musicians and lyricists—may have been the determining catalyst for re-gathering his former bandmates. Or perhaps, as it has been rumored, it was done at the strong suggestions of his new label's leader David Geffen.

Ultimately, who cares how it happened? It did, and that made all the difference. *Too Low for Zero* firmly placed Elton within the consciousness of the emerging MTV generation—not as a dinosaur relic from the seventies, but as a viable and contemporary artist of the time.

In addition, the album's liner notes mark the first mention of a certain dark-haired engineer and future wife, Renate Blauel, a name that would come to mean more in Elton's personal life less than a year after the album's release. From the album's first song, the atmospheric and wondering "Cold as Christmas (in the Middle of the Year)," it was jubilantly obvious that the John-Taupin partnership was back with a vengeance. And "I'm Still Standing" cinched it. The pumped-up pop/rocker has become both a concert favorite and a personal anthem for Elton, who has gone through enough ups and downs to keep the song's joyous proclamation relevant every decade or so. A great song? No. A fun song? You bet.

The only ingredient of Elton's classic sound missing from the album was his crisp piano.

Following the trend of the times, Elton instead tinkled that synthesized sound of an electronic keyboard, giving most of his solos a muted, condensed sound that kept them from standing out in the mix. The album's standard, "I Guess That's Why They Call it the Blues," (with co-writing credit to Johnstone) deserves its place among Elton's classics. The song endures thanks to a deliciously longing, lusty lyric from Taupin, an infectious, chugging melody, sweet harmonies and a gleeful harmonica solo from Stevie Wonder.

However, for all its strengths, *Too Low*'s enveloping and most memorable moments are the album's last two songs. "Saint" blithely billows on the sound of synthesizers (again, the electronics work) and some out-and-out fantastic bass playing by Dee Murray. His instrument at times takes on a lead position, making its presence and style noticeable. But it's the desperately touching "One More Arrow" that qualifies as another one of those timeless John-Taupin tunes that only a handful of fans will ever know and fully appreciate. This emotional tribute to a dead father is chilling, with vintage harmonies and James Newton-Howard's compassionate string arrangement.

Too Low for Zero re-ignited Elton's career and found him singing, playing and writing with the same type of confidence that he and this musical unit had during those amazing days at the chateau. Oh, if Gus Dudgeon were only there, too. Because his ear and creativity might have taken this from being just a great album to perhaps making it a classic. It's still damn close.

▲●▲●▲●▲●▲●▲●▲●▲●▲●▲●▲●▲●▲

BREAKING HEARTS

Originally released on Geffen, June 1984

In February of 1984, still enjoying reawakened popularity from *Two Low,* Elton threw the entire world (and especially his family and friends) a huge curveball by marrying recording engineer Renate Blauel (who also worked on *Too Low for Zero*). The marriage, which took place in Australia on Valentine's Day, was a desperate, selfish move to give his life a sense of normalcy. It was a temporary act to hide an inner struggle of a gay lifestyle washed down with a cocaine and alcohol chaser.

To meet and hopefully exceed the internal and external expectations created by *Too Low for Zero,* Elton again relied on his recently reteamed bandmates of Davey Johnstone on guitar, Nigel Olsson on drums and Dee Murray on bass. And naturally, he his most trusted collaborator, Bernie Taupin, to supply all the lyrics. With this lineup in place and *Too Low* producer Chris Thomas returning as well, Elton obviously believed he had the people needed to duplicate the magic he'd re-captured with his last release. He came close.

Musically, *Breaking Hearts* suffers from being the first in a long line of albums released throughout the eighties and into the nineties that took the emphasis away from the most important sound, Elton's piano. He succumbed to the eighties "electronic fever," overusing synthesizers and other new studio gadgets.

The first track, "Restless" (the working title of the album) kicks things off with an aggressive edge that gives Elton a chance to sing Taupin's societal rants with gusto and authority but never gets passed its initial Rolling Stones guitar riff. The bright and boppy, "Slow Down Georgie (She's Poison)," changes the mood, thanks to some nice acoustic guitar strummings and cheery, layered harmonies. But the hummable hit, "Sad Songs (Say so Much)" is a glorified drum machine creation Elton and Taupin could write in their sleep.

Breaking Hearts at times is able impress only during its share of charged ballads. The title song, "Breaking Hearts (Ain't What it Used to Be)" is classic Elton—just his piano and angelic backing harmonies heard as he sings as an aging lothario agonizing that the chase and conquest had lost their thrill.

If anything makes you take another listen

to *Breaking Hearts,* it's the album's two soaring ballads, "In Neon" and "Burning Buildings." "In Neon," with its Jim Reeves country flavor, tells the story of a naive, young, movie star wanna-be. Elton's impassioned vocal is what brings Taupin's story to life and the entire band shines on the track, most notably Johnstone's guitar, which carries the melody, and again, the great backing vocals, which in many ways are *Breaking Hearts*'s greatest assets throughout. And finally, there is "Burning Buildings," another one of those great John-Taupin ballads that are known by just a handful of loyal fans. Classic Taupin is sprinkled throughout each verse, as he translates love's desperation in a series death-defying acts. It offers Elton the opportunity to cry out in anger and depression with the same emotional overload that makes the chestnut "Don't Let The Sun Go Down on Me" still bristle with pathos almost thirty years later.

Though it has an outward sound of confidence, a close listen to *Breaking Hearts* reveals that Elton is trying too hard to sound like Elton John, whereas *Too Low For Zero* sounded like it flowed effortlessly. During this difficult time in Elton's personal life, on *Breaking Hearts*, he faced the realization that the ease of dealing pressure ain't what it used to be.

ELTON JOHN

ICE on FIRE

Originally released on Geffen, November 1985

Ice on Fire? More like *Ice on Lukewarm.* As were most of Elton John's 1980s musical efforts, his 1985 release, *Ice on Fire* was as confused and inconsistent as his personal life at the time. During this period, change was a constant. After reuniting his seventies band of Davey Johnstone, Dee Murray and Nigel Olsson for both *Too Low for Zero* and *Breaking Hearts* and their supporting tours, Elton—as he did ten years earlier in 1975—disbanded the group in favor of a large, more rocking sound. Johnstone was retained

to be part of Elton's new fuller musical ensemble, but Olsson and Murray were cast away, making *Breaking Hearts* album and tour the storied rhythm section's last as full-time band members.

Overall, the album relied too much on the popular electronic gadgetry of the time, and the synthesizer's great versatility replaced a more organic, human sound. Ultimately, the album sounded distant musically, and thus made Elton sound removed from the music. It felt like was merely a piece of the songs, rather than the driving force. This feeling blocked him from making a true connection with the listener—one of Elton's greatest recording assets.

For longtime fans, the arrival of *Ice on Fire* brought initial anticipation because Elton tapped Gus Dudgeon to produce (Chris Thomas was reportedly already booked on another project) for the first time since 1976's epic *Blue Moves.* Sadly, the excitement dimmed after a listen.

From the first funky beat of "This Town," it was clear this wasn't the reunion most fans were hoping to hear. The biggest disappointment was that you didn't hear Dudgeon. Song for song, it sounded like almost anyone could have been producing rather than someone with the history, track record and influence Dudgeon had with Elton. And aside from a few songs featuring Elton's piano—the album's best—the piano was low in the batting order rather than in the clean up spot.

It's unfair to say that *Ice on Fire* is a bad album, because there are a few moving songs and performances. Buried somewhere beneath dense or distracting production, songs like "This Town" and "Satellite," have potential but get lost in studio trick indulgence and become simply repeated choruses. Ballads like "Cry to Heaven" and the aching "Shoot Down the Moon" are especially well-crafted and executed moments. And for what it is— a wild, everything-including-the-kitchen sink rave-up— "Wrap Her Up" is even digestible.

There are just too many one-trick throwaways on *Ice on Fire* that impede its flow just when the listener senses it might be going somewhere. These roadblocks include the repetitive, pseudo-soul take, "Soul Glove," the "Lolita" languishing, too-long "Too Young," and the sugary, chocolate-dipped popish "Candy By the Pound."

Only on the mesmerizing synthesizer-based "Nikita" do the production and Elton's voice meet to create one of his most infectious pop singles ever. The subtle gay/Cold War love song (in Russian, Nikita though a feminine sounding name is actually a masculine name, as in former Russian leader Nikita Khrushchev) features a vocal performance that maybe only Dudgeon is able to draw from Elton.

With the passage of time, some of the immediate chill of *Ice on Fire* somehow has melted. Perhaps because it wasn't the album so many wanted it to be. One fact that remains, *Ice* held little fire, just a few errant sparks.

▲ ● ▲ ● ▲ ● ▲ ● ▲ ● ▲ ● ▲ ● ▲ ● ▲ ● ▲ ● ▲ ● ▲ ● ▲ ● ▲

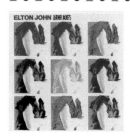

LEATHER JACKETS

Originally released on Geffen, November 1986

If the sound and direction of 1985's *Ice on Fire* were a disappointment, it's hard to describe the feeling among Elton John fans in November of 1986, when its weaker, bastard stepchild, *Leather Jackets,* was released. It's not fair to say *Leather Jackets* was a complete abomination. But it would be tempting.

Created by piecing together previously written songs, along with some new ones, *Leather Jackets* reflects a makeshift process. In fact, after successfully solidifying his writing partnership with Bernie Taupin and rediscovering their magic back in 1983 with *Too Low for Zero*, Elton again broke ranks by including collaborations with former short-term lyricist Gary Osborne and, believe it or not, Cher.

Overall, you get a sense that Elton just didn't care. Producer Gus Dudgeon clearly did not

have the material to pull off a better record, but he certainly could have kept many of these songs, such as the Cher's "opus" "Don't Trust That Woman" and the frantic "Heartache All Over the World," from degenerating into little more than over-blown, chorus-repeating, never-ending musical jams.

For these stated reasons, *Leather Jackets* stands as Elton's career creative low point. What's most sad about it is that Elton's drug problems obviously not only clouded his talent but dulled and destroyed his sense of artistic and personal pride.

The title and kickoff cut provided the first hint of danger. The song featured a throwaway lyric. Musically, it's all dressed up with nowhere to go. Yet, an *Ice* sessions holdover, "Hoop of Fire," offered hope for redemption. A steamy Taupin lyric of dangerous, risky love is matched by a flaming, effective Elton vocal. It's a shame this song got exiled to this album, because it's actually one of Elton's better recorded performances. But it will forever be known only to the seventeen people who own this album. "Gypsy Heart," with a rollicking, "Elton John-sounding" chord progression, was simply proof that Elton can write a good melody when not even trying. The trickling duet with Cliff Richard—a little over a decade later, this would provide to be perhaps the first song sung by two British knights—"Slow Rivers" wanted so much to be more than it is, and Dudgeon did a credible job of helping it move upstream. "Angeline" may be one of the worst songs Elton's ever put his name and voice to, and the lone Osborne cut, "Memory of Love," had a melodic chorus that can draw you in with enough listens, but he was lyrically shallow and mundane.

Closing *Leather Jackets* are its two best moments. The unfortunately overlooked and mostly unknown "Paris" is the best motivation to even play this album. Taupin captures the longing for escape and the anticipation of living the artist's life in the "City of Lights." Elton accompanies this brief daydream with a fittingly gentle, infectious melody that enables the listener to share in the narrator's Parisian fantasy.

The album's finale, "I Fall Apart," in many ways represents Elton's dark demeanor and emotional state at the time, and that's probably why he sings it with an emotion and strength not heard anywhere else on the album.

With a title that connotes excitement and rebellion, *Leather Jackets* instead is uneventful and devoid of risk or edge, making it nothing more than musical corduroy at best.

▲ ● ▲ ● ▲ ● ▲ ● ▲ ● ▲ ● ▲ ● ▲ ● ▲ ● ▲ ●

 **LIVE in AUSTRALIA WITH THE MELBOURNE SYMPHONY ORCHESTRA**

Originally released on MCA, September 1987

The hell with *Survivor*'s Colby or Tina. Fifteen years before those two braved the Australian outback, Elton John was proving he was indeed a true survivor down under. Professionally, the most crucial career "bounce back" Elton ever orchestrated occurred in 1986 with the help of the Melbourne Symphony. He performed a series of twenty-seven shows that traversed all of Australia, and culminated in an awe-inspiring final concert on December 9 that ultimately became Elton's best live album to date, 1987's *Live in Australia*.

Emerging from his artistic gutter (better known as the album *Leather Jackets* released in November 1986), Elton's wise decision to barnstorm Australia in December might have been one his greatest career masterstrokes that again proved his resiliency. It also provided Elton with a serious health scare that would put his career in jeopardy. His voice, tested by years of touring and self-abusing addictions, was literally in threads. During the recording of *Live in Australia,* which took place on the tour's final night, Elton's voice was in its most ravaged state. What you're hearing then, on this illuminatingly recorded and performed

fourteen-song collection, then, was Elton John's bravest performance.

Live In Australia reaches its myriad peaks on several fronts. James Newton-Howard's masterful conducting, the ever-powerful jolt of Paul Buckmaster's graceful and charging arrangements that will never be topped, the artful mixing and engineering of Gus Dudgeon and stalwart soundman Clive Franks, the Melbourne Symphony Orchestra, and of course, Elton's unrelenting performance.

A close listen makes this all so apparent. The album begins with the stirring string introduction of "Sixty Years On," and continues through Elton's dour vocal in which he conveys Taupin's disgust of old age. This is immediately followed up by the childlike devotion of love expressed in the emotional, "I Need You to Turn To." Elton's voice elevates with the swirling power of the orchestral backing to make this the definitive recording of this song. And can this album get any better than it does than on the performance of "The Greatest Discovery"? Elton he teasingly leads the listener to the heartwarming and glowing discovery that emerges in the song's final lyric passage.

This album also made a new hit out of "Candle in the Wind," which became a huge selling single in the United States despite rising to classic status ever since its release on *Goodbye Yellow Brick Road* in 1973. The song re-established Elton's stature with his original fans and introduced him to a new generation of record buyers.

Still, all the performances on this album have their moments of endearment. Thanks to the roughness of his voice, the pain of "Tonight" bonechilling, his strained proclamations in "The King Must Die" add nuance of outrage and desperation not even hinted at on the recorded version, and "Have Mercy on the Criminal" finally gets its recognition in its grand and escapist performance by the Melbourne Symphony. And though they've been played and heard thousands of times, the power-packed renditions of both "Your Song" and the album's closer, "Don't Let the Sun Go Down on Me" here are more evidence of Elton's survival instinct. He sings both with such careless disregard for the damage it can do to his crippled vocal cords, it's as if he's actually singing these longtime friends for the last time—ever.

Live in Australia is musical, emotional, passionate, courageous, tender, arrogant, stubborn, indulgent, humorous, poignant, contradictory, entertaining, unique and ultimately satisfying. Everything we know as the creative enigma, Elton John.

▲ ● ▲ ● ▲ ● ▲ ● ▲ ● ▲ ● ▲ ● ▲ ● ▲ ● ▲ ● ▲

REG STRIKES BACK

Originally released on MCA, July 1988

By having his personal life shamelessly exaggerated and slandered in the British press, ending a misguided marriage, and with many wondering if he'd ever rise to his previous status in the entertainment world, the period of 1987-88 derailed Elton John. But then, Reg struck back. Only a stubborn, workaholic like Elton John would think about creating music through amid so much personal turmoil. But he did with a vengeance. *Reg Strikes Back* was his most perfectly titled album.

Produced again by Chris Thomas and featuring the first full set of Taupin-penned lyrics since *Ice on Fire*, the album was Elton's only way of boldly stepping back into the ring and showing the world and himself he wasn't done just yet.

Reg Strikes Back was a misunderstood and overlooked album. It contains the smash hit "I Don't Wanna Go on with You Like That," a macho mix of rock and dance music that enabled Elton to show off his keyboard skills in the old tradition and fit nicely into radio formats of the day. However, aside from the semi-hit follow-up "A Word in Spanish," one of Elton's more under-appreciated singles given his outstanding vocal, and Davey Johnstone's

Spanish-flavored acoustic guitar solo, the album failed to get its full due.

While it is uneven in that it isn't a top-to-bottom succession of songs that build, there are enough exceptional standouts that push *Reg* toward one of Elton's better long playing releases of the eighties. Opening the album with the buoyant synthesizer bounce of "Town of Plenty," the album bursts, and Taupin gives Elton a chance for revenge with a song that celebrates art and attacks the media. And Pete Townshend's acoustic guitar helps the song's chu-chunging beat.

Some songs have aged better than expected including "Poor Cow," Taupin's white trash tribute exposing the *Jerry Springer* guest line-up when the schlock show host was still hanging in Ohio obscurity.

Both "The Camera Never Lies" and "Heavy Traffic" are the album's buried gems. Both have infectious grooves and targeted vocals that add to the each of the song's attitude and mood. "Camera" opens with a Philly soul beat and a whispered "Hey, girl," which is one of those little obscure touches that make an Elton John song special. Though Elton doesn't play the piano on the album, his keyboard solos are more frequent than on previous Thomas-produced albums, and this song give him a chance to do some pounding. "Heavy Traffic," Taupin's tour to the L.A. late night street life and drug scene, has a tempting Latin/salsa feel, and again, Elton's keyboard solo is masterfully played and sounds like the impromptu jam that it is.

The major disappointment is the outlandishly elaborate "Mona Lisas and Mad Hatters Part 2." Connecting this heartless, bombastic, studio concoction with the sweet, lost innocence of "Mona Lisas and Mad Hatters" from Honky Chateau borders on blasphemy.

"Since God Invented Girls" a clear Beach Boys tribute in music, while with words Taupin tries his hand at his own version twisted version of "California Girls." Elton's melody and chord structure again bows to his hero, but this one is a forced homage.

Elton views *Reg Strikes Back* as an important album for him and his career not so much for the overall quality of the songs, but because it got him back into the studio when he needed to be. After taking a public pounding for being Elton John, this record is proof that Reg Dwight could still write, sing, perform and strike back on demand.

▲ ● ▲ ● ● ▲ ● ▲ ● ▲ ● ▲ ● ● ▲ ● ▲ ● ▲ ● ● ▲ ●

THE COMPLETE THOM BELL SESSIONS

Originally released on MCA, March 1989

Looking to retreat from the career pressures and trappings of fame that made his life a confining existence, and dealing with the public fallout from his self-outing proclamation in *Rolling Stone* that he was bisexual, Elton John indulged himself in 1977. A lifelong devotee of soul/funk music and its artists, Elton decided to try his hand—or more accurately, his voice at making a record that celebrated the style of rhythm and blues known as "the Philly Sound." Groups including The Spinners and The Stylistics excelled with a feel that combined bass-driven beats, funky guitar parts, hook-driven melodies, pecks of percussion and horns, and gliding orchestral arrangements. Elton admired the sound, and having dabbled with it on "Philadelphia Freedom" and "Don't Go Breaking My Heart" few years earlier, Elton decided to pursue it in full force.

Teaming with producer Thom Bell, one of the key architects of the Philly Sound, Elton embarked on a series of recording sessions in which he allowed Bell to craft a similar sound for his music and voice. It almost worked.

For the recording sessions, Elton contributed two new songs: a Taupin composition, "Nice and Slow" that is repetitive and flat; plus a song written with his "new' lyricist at the time, Gary Osborne. The song, "Shine

on Through" was forced into "Bell treatment," here, with an extended, rambling ending where it just didn't work. It would later appear as a simple, quiet piano ballad on *A Single Man,* and it was one of the best on the album.

Bell wrote three songs, the peppy "Three Way Love Affair," "Are You Ready for Love?," and only true salvageable song, "Mama Can't Buy You Love," which in 1979, was released and became a surprise hit single. The other song, Joseph Jefferson's "Country Love Song" was a derivative, laborious ditty that went nowhere.

On all the songs here, Bell pulls out all his usual production stops, which eventually made the songs sound too formula and familiar. Instead of delivering a new, fresh, different breezy sound for Elton to spread his artistic wings over, the six songs recorded sounded like rewarmed Philly steak sandwiches. Elton was not pleased with the initial recordings, and to make things worse, Bell had The Spinners replace many of Elton's vocals, making "Are You Ready for Love" or a Spinners song with Elton guesting. What began as a potentially exciting project personally and professionally for Elton, quickly faded from memory. The entire project was never released until 1989, as when it came to light as *The Complete Thom Bell Sessions.*

One lasting lesson Bell did impart on Elton, which has served him well to this day, was the urging for him to sing in a lower register. So much of Elton's vocalizing up to this point was done in a high or even exaggerated falsetto, but here he let his lower register dominate, and it gave him a more warmer sound. This technique was most evident on "Mama Can't Buy You Love" and "Three Way Love Affair," which were the two best outings on the record. He later used it to give the hit "Blue Eyes" a mysterious quality, and after his throat surgery in 1987, he has sung more often in lower tones with resonating results.

The Complete Thom Bell Sessions were not a complete failure, just an experiment that might have been more of a whim than a committed effort.

▲ ● ▲ ● ▲ ● ▲ ● ▲ ● ▲ ● ▲ ● ▲ ● ▲ ● ▲ ● ▲ ● ▲

SLEEPING WITH THE PAST

Originally released on MCA, August 1989

As 1988 came to close and Elton was finally putting the scandalous *Sun* tabloid fiasco behind him and officially ending his marriage, he and Taupin came together to decide how they wanted their next album to sound. Renewed by the positive response to *Reg Strikes Back,* Elton and Taupin were energized to make an album that pleased them as well as the masses. With this focus and determination, Elton and Taupin sought to make an album they wanted to make. The Captain and the Kid, both nearing middle age, wanted to do it for themselves after doing it for so many other reasons for so long. This wasn't so much an autobiographical album like *Captain Fantastic,* but a tribute to the music and artists who influenced them.

Reminiscent and evoking the influence of Ray Charles, The Impressions, Smokey Robinson, Marvin Gaye, *Sleeping with the Past* was a valentine to the past and their past. Recorded in late 1988, with radio play of the singles from *Reg* still strong, and released in August 1989, the album featured words and music blended together on *Sleeping with the Past* as proof the good things happen with a tighter writing process. Producer Chris Thomas obviously understood the concept and sound the boys were aiming for and created an overall a sound that both harkens back to the influences and remains strong and in the moment. It was probably Thomas' best work for Elton.

Backed with a black rhythm section of Jonathon Mofett on drums and Romeo Williams on bass, as well as Davey Johnstone, Fred Mandel, Guy Babylon and background singers Marlena Jeter, Mortonette Jenkins and Natalie Jackson, Elton surrounded himself with a band able to execute the musical vision. The fulfillment of the album's promise came alive with the second cut, "Healing Hands," a gospel rave that was complete with the power and the glory of its redemptive lyric. There was an urgency in Elton's vocal that brought out the song's best traits: longing, energy, enlightenment. For a stroll under the boardwalk, "Club at the End of the Street" created the vibe of the urban landscape teeming with people drinking in life's rich pageant. The Drifter's classic summertime ode "Under the Boardwalk" was embedded in this song's structure and soul.

On a first listen to "Stone's Throw from Hurtin'," you wonder whom Elton brought in to handle the lead vocal. After a few moments, you realize it was Elton. If there was one song that personifies *Sleeping*'s R&B concept it was this one. "Sacrifice" might not be as in line with the album's overall concept in terms of sound, but what a classic. It was almost an anti-love song wrapped into a love song. With touches of a marital discord, infidelity and hurt, it somehow offered a sense of salvation. The slow way of "Amazes Me" couldn't help but bring Ray Charles to mind. It's thick with the heat, humidity and blues of the Old South, as Taupin dropped in touches of the Southern tradition including Cajun voodoo, the mighty Mississippi River and that ever-present yellow moon hanging in the sky. Johnstone contributed an aching blues solo to give the song its bite and Elton again got to play with the Jim Reeves-country style of singing, which he had been doing since the pubs in Pinner.

To end this diversely delightful set was "Blue Avenue," a veiled epitaph to Elton's failed marriage and lost love, and without question, one of the best John-Taupin songs ever. Period. No discussion. *Sleeping with the Past* was just how good Elton and Taupin can be when they want to.

TO BE CONTINUED...

Originally released on MCA, October 1990

The four-CD, sixty-seven-song collection, *To Be Continued...*certainly does a solid job of compiling his two decades of hits and impressive album tracks up to that time, and tosses in a some early song, B-sides, unreleased songs and even four new originals. However, most longtime fans had hoped this collection would be less of an extended greatest hits album and dig deeper into Elton's career to become more of a prized treasure trove of first recordings of the John-Taupin partnership, album outtakes that never became B-sides and some "lost songs" from Elton's previous twenty years.

But for the average fan, it does represent a comprehensive overview of Elton's career up to 1990, and does include a good number rarities the masses probably never heard, including one of Elton's first singles released in the United Kingdom, "Lady Samantha," and other early songs that never made the *Empty Sky* and *Elton John* albums including "It's Me That You Need" and "Bad Side of the Moon." It also features several excellent songs that were relegated to B-side status including "Young Man's Blues" and "The Retreat."

Even for the serious Elton John fan, *To Be Continued...* does provide some worthy "lost" moments. For instance, there is the original demo version of "Your Song," which features a naive and timid-sounding Elton playing this eventual standard. Yes, the foundation of the song is there, but here Elton is singing less confident and emotive—the too ingredients that make "Your Song" a classic. Also, there is a beautiful live rendition of the orchestral instrumental "Carla/Etude," left off the *Live In Australia* album, and a moving solo live performance of "I Feel Like a Bullet (in The Gun of Robert Ford)" from 1976 that up to this point only appeared on bootleg recordings.

Of the four new songs Elton included on the set, only two make the grade. All produced by Don Was (a collaboration that deserved to be further explored), the best of these songs carry the bluesy, funky feel Was is known for, but remain true to the Elton tradition. "Easier to Walk Away" moves to a chugging beat and is highlighted by one of his most soulful vocals and deserved to be a single in the U.S. (It was released in the United Kingdom).

But it's "You Gotta Love Someone" that is one of the best songs—in production, melody, lyric and vocal that Elton has ever recorded. It remains largely unknown but should have been a huge hit (it also appears on the *Days of Thunder* movie soundtrack). On a backdrop of a gospel-like tune, Elton sings about prioritizing life, putting love above all else. It is a song of redemption and life-affirming energy, appropriately highlighted at the end with a gospel choir that enables Elton to join in triumphant unity. This one song alone is almost worth the $50 bucks for this 4-CD set.

In the United Kingdom, the set was released with a different, more subdued design packaging (the newly-sober Elton reportedly disliked the U.S. packaging at the time, which he felt was gawdy and celebrated too much of his past), and oddly, it also dropped two of the Was songs, replacing them with two songs from *The One* session (including an outtake, "Suit of Wolves").

*To Be Continued...*delivers all the hits and more. It's just too bad there isn't a little bit more of the "more" and little less of the previously-released "hits."

THE ONE

Originally released on MCA, July 1992

From a critical perspective, *The One* can be compared to 1988's *Reg Strikes Back*, important in his history because it got Elton back into the studio, back atop the music charts and back into the fans' consciousness. Great? No. Pretty damn good, though.

Musically and lyrically, *The One* reflects Elton's newfound drive and persistence after recently getting clean and sober and beating his drug, alcohol and eating addictions. Like his new outlook on life and his career, the melodies are bold, his keyboard (still no return to piano) playing revived and robust.

Taupin again does well by his mate, delivering lyrics that instinctively zoned in on Elton's state of mind. The songs revolve around self-realization, redemption, spirituality, prioritizing, compassion and care for others. The biggest drawback is the album's overall dependence on electronic programming, still clinging to machines rather than organic sounds.

The One is, however, able to overcome this misguided production decision thanks to the strength of the material and Elton's overall performances. "Simple Life" is the official introduction of the new, sober, less complex lifestyle that Elton John so sorely needed, sought and achieved. It's chugging rhythm is an instant hand-clapper, carrying the message of personal realignment.

The title track, "The One," deserves its almost instant ordainment as an Elton John standard. The song shifts between metaphors of a relationship between two lovers and to a higher power. And it includes so many great lyric lines.

Two intriguing selections, "Emily" and "On Dark Street" has Elton bucking the expected melodic course one would expect. The results are noteworthy. "Emily," the somber and hopeful tale of a lonely octogenarian about to pass on is placed on a peaceful, but almost too happy synthesizer line. Same with "On Dark Street," which glides on a carefree Motown beat while the protagonist struggles with unemployment, homelessness and a way to keep his family together. Just the stuff of a happy tune, huh? The odd thing, in both instances, the choices work.

Another standout is "The North," one of Taupin's autobiographical lyrics, describing the "cold, gray place" of his birth and how his inner wanderlust gave him no choice to look South for a better life. The album ends with a challenging, gripping, passing note, the revealing hope of "The Last Song." Again, Taupin inspiringly captures the reality, pain and struggle of a difficult issue. Here, Taupin examines the emotions inherent with a young man with AIDS on his deathbed reconciling with his father. These feelings are transformed into a universal anthem for tolerance and care. His moving imagery of the young man dying and the tidal wave of emotion are what songwriting is all about. Elton also delivers one of his most passionate vocal performances, and you can hear the care, love and devotion in his voice. "The Last Song" has fittingly become a song of hope for the AIDS fight, and with Bruce Springsteen's "Streets of Philadelphia" are the most tender and inspiring songs dealing with this difficult disease and personal and social issue.

The One told the world Elton John was, finally, still standing because this time he meant it.

▲ ● ▲ ● ▲ ● ▲ ● ▲ ● ▲ ● ▲ ● ▲ ● ▲ ● ▲ ● ▲ ● ▲

RARE MASTERS

Originally released on PolyGram, October 1992

Rare Masters may be considered a compilation more than an original album. But because it includes a comprehensive sampling of many vintage and hard-to-find Elton John-Taupin recordings from the late sixties in addition to several quality B-side or discarded songs that were written and recorded for many of Elton John's most prominent albums of the '70s, it seems appropriate to add them to our discussion.

Released in 1992, and spearheaded by Elton's then-longtime manager and confidant, John Reid, *Rare Masters* was a rare treat for die-hard or casual fans because it collected for the first time in one place, a series of worthy songs that somehow got away. It also featured the soundtrack album *Friends* in its entirety on

CD for the first time.

A double-disc set such as *Rare Masters* is important and fulfilling because it helps fill in the blanks of a sustained artistís career, while unearthing meritorious music that failed to make the final vinyl cut. Disc One of *Rare Masters*, which was compiled by Bill Levinson and includes liner notes by Bernie Taupin, looks back at some of the earliest Elton John recorded music. Some of its is naive and amateurish on its face, but does contain the smoldering sparks of what would become a firestorm of hit-making talent.

"I've Been Loving You," (with lyric written by Elton is proof why he needed a lyricist), though a corny late-sixties, Tom Jones-like ballad, does hint at the ability for Elton to write the melodies he would be later known for. "Lady Samantha," and "Just Like Strange Rain" both bask in 'sixties psychedelia, and "It's Me That You Need," "Bad Side of the Moon" and "Grey Seal" (later re-recorded for *Goodbye Yellow Brick Road*) are all solid examples these upstarts demanded attention. These songs contain the first blushes of the imaginative, emotional Taupin lyric colliding with and the driving and infectious Elton John musical bed.

Disc Two is a treasure trove of missed opportunities and rarities. A bolder, screeching version of "Madman Across the Water" featuring a Mick Ronson guitar solo is provocative; a steamroller rocker from the *Madman* era, "Rock Me When He's Gone" charges, and a sped up "Slave" from *Honky Chateau* offers a different look. A few B-sides that easily could have been album cuts include and pop/rocker "Sick City" and the contemplative "Cold Highway" both left off of *Caribou*. The nine-song *Rock of the Westies* could easily have benefited from both "Sugar on the Floor," a pretty Kiki Dee-penned ballad that Elton delivers in fine morose fashion, and "Planes," a quiet, acoustic reflective ballad that may be the best revelation on *Rare Masters*. In fact, for this song alone *Rare Masters* earns its right to exist.

Other hard-to-find favorites are found here, including Elton's 1973 Christmas single, the joyful, cheery Phil Spector-inspired "Step into Christmas," his live recording of "I Saw Her Standing There" with John Lennon from Madison Square Garden in 1974, a beautiful cover version of Lennon's simple rhyme classic "One Day at a Time," and a re-worked, more expressive version of one of the earliest John-Taupin compositions, the gliding "Skyline Pigeon."

All great songwriters have to start somewhere, and on *Rare Masters* some of the best and most telling early glimpses are offered for your "viewing."

▲ ● ▲ ● ▲ ● ▲ ● ▲ ● ▲ ● ▲ ● ▲ ● ▲ ● ▲ ● ▲ ● ▲ ● ▲ ● ▲

DUETS

ELTON JOHN

DUETS

Originally released on MCA, November 1993

On paper, it sounded like it could be a masterpiece. Elton John teaming with a slew of superstars including k.d. lang, Don Henley, Bonnie Raitt, Paul Young, Gladys Knight and a few of his own personal idols, like Little Richard and Leonard Cohen, on a collection of originals and some classics. How could Elton's Duets possibly miss?

Almost eight years after its November 1993 release, fans are still struggling for an answer. Is *Duets* a subpar album or simply a disappointment because it could have been so much more? Originally, *Duets* was slated to be a quasi-greatest hits package, compiling some of his classic *Duets* in order to feed the Christmas season CD bins and take advantage of the "duets craze" that was filtering through the record industry at the time. Elton insisted on adding some new songs to the collection, and it was soon transformed into a full-fledged "new" album of "duets" with many of his famous friends. Like many of Elton's career moves, though, this one didn't seem to have to follow-through or in the correct direction. Elton's contributions for the most part on *Duets* are mostly vocal and production-related. Recording in-between his sixteen-date fall Cooper tour in the United States, he was in and out of the studio laying down vocal tracks in quick fashion as is his style, and allowing producer Greg Penny to supervise the overall project. Penny was either intimidated by Elton's star stature or didn't feel it was his place to restructure the entire concept.

Whatever is the true cause, *Duets* failed to hit the mark it was recorded in a hodge-podge, slapped together fashion, and you can hear it. Yet, for all its flaws, *Duets* is still listenable, at time enjoyable and, in a few places, downright extraordinary.

For instance, the appearances by k.d. lang, Henley, Little Richard, Gladys Knight and RuPaul as missed opportunities. The songs they perform here all have their moments of merit, but if they sang the correct types of songs, these collaborations could have made *Duets* great. Thankfully, Elton's reunion with Kiki Dee on "True Love," the delicate and whimsical Cole Porter classic, is the perfect vehicle for these two to share their friendship and talents.

The three best songs on *Duets* feature Elton and his friends firmly in their areas of expertise. His scorching duet with Bonnie Raitt on "Love Letters" includes a powerful production job by Don Was, who gives the song a nostalgic tone but plants it in the present. He gives the floor to Raitt's sexy slide guitar solos, her come-hither vocals and Elton's sorrowful but hopeful responses. With one of his idols, Leonard Cohen, Elton wisely selects Ray Charles's "Born to Lose" with a Cohenesque arrangement. The Canadian crooner's deep voice and spoken style enchants, as Elton matches with an equally deep register while occasionally going to a higher register to give the song a bluesy/soulful feel.

Which leaves us with the album's centerpiece and "should have been classic," the Tammy Wynette duet, "A Woman's Needs." This engulfing, countryish ballad is the answer to Wynette's trademark hit, "Stand By Your Man," and she sings with the same gusto and love. The biggest waste is it's one of the greatest Elton John songs that most people will ever

hear, and Wynette could have had one last deserving success before her untimely death a few years later.

Like its title, *Duets* has two distinct personalities. The haunting question remains, "Can all that's good and sometimes great with *Duets* overcome what's bad and sometimes terrible with it?"

▲ ● ▲ ● ▲ ● ▲ ● ▲ ● ▲ ● ▲ ● ▲ ● ▲ ● ▲ ●

THE LION KING

(Motion Picture Soundtrack)
Originally released on Walt Disney Films, June 1994

Elton John writing the music for Disney animated feature? Whose Mickey Mouse idea was that? According to reports, it was lyricist Tim Rice's, and it turned out to be a fortuitous suggestion for Elton, Rice, Disney, Jeffrey Katzenberg, Michael Eisner, Nathan Lane, Julie Taymor, Hans Zimmer and just about anyone who has come within a whicker of being associated with the blockbuster animated feature *The Lion King*, and its spin-off projects.

Certainly, the John/Rice musical compositions aren't the only reason *The Lion King* has dominated the entertainment jungle, but their influence cannot be discounted, either. However, without question, the power and popularity of the film's major songs, including "Hakuna Matata," "Circle of Life" and the Oscar-winning "Can You Feel the Love Tonight?," are major reasons for the film's huge crossover audience appeal. The Elton John we know today would not be in place if not for *The Lion King*. Elton's connection to the film has been responsible for much of his musical output, renewed status and overall success he enjoys today. It helped to introduce him to a new audience and spread his creative wings into film and stage scoring, as well as solidify his legend.

Though Elton wrote all the original songs on *The Lion King* soundtrack, it's not a true Elton John studio release, "Hakuna Matata" became the bane of most parents' existence in the summer of 1994, as their kids sang the song's jumpy lyrics for three months straight. And while "I Just Can't Wait to be King" is something of a rock, it's tame even for a lion's tale. However, Elton does perform most of the film's best songs ("Circle of Life" and "Can You Feel the Love Tonight?") and these two songs have endured to be among his most popular of the last ten years.

Elton initially believed that "Circle of Life," the affirming hymn that sets the stage for the film's action and is among the most visually inspiring scenes in any animated film, would be the song that would win the Academy Award. He rightfully reasoned that the song established the tone for the story (the film version includes the dramatic drum slam ending that leads into the film's opening credits). However, he miscalculated the effect the video for "Can You Feel the Love Tonight?" would have on the popularity of the song (especially with youngsters), which made this a shoo-in to win the top Oscar prize. Elton's version of "Can You Feel the Love Tonight?" is a big, bold, over-the-top ballad that strikes on every chord it's meant to (the movie version is a more light, character-driven and even humorous take), and it does include a moving, sentimental Tim Rice lyric.

On the other hand, "Circle of Life" is easily one of Elton John's best songs. Like the perfect marriage of John melody and Taupin lyric, on "Circle," Elton and Rice capture that special magic. The song starts slow and solemn and gains a power and strength that's inherent in both the words and the melody. Elton's vocal soars from the middle of the song until its exciting crescendo coda, where you can also feel Elton straining and swaying as he sings the triumphant refrain.

The Lion King was a "mane" event in Elton's career that must be recognized and applauded. Some may dismiss it as simply cartoon music, and if that's the case, all we can answer is, "Hakuna Matata."

▲ ● ▲ ● ▲ ● ▲ ● ▲ ● ▲ ● ▲ ● ▲ ● ▲ ● ▲ ● ▲

MADE in ENGLAND

Originally released on Rocket /Island, May 1995

Made in England is Elton John's best studio album since *Captain Fantastic and the Brown Dirt Cowboy.* It comes oh-so-close to being in the category of a "classic Elton John album" due to a few unfortunate song exclusions. If outtake songs such as "Live Like Horses" and "Hell," both recorded during these sessions, were included rather than the tepid "Lies" and "Man," *Made in England* might have even eclipsed *Captain Fantastic* (even including the poster and lyric book!).

Fighting words? Perhaps, but *Made in England* featured orchestrations by Paul Buckmaster and George Martin, Beatle-sounding influences, a set of taut, introspective Taupin lyrics that evoked the style and spirit of John Lennon, a strong, organic sound punctuated by real instruments, including banjos, accordions, flutes, mandolins and violins—things with strings and airholes, not electronic buttons. It even had Elton himself taking an active role in the production, a fact that cannot be discounted or under-valued.

Though *Duets* producer and acknowledged Elton fan Greg Penny was pegged to handle the chores, as the album continued, Elton played more of an active role and his involvement made a difference. Originally titled *Believe*, *Made in England* begins like vintage Elton John—steeped in drama with the string-driven dirge to love, "Believe."

It can at times be compared to Lennon's "Imagine" in its lyrical simplicity and steady melody, but Buckmaster's dark string arrangement propels it to another plain.

The title cut begins with a crashing guitar chord reminiscent to the one that bellows at the beginning of The Beatles *Hard Day's Night*, and continues on a straight rocking course. Another Lennon-inspired ballad, "House" is a beautifully crafted free association that wafts gently on a simply melody that gains power as it continues. This song floats to an almost out-of-body feel, giving it an instant timelessness. This too might have been a possible choice for a single down the road. "Belfast" is highlighted by a reprise of the strings from "Believe" and Elton's vocal is the star here, conveying the pain and sadness that continually plague this embattled emerald city. A distant sound of Irish music can be heard as the song fades, yet another hint of the creative care that went into the production.

On the somber and soothingly sad "Latitude," Elton and Taupin again work their magic of combining lyric with melody. The song has the sway of The Beatles' "You've Got Hide Your Love Away," the crispness and hope of "Yesterday," and a gorgeous George Martin string arrangement. One of the mysterious blanks in Elton's career is why he never used Martin to produce a full album.

"Live Like Horses" is perhaps among the top five songs Elton and Taupin have ever written. Unfortunately, rather than treating it to a simple, organic, piano-only treatment in the feel with the rest of *Made in England,* it appears later on *The Big Picture* with a pompus production that overtakes the song's simple but powerful plea of freedom.

"Hell," a dark, brooding tale engulfed by Buckmaster strings is a song so different from what Elton has offered since 1973's "Funeral For a Friend/Love Lies Bleeding" in its bravery and abstraction, the public deserved to hear it and it would have fit within this album's tone.

Made in England will remain as Elton's best studio output and shows enough brilliance despite his age, he has at least one more masterpiece in him left to record if he wants to.

▲ ● ▲ ● ▲ ● ▲ ● ▲ ● ▲ ● ▲ ● ▲ ● ▲ ● ▲ ● ▲ ● ▲

LOVE SONGS

Originally released on MCA, September 1996

The title of 1996's commercially-driven greatest hits package boasts this col-lection should be filled with *Love Songs*. And while the fifteen songs included are legitimate choices for a greatest hits album, some seem to be stretching the definition of "love song."

For instance, when you think of an Elton John love song, you think of "Candle in the Wind"? It's a stinging condemnation of fame and the price it demands. "Someone Saved My Life Tonight"? The desperate telling of how Elton was thankfully seized from the clutches of a misguided potential marriage. "Daniel"? A somber song of the isolation surrounding a returning Vietnam vet who flees a country that views him as an enemy rather than a hero. "Believe"? More of a rant about a world devoid of love, rather than an emotional tribute. These are all excellent songs worthy of inclu-sion as among Elton's greatest hits, but are hardly the kind of love song you'd play as mood music to go along with the blazing fire-place, bottle of wine, candlelight and rose petals scattered on the floor. The U.K. version, with its seventeen songs, also has some odd choices, like the bouncy, singalong, "Please" and the eerie elegy, "Song for Guy."

Love Songs does include two previously unreleased songs, he reflective "You Can Make History (Young Again)," and the sarcastic "No Valentines," both new John-Taupin composi-tions used to slyly sell this collection to those who already owned all the previously-released hits on the album. The U.K. version is less cal-culated, by adding two more songs than the U.S. version but eliminating the two new songs. "No Valentines," despite the reference to Hallmark holiday love cards, is hardly an ode to Cupid's favorite pastime. In it, Taupin decries all signs of obligatory outward love, like valen-tines and birthday cards, and claims these dime store tokens of affection are filled with "empty lines. Wow, your heart just melts with that kind of sentiment, doesn't it? Again, an interesting insight and, overall, not a bad song, but as part of an album purporting to be full of love songs?

"You Can Make History (Young Again)" is more fitting. The lyric contains a touching hope for love and commitment, as the narrator confronts his aging, his past and his mortality. However, rather than wallowing in self-pity, he looks to his lover as the one person who can keep his life moving forward with hope for the future. Unfortunately, the song's over-produced, sappy production deflates all the lyric's poignancy, and even Elton's convincing vocal can't overcome the bland, cliched production. A more stripped-down version, with only piano has surfaced on radio promotional discs, and in this version the song is a strong, emotional and loving tribute to the power of love. On *Love Songs*, though, it's pure pap. Another example of a potentially solid song lost in the muck and mire of production Hell.

Ballads would have been a better title for this collection of strong, slower songs of feeling and emotion. But feeling and emotion doesn't always mean love. And there are plenty of real Elton John love songs that could have been included (where's "Little Jeannie"?), but probably wouldn't have struck an immediate, recognized chord with the casual music fan, who is the only target audience for this album.

▲ ● ▲ ● ▲ ● ▲ ● ▲ ● ▲ ● ▲ ● ▲ ● ▲ ● ▲

ELTON JOHN

THE BIG PICTURE

THE BIG PICTURE

Originally released on Rocket, September 1997

With the mainstream in mind, Elton and Taupin play to their strengths on *The Big Picture* with a collection of dramatic ballads and mid-tempo popsters that embrace the adult contemporary sound to a fault, but on occasion do find inventive ways to attract. Producer Chris Thomas again fills every possible inch of open space with some sort of sound, which gives the entire album a dense, overwrought feeling, only magnified by the dominating slow, serious song content.

The album was released on the heels of Elton's greatest public moment—his moving tribute to Princess Diana at her funeral with the re-worked "Candle in the Wind 1997"—and there was great expectation before this album's release, and great disappointment after. Lyrically, Taupin's themes revolved around questions of love, relationships, inner reflection and little else, giving the album a same-sounding personality. His third marriage found trouble and ended soon after this album's release, and a close reading of the words today does reveal introspection concerning a relationship in question or peril.

Though the feeling is somewhat moody throughout, there is a grandeur on many of the songs that help to make them more than forgettable fare, including "Live Like Horses," "The End Will Come" and "If the River Can Bend." "Horses" sadly is put down with this elaborate Thomas production, which suffocates the song's impassioned lyric and Elton's pleading performance. This is one of the best songs Elton and Taupin have ever written, but this studio version gallops without direction. In a live, piano-only setting, the song is momentous and inspiring. Similarly, "Recover Your Soul" is elevator music here, yet when performed live with just a piano, it's a strong motivator.

The straight ballads including the hymn-line "Love's Got a Lot to Answer For" and "Long Way from Happiness" on a hasty listen would seem like usual slow song drivel. But, there are few that can sell a ballad like Elton John and though the lyrics don't elevate, his vocals do, enabling both these songs to rise higher than they deserve. And "I Can't Steer My Heart Clear of You," though admittedly bloated and overly-dramatic pop, is again saved by Elton's delivering Taupin's turbulent lyric with tortured feeling.

The title song is the album's most realized moment, as Taupin is more on track lyrically and the *Abbey Road* musical influence adds a nostalgic touch. "January" is the most creative and adventurous, with quirky keyboard effects, a driving string arrangement and a sassy vocal. The lone hit, "Something About the Way You Look Tonight" may be Taupin's most lazy lyric of his career, with school boy metaphors like "beacon on the bay." But, somehow, with Elton's invigorated melody and vocal, this sappy sentiment works.

The Big Picture is an album that's trying too hard to make up for a collection of average material at best. It may be Taupin's weakest outing on record. And when there are hints of some excellent songs, the production overcomes them in repeated, foolish attempts to pump them up rather than let them stay simple and strong. The big production on *The Big Picture* makes it hang a bit crooked.

▲ ● ▲ ● ▲ ● ▲ ● ▲ ● ▲ ● ▲ ● ▲ ● ▲ ● ▲ ● ▲ ● ▲ ●

ELTON JOHN AND TIM RICE'S AIDA

Originally released on Island, March 1999

The best Elton John album of the nineties most likely will never be officially released. And that is a shame, because his collection of fourteen original demo recordings that became the foundation for his Tony Award-winning stage musical, *Aida*, rank among the best music Elton John has written and performed—ever—in his entire thirty-plus year career.

Regrettably, rather than release these finely arranged and produced compositions (they should hardly be categorized as "demos") an ill-conceived all-star "concept" album, which featured Elton and a host of mismatched guest stars singing interpretations of the show's stirring musical score, was created. This odd collection, which "starred" among them Sting, James Taylor, The Spice Girls, Tina Turner, Lenny Kravitz and two of the show's stars, Tony winner Heather Headley and co-star Sherri Rene Scott, failed to correctly represent the emotion, angst and romance instilled in the show's songs.

Released almost a year before the show premiered on Broadway, this official collection did nothing to create a buzz for the show, and if anything raised more questions surrounding its difficult trek to the Great White Way. The show and the music finally was vindicated when and Elton and Rice won the Tony for the score and later, the cast album won a Grammy Award.

Clearly, great music was there, but the concept album *Elton John and Tim Rice's Aida* failed to expose it.

That's why it's a travesty that Elton's demo recordings, which collectively are the realization of the previously-hinted at potential of the John/Rice tandem have never been released to the public. On songs like "How I Know You," "I Know the Truth," "Trio" (later re-titled "A Step Too Far") and "Written in the Stars," Elton sounds connected to the material and adds the exact amount of drama and pathos.

His vocal performance is delicious and delicate on "Enchantment Passing Through," he extracts a Cole Porter-like style in melody for the stirring showstopper "Elaborate Lives," offers a tender little love note washed in tears on "Amneris' Letter" and has some high camp hijinks on the Motown beat of "My Strongest Suit." The best song of the show *Aida*, and one that had a more prominent placing in earlier stagings, is the reflective, "Not Me." It's Elton's best "big" ballad since "The One," and its triumphant declaration of love in exhilarating at the coda. Pure Elton John.

In addition to the power and drama these songs contain in there own right, the main reason these demo versions are so captivating is due to the production. These are almost fully-realized productions. Much of the credit for the amazing quality of these demos goes to longtime Elton band member, keyboardist Guy Babylon (who also won the Grammy for the cast album). He produced and arranged them, and much of the sound and direction he added at this early phase of development made its way to the finished product onstage. In addition, band members Davey Johnstone and Bob Birch also played on all the tracks, and it's the highest compliment to these four musicians (Elton, Babylon, Johnstone and Birch) that despite several incarnations, their first crack at these songs arguably remain the definitive recorded collection of the music of *Aida*.

Someday, perhaps, these *Aida* demos will be released in their entirety, and the world can not only get a glimpse of the birth of this endearing music, but also hear how it was meant to sound and be performed. The *Aida* demos deserve a curtain call.

▲ ● ▲ ● ▲ ● ▲ ● ▲ ● ▲ ● ▲ ● ▲ ● ▲ ● ▲ ● ▲ ● ▲

THE MUSE

Originally released on Island, August 1999

In 1990, when recalling his experience in composing the score and soundtrack for the early-1970s film, *Friends,* Elton John stated he would never write for a movie again, saying the format was too limiting and structured. However, he often changes his mind when the mood or the muse moves him.

The muse literally did inspire him back to film scoring—the 1999 Albert Brooks film, *The Muse,* that is. Reportedly asked to get involved in the project by starlet friend and star of the film, Sharon Stone, Elton found some spare time to compose and perform the comedy's score, as well as contribute a new John-Taupin composition with the same title of the movie. The new original song was played over the film's closing credits.

Much of *The Muse*'s score found Elton returning to his more orchestral and classic roots. Elton chose a more formal but flighty backdrop to Brooks comic story of a successful screenwriter who has hit a serious writer's block and turns to the supposed magical and inspirational powers of a modern-day muse (played by Stone). The music Elton wrote for *The Muse* was a mix of bright and bouncy orchestral bursts, which nicely enhanced or mimicked the film's often comically frantic or gently reflective scenes. Most of Brooks' comedies are more "thinking man's comedies," based on witty dialogue, clever one-liners and observations and occasional slapstick stunts. His comedy is more subtle and stinging rather than over-the-top and bawdy, and Elton did a dutiful job of composing a score that matched Brooks' comedic style and the film's pacing, story and playful plot twists.

Musically, one can hear many of the Elton John melody signatures, and his classic training and a Mozart influence were obvious throughout. As a listening experience, the music pleasing as background music for a nice dinner or when seeking some Sunday afternoon solitude. Many of the songs were brief, as they were written either to fit short parts of scenes or to augment transition scenes and establish shots. One song though, "Better Have a Gift," did turn the ear, with its changing tempos and quiet piano solo. Elton injected a sense of folly and fun throughout the score, which did a solid job of adding to the whimsical mood of the amusing comedy.

The song, "The Muse" was a pleasant enough ballad, more impressive due to Taupin's lyric, which echoes the film's angst of looking for creative and life inspiration. Elton's voice sounded a little gruff and scratchy here, and the melody didn't dip or soar, but stayed relatively even throughout. The catchy chorus, though, helped to give the song its only lasting spark.

The film *The Muse* was not a huge hit, and this soundtrack didn't draw much attention or Academy Award consideration, but it was a nice diversion to hear Elton composing some instrumental, classical music, even if most of the songs weren't more than two minutes long. Maybe the muse will strike him again and it won't take almost thirty years to score another film.

▲ ● ▲ ● ▲ ● ▲ ● ▲ ● ▲ ● ▲ ● ▲ ● ▲ ● ▲ ● ▲ ● ▲

THE ROAD TO EL DORADO

Originally released on Dream-Works, March 14, 2000

Cartoon scenery or a legitimate album? That's the intrinsic battle that *The Road to El Dorado* fights with itself from beginning to end. Written as the soundtrack to the 2000 Dreamworks' ho-hum animated feature about two vagabonds searching for Aztec riches, Elton teams up with *Lion King* and *Aida* partner Tim Rice aiming for a musical trifecta.

They come down to the wire, but they lose by a nose. This is unquestionably a soundtrack in its sound, production and overarching story-telling theme, but it also is a promising step forward toward the type of energy and life that were missing from Elton's last official album release, *The Big Picture*. Given the film's rustic buddy/on-the-road/comedy/love story plotline, the melodies and lyrics do alternate between bouncy, upbeat pop songs and moving ballads. And this adventurous aspect could have allowed Elton to return to his *Tumbleweed Connection* roots. Alas, it doesn't reach that hopeful pinnacle, but itís not bad for a shot at making a good-sounding Eagles album.

Rice is not as creative lyrically as he could be because he's restrained by a specific story script, and Elton sings in a "character voice" on each song. There are several excellent tunes here, but none that will ever become Elton John-Tim Rice standards like those that emerged from *The Lion King* and *Aida*.

El Dorado succeeds and fails due to producer Patrick Leonard, who helms the board for the first time on an Elton John album. Leonard is a proven studio whiz, and while he brings a refreshing breath of fresh air to the proceedings, he also eliminates any organic or acoustic tone the songs may have had, and instead allows his studio tricks and electronic leanings to rule the day. Much of Elton's and his band's playing is replaced by machines or Leonard's studio croanies, which may be why it feels less than a true Elton John album and more of a Patrick Leonard project. The title and first-track song begins the journey with a spirited opening, complete with a tasty, appropriate Spanish trumpet and openness, and Elton's vocal is enthusiastic and hopeful. The album's single, "Someday Out of the Blue," though catchy and forceful, does sound a bit mechanical and manufactured and it's Leonard—not Elton—playing the piano. What's that about?

The up-tempo songs are hit and miss. The tumbling and bumpy "The Trail We Blaze," is fun and light, and "16th Century Man" rocks harder than Elton has in many years on record, making it an overdue treat. However, the duet with Randy Newman on "It's Tough to Be a God," is so wrong for so many reasons, it's a shame these two great singers couldn't have better material to work with.

The best songs here are all ballads, including the Backstreet Boys-backed, "Friends Never Say Goodbye." Their harmonies take center stage and nicely add strength this overt power ballad. "The Panic in Me," offers a haunting Elton vocal and swirling mood that takes it to another level, and "My Heart Dances" is strong with its melancholy and pumping flutter of love. The best is the closer, "Queen of Cities," with its quiet longing that takes the listener into a peaceful sunset. A simple song with a breadth of majesty.

The Road to El Dorado soundtrack is yet another interesting musical detour for Elton working with Tim Rice, but not a substitute for a true Elton John-Bernie Taupin album. *Road* is a nice side trip, but doesn't deliver the delights of the preferred destination.

▲ ● ▲ ● ▲ ● ▲ ● ▲ ● ▲ ● ▲ ● ▲ ● ▲ ● ▲ ● ▲ ● ▲ ● ▲

ONE NIGHT ONLY

Originally released on Universal Records, November 2000

Admittedly, a new live Elton John album in 2000, the first since the triumphant *Live in Australia*, to be recorded to commemorate his fiftieth and fifty-first shows in his favorite venue, Madison Square Garden and also be taped for a television special, did at first sound promising. Unfortunately, as the as the project continued to develop, it was clear that rather than an important creative and career-defining enterprise, this was really just a quick commercial grab to fill holiday CD bins. *One Night Only: The Greatest Hits* produced a few redeemable highlights and made its mark more for the opportunities missed more than gained: it's a disappointment not so much for what's on it, but what isn't. Even

125

from a commercial standpoint, is there anyone who doesn't have every song included here on one album or another? Rather than reflecting some of the genuine creativity injected into the live shows' setlist, the album sounded like any other Elton John greatest hits collection with occasional crowd noise.

If the goal was to make a solid live album that made a statement as well as pleased listeners—as it should have been—the album would have kicked off the same way the live shows did with the songs from the first side of *Goodbye Yellow Brick Road* in its original running order followed by "Goodbye Yellow Brick Road," which was the first song on the second side of the original album. Although the stage was dominated by percussion (separate drum kits from Olsson and Bisquera, plus John Mahon's own musical menagerie), its synergy was never more prominent and impressive than on the evenings first song," Funeral For a Friend/Love Lies Bleeding." Olsson and Bisquera were in perfect sync throughout, adding power and nuance when needed. Unfortunately, this blazing performance didn't make the album. Guess this innovative, eleven-minute masterpiece didn't make the cut of "greatest."

Other highlights, including the seldom-played "Little Jeannie," which was gently performed with a tasteful break toward the end making it leap like an acrobat, is not on the CD, even though as a single it peaked at number three. In addition, Elton gave an emotional "Someone Saved My Life Tonight," which stayed on the cutting room floor. And two of the concerts' best song selections, the breezy "Club at the End of the Street" and the explosive and surprising cover of the Beatles "Come Together," may have fudged with strict "the greatest hits" concept, but would have made the album stronger and richer.

These interesting moments had to step aside so we could get to hear standard, studio-like versions of "Daniel" and "Sacrifice," "Philadelphia Freedom," all the all-too familiar concert warhorses, or unremarkable duets with Ronan Keating, Bryan Adams or Anastacia.

Which all lends to the bigger question, "Why couldn't this be a two-CD package?" Two CDs would have pleased both casual and serious fans and could have included some if not all of the great but overlooked songs performed during the shows. It also would have helped to make this album sound and feel less than a quick money-grab, which it was or has become. The unfortunate result of this quickie live album is that now we may never get the legitimate successor to *Live in Australia*.

While he's still at the top of his game, Elton needs a live album of two or three CDs and spans his entire career, with a classic mix of hits, covers and album cut classics, is *One Night Only* definitely not it.

▲ ● ▲ ● ▲ ● ▲ ● ▲ ● ▲ ● ▲ ● ▲ ● ▲ ● ▲ ● ▲ ● ▲ ●

*SONGS FROM THE WEST COAST

Originally released on Universal Records, October 2001

Elton officially came back to the basics with 2001's *Songs from the West Coast*. After recent forays into film and theater, it was a welcome return to the sounds that made him a star in the 1970s. Elton himself touted the new work as an organic, simple album, one that harks back to his heyday.

Songs from the West Coast, Elton's 40th release, featured a collection of twelve songs that were indeed reminiscent of the singer /songwriter's early days. Stripped down to just piano, guitar, bass and drums, most of the songs had a true seventies feel. There was no fancy technology to get in the way. Only the bare necessities, with organ and strings as embellishment on a few songs.

After a four-year hiatus from collaborating with Bernie Taupin, Elton and his longtime lyricist reconnected for the album. Elton and Bernie hadn't written together since 1997's *The Big Picture*. Elton and lyricist Tim Rice had collaborated on Elton's most recent projects *The Road to El Dorado* and *Aida*.

Bernie's return to the pen with this offering proved a pivotal element in the seventies feel of the album. In the summer of 2000, Elton and Bernie sat down and discussed the kind of album they wanted to create. Both men agreed they sought to make an album as good as any from the early-to mid-seventies. So therein lie the challenge for Bernie. It would be up to him to compose the words with enough depth to inspire Elton to compose legendary music.

Bernie rose to the occasion, with lyrics as vivid, rousing and astute as any from the mid-seventies. In the track "American Triangle," Bernie told the horrific story of the death of gay Wyoming college student Matthew Shepard with sorrowful, poignant words. Elton, too, stepped up to the challenge, composing lush melodies, bluesy rockers, catchy pop tunes and soulful strains. With "American Triangle," Elton created a stirring portrait with a somber piano introduction and ensuing melancholic verse and chorus. Singer Rufus Wainwright provided harmony vocals on the track, beautifully complementing Elton's vocals on the chorus.

Producer Patrick Leonard was also instrumental in securing the sound Elton and Bernie strived for on the album. Formally a producer of Madonna, Leonard stepped in with *Songs* (as he did with *The Road to El Dorado*) and gave the songwriters exactly the sound they were looking for. Also germane to the project were the background vocals of Davey Johnstone and Nigel Olsson. The duo contributed a mellifluous sound to tracks such as the Beatles-esque "I Want Love," the heavyhearted "Ballad of the Boy in the Red Shoes" and the light-hearted "The Emperor's New Clothes." Their background vocals on "The Emperor's New Clothes" were so reminiscent of "Someone Saved My Life Tonight," it's surreal.

Orchestral arranger Paul Buckmaster was brought in to work his magic on five of the album's tracks. Buckmaster had been the arranger behind the orchestral pieces on *Elton John, Tumbleweed Connection, Madman Across the Water* and *Made in England*. With *Songs*, Buckmaster crafted his art on "The Emperor's New Clothes," "Original Sin," "Ballad of the Boy in the Red Shoes," "Mansfield" and "This Train Don't Stop There Anymore." On "Original Sin," with its affecting, hypnotic chorus and tender melody, Buckmaster utilized the strings as profoundly as he did on 1970's "The Greatest Discovery."

Celebrated as a return to Elton's 1970s style, *Songs from the West Coast* lived up to its intention. Musically, lyrically and vocally, the album delivered. Elton proved himself a masterful songsmith, as always.❖

—Album reviews courtesy of Jim Turano, *East End Lights* (except for those noted, which were provided by Lori Sears).

Elton and Kiki Dee, circa 1993.

CHAPTER TEN

Scraps
What Others Say About Elton

Ask anyone who's anyone in the music biz, Hollywood or the press what they think of Elton John, and they'll tell you he truly lives up the legend, both onstage and off. Over the years, he has fought for the rights of his band and made sure they had the most excellent salaries in the music business, introduced new artists to rock fans by getting them record deals, sponsored soccer teams, done immense work for AIDS research and even sold his clothes for a multiple of charities. Everyone who has come in contact with Captain Fantastic describe him not only as a seminal rock influence, but also as a caring human being who does not let his stardom turn him into an egomaniac. He might live lavishly, but Elton is anything but selfish. People who have met him via the music business, sports or charity work have been impressed by how he's always Johnny-on-the-spot, willing to help out with their latest projects. Elton will always been known as musician who couldn't say no to a good cause. All it takes is one call and assistance is given. He's always willing to give a helping hand even when his own life seems out of control.

Ever notice that Elton doesn't seem to have any enemies? There's a good reason for that. He's open-minded, progressive and loving. Now let's see what happens when we poll some famous Elton associates about their most unique and interesting experiences with the master of the eighty-eights.

"It must be frustrating for Elton John to hear everyone talk about his seventies hits when he turned out some of the most finely crafted and appealing singles of the eighties."—Robert Hilburn (Los Angeles Times music critic)

"Things sort went full circle for me because I saw this interview with Elton John and he has

Detroit was just wonderful. There was band called Redbone that we used to listen to, and the drummer in the band was so off the wall. I remember sitting down with Elton and Bernie and listening to this record at the time in England and how amazed I was. We also used to listen to a lot of the Band, too. So, Elton John brought me to a phase of my own."—Nigel Olsson

"When I was recording the vocal for "I've Got the Music in Me," I was getting very uptight because I couldn't get the expression that I thought the song needed. Then Elton streaked through the studio with his trousers around his ankles. He lightened the mood, and I did the master vocal on the next take."—Kiki Dee

Davey Johnstone.

Axl Rose.

"Elton is truly one of the great musicians of the 20th century, and his magnificent voice is an important an ingredient in his success as his peerless songs are. I am honored to have written with Elton and to have a small part of his legend."—Tim Rice

"It seems that every couple of decades there is a phenomenon in the recording world. Someone bigger than life. Elton John is that bigger than life entertainer, part due to the incredible lyrics of Bernie Taupin. I have always been a huge fan and i'm proud to be a friend."—Neil Sedaka

said something really complimentary things about me. I got chills hearing about this. Hearing that from Elton meant a lot to me because Elton's music always meant a lot to me."—Bruce Hornsby

"Elton is one of the most talented people I have ever worked with in this business who is big. Elton is so talented, he leaves everybody standing. You can't equal that."—Davey Johnstone

"He's been a very, very large inspiration. In the early days, the stuff he was listening to, like the soul records, the stuff out of Memphis and

"If I had to make up a list of the greatest pop artists of all time, Elton would be near the top. He a perennial for me. He's one of the easiest artists to that I've encountered…recordwise. He always knows what the next step is going to be. He's very comfortable in the studio.—Phil Ramone (record producer)

"Elton and I are still total opposites—town mouse and country mouse. But we've both carried on being terrific pop fans. That's the whole basis of it. The first thing we say when we meet or talk on the phone is. 'Hey, have you heard such and such.' I think we've put a lot of intelligence back into pop."—Bernie Taupin

"I admire Elton John's music immensely. He's one of the best songwriters there is. "Candle in the Wind" is a great song. It's one of my favorites. A good song deserves to be heard." —Bono of U2

"When I first heard "Bennie and the Jets," I knew at that time I had to a performer. Here is a man who is responsible in a way for more things than he ever planned."—Axl Rose

"I've been on Elton's private boat while in

Elton John and Bernie Taupin: One of the most successful and influential songwriting teams of our time.

131

Australia and to one of his birthday parties in London. He's a big part of my life. The most outrageous costume I designed for him involved the use of 50 different types of fur. The ranged from being lighter around his face to darker at the bottom, towards his feet. I also made him fur glasses to match. It took a couple of months to make. I also did a feather peacock outfit he wore during his tour in 1987."—Bill Whitten (Hollywood clothing designer)

"Elton is one of the greatest artists that ever lived. He was an absolute dream to work with (on his American debut). Very much a gentleman. I remember arranging the press for his famous North American debut at the Troubadour. I hired one of those English double-decker buses to pick him up at the airport.

Initially, he was nothing like the flamboyant star he is today. He only became that way on stage."—Norman Winter (famed Los Angeles-based publicist)

"Elton is an unabashed Beach Boy fan. He's always coming up to us after shows to tell us how much he loves our music."—Al Jardine of the Beach Boys

"Elton is one of the most extraordinary vocalists, and he arguably is one of the finest piano players I've ever heard, and writers, and performers, and if I come off sounding like his biggest fan, it's probably because I am."—Bernie Taupin

"It's been very positive working with Elton all

Billy Joel on Elton: "Elton's a great piano player."

Elton, Sylvester Stallone and Tim Rice at the 67th Academy Awards. Elton won the Oscar for "Can You Feel the Love Tonight?" from *The Lion King*.

these years. With him being the keyboardist and me being the guitarist, he has never told me what to do. I have been a guitar player in the band for such a long time that he has given me a free hand at everything. It's great working with him, he gives me a lot of free rein."—Davey Johnstone

"People like to think that the Troubadour was the creation of Elton John. It was many things added up to that."—David Rosner (early Elton insider)

"I am proud to be part of the original and in my opinion, the best ever Elton John Band for

almost twenty years and have been inspired by Elton and Bernie's music."—Nigel Olsson

"Looking back, Elton's music has truly stood the test of time. Having arranged "Your Song," "Tiny Dancer," "Come Down in Time," "Madman Across the Water," "Sixty Years On," among many other wonderful pieces, I'm proud to have had the opportunity to collaborate on such important recordings. It's been a very special experience, and I'm glad to have taken part in it."—Paul Buckmaster (musical arranger)

"I have a lot of fun being Elton's musical direc-

David Furnish.

tor. There's so much to do when a show comes, like putting the band together and thinking about what songs to include in the show. That's tough to do sometimes. You know there are always people who want to hear songs that are not played. I know that a lot of people are going to be disappointed because there are songs they want to hear. You can't play them all at one concert."—Davey Johnstone

"We've written a couple of songs together. But when there's three different lawyers from each side involved, it's not going to happen right away. We've written a song together, but haven't recorded it yet. Maybe if we get one set of lawyers out of way. Elton's a very funny guy. He's completely professional. Always on time. I never saw him throw any hissy fits. Elton's a great piano player. We had a great time working together on the Face-to-Face

tour. He's a good man and a good friend. On one of the tours I having a hard time personally and he kept me up."—Billy Joel

"Elton John is unbelievable!" He's just phenomenal. He has a genius for singing. He always blows my mind."— Brian Wilson of the Beach Boys

"It's important when your involved with someone like Elton, who has a super-persona, that you retain your own identity. I didn't want to walk into the room and be known as 'the Boyfriend', and all I've got to talk about is everything I do with Elton."—David Furnish (film maker and Elton's current boyfriend)

"For myself and many others, no one has been more of an inspiration than Elton John. When we talk of great duos like Jimmy Page and Robert Plant, John and Paul, and Mick and Keith, I'd like to think of Elton John and Bernie Taupin. But also, I think Elton should be honored for his great work and fight against AIDS, and his bravery in exposing all triumphs and tragedies of his personal life. The knowledge of these things helps ups get through things every day."—Axl Rose

"The guy's a genius. people don't rally know, maybe because the glitzier aspects of his persona overshadow his musical talent. But he's one of the most talented people I have ever met in my life. I hope that doesn'r get lost in what he does."—Don Was (record producer)

"When I stopped working with Elton, all I was offered to work with were piano players."— Gus Dudgeon (record producer)❖

Elton Goes Gold

How many Elton John albums have gone gold and platinum in the United States? Too many to keep track you may think. According to the Recording Industry Association of America all albums that went gold, which means selling over 500,000 copies in the U.S. are recorded for history. Platinum albums weren't recognized by the RIAA until early 1976. Those albums which sold over one million were indicated with an asterisk as seen in *Billboard*.

In the following list, many Elton John albums are acknowledged more than once meaning the album went gold and then progressed to platinum and/or multi-platinum sales (some including the combined sales of vinyl, cassette and CD). Each progression is signified by the date the award was issued.

The following is a list of gold-certified Elton John albums from 1971 to 2001.

Elton John, February 19, 1971
Tumbleweed Connection, March 22, 1971
Friends, April 6, 1971
Madman Across the Water, February 18, 1972
Honky Chateau, July 24, 1972
Don't Shoot Me I'm Only the Piano Player, February 12, 1973

Goodbye Yellow Brick Road, October 12, 1973
Caribou, July 5, 1974
Greatest Hits, November 8, 1974
Captain Fantastic and the *Brown Dirt Cowboy,* May 21, 1975
Rock of the Westies, October 21, 1975
Here and There, May 6, 1976
Blue Moves, October 29, 1976
Greatest Hits Vol. II, September 30, 1977
A Single Man, October 24, 1978
21 at 33, September 22, 1980
Jump Up!, November 22, 1982
Too Low For Zero, January 18, 1984
Breaking Hearts, September 12, 1984
Ice on Fire, June 26, 1986
Live in Australia with the Melbourne Symphony Orchestra, January 5, 1988
Reg Strikes Back, July 19, 1988
Greatest Hits Vol. III, February 14, 1989
Sleeping with the Past, October 30, 1989
To Be Continued..., June 23, 1992
The One, July 27, 1992
Decade: The Greatest Hits 1976-1986, January 1, 1994
Duets, January 26, 1994
Made in England, May 23, 1995
Love Songs, December 1, 1996
The Big Picture, August 19, 1998
One Night Only, July 27, 2001
Songs from the West Coast, November 5, 2001

The following is a list of platinum-certified Elton John albums from 1976 to 2001.

Blue Moves, December 9, 1976
Greatest Hits Volume II, November 9, 1977
A Single Man, November 15, 1978
Sleeping with the Past, April 2, 1990
Greatest Hits Vol. III 1979-1987, November 8, 1991
The One, September 18, 1992
Captain Fantastic and the Brown Dirt Cowboy, March 23, 1993
Caribou, March 23, 1993
Don't Shoot Me, I'm Only the Piano Player, March 23, 1993

Goodbye Yellow Brick Road, March 23, 1993
Greatest Hits, March 23, 1993
Madman Across the Water, March 23, 1993
Rock of the Westies, March 23, 1993
Duets, January 26, 1994
Made in England, May 23, 1995
Honky Chateau, October 11, 1995
Decade: Greatest Hits, 1976-1986, October 13, 1995
Live In Australia with the Melbourne Symphony Orchestra, October 13, 1995
Too Low for Zero, October 13, 1995
Love Songs, March 28, 1997
The Big Picture, August 19, 1998
Here and There, August 25, 1998
Tumbleweed Connection, August 26, 1998
Breaking Hearts, August 28, 1998

The following is a list of multi-platinum-certified Elton John albums from 1993 to 2001.

Captain Fantastic and the Brown Dirt Cowboy, March 23, 1993
Caribou, March 23, 1993
Don't Shoot Me I'm Only the Piano Player, March 23, 1993
Goodbye Yellow Brick Road, March 23, 1993
Greatest Hits, March 23, 1993
Greatest Hits, Volume II, March 23, 1993
The One, May 18, 1993
Greatest Hits, September 11, 1995
Don't Shoot Me, I'm Only the Piano Player, October 11, 1995
Greatest Hits: Volume III 1979-1987, October 13, 1995
Greatest Hits, August 21, 1998
Greatest Hits, Volume II, August 25, 1998
Decade: Greatest Hits 1976-1986, August 26, 1998
Goodbye Yellow Brick Road, August 26, 1998
Madman Across the Water, August 26, 1998
Love Songs, December 11, 1998

Top 8 Most Memorable Elton John Concerts of All Time

Percussionist Ray Cooper accompanied Elton's 1979 *A Single Man* Concert Tour which included eight shows in Russia.

Though Elton John toured extensively around the world for more than three decades, a few special concerts remain as historical. These concerts include:

1. The Troubadour, Los Angeles, August 25, 1970

Elton's U.S. debut and the night that changed his career and his life forever. He arrived an unknown and left a superstar in the making. His stand at the club eventually drew crowd and some of the day's biggest music stars, including one of Elton's influences and idols, Leon Russell.

2. The Hollywood Bowl, Los Angeles, September 7, 1973

This show was rock at its most flamboyant, with Elton taking the stage with five grand pianos filled with white doves, Hollywood legend look-alikes, engineer Clive Franks playing organ on "Crocodile Rock" in an alligator costume and Elton wearing several wild costumes.

3. The Hammersmith Odeon, London, December 23, 1973

These holiday shows in Elton's homeland remain historic for their spectacle and tradition (he repeated the event the next year). Elton was experiencing his first wave of super fame with the release of the album, *Goodbye Yellow Brick Road* and was finally being accepted by his country. His impromptu version of "Rudolph the Red-Nosed Reindeer" made the show stand out.

4. Madison Square Garden, New York, November 28, 1974

This Thanksgiving concert may be the most memorable of all Elton John concerts due to the special guest appearance of John Lennon, who appeared for three songs, "Whatever Gets You Through the Night", "Lucy in the Sky with Diamonds" and "I Saw Her Standing There". The night was historical because it not only turned out to be Lennon's last concert appearance, but was also the night that Lennon and Yoko Ono reconciled after a separation. Less than a year later, Sean Lennon was born and Elton was chosen as the boy's godfather.

5. Dodger Stadium, Los Angeles, October 25, 1975

Not since The Beatles had a rock concert been held at the huge arena that housed Los Angeles's famed baseball team. Elton was experiencing the height of his fame, and these special concerts (another took place on October 26) featured Elton wearing a spectacular sequined Dodgers uniform.

6. Rossya Concert Hall, Moscow Russia, May 28, 1979

Elton was the first major entertainer for the West to tour Russia. But despite all the hype, he was really not the first performer to visit Russia. British Cliff Richard, and blues great B.B. King proceeded him. Elton viewed the eight-show tour as one of the biggest accomplishments of his career at that point in his life, and rightly so. The historic concert was filmed for a television documentary that was later released as a home video, *To Russia with Elton*.

7. Central Park, New York, New York, September 13, 1980

A record-breaking crowd of over 450,000 came to witness Elton's historic free concert in the Big Park. Thousands of fans camped out on the lawn two days prior to the concert to secure a good spot. Memorable highlights included Elton singing "Imagine" and dressed as Donald Duck for "Your Song". Bernie Taupin, along with many celebs—including Carly Simon, Susan Anton and Dudley Moore—watched from the wings. The concert was also filmed by HBO and shown on TV at a later date.

8. Syndey Entertainment Center, Australia, December 14, 1986

This amazing concert featured Elton backed by a world-renown orchestra. No rock star since has completed such a daunting major tour. It took two years of discusson and rehearsals for the ambitious event to occur. Though, Elton's voice wasn't quite up to par, the concert was rousing success. The concert was recorded for album and for a later home video. Highlight—and there many—included "Candle in the Wind" which was released as live single from the album.

Breaking the Mold

Musician, composer, actor, and comedian, Stephen Sorrentino has been doing impressions since the age of five. For over the past decade Sorrentino has performed as Elton John in 18 countries and 37 states. According to hundreds of published stories on him from various newspapers and magazines around the world, he is considered the best in the business. There are several other "working" Elton John impersonators, but only two besides Sorrentino do the gig on a full-time basis, and those impersonators don't actually sing or perform musically like he does. "I sing, play piano, act, walk, and talk like Elton. This is a true acting performance as well as musical and mimicry," Sorrentino said. He has been a Captain Fantastic fan since the '70s and briefly worked for Rocket Records in 1979 before the label folded. No other impersonator has had his own full concert, and plays internationally. "Stephen's the only one," says his press representative. "In costume, mannerism, speaking voice, singing voice and even

The many faces of Stephen Sorrentino including one of Captain Fantastic.

sometimes in his temperament. So for that time when the show is on, he "'is' Elton John."

Sorrentino has played Elton in the famed Legends in Concert as well as Disney and Dick Clark Productions, and also performs hundreds of Elton shows a year on his own. He sings songs from the '70s to the present and tries to manage at least three costume changes and no less than 10 pairs of flamboyant trademark glasses per show. But don't expect this multi-talented entertainer to portray Elton John in concert for the rest of his career. These days Sorrentino is making a name as himself. "I don't want to be Elton John when I grow up. There's only room for one in the world," he says. "I want to be noted for my own originality and abilities." Being seen as an individual talent, Sorrentino has made *seven* films, appeared on six TV shows, and done over 100 radio and television voice-overs. Currently he stars in his own show, "Voices in My Head" in Las Vegas, where he performs over 150 different celebrity vocal impressions, does a hilarious stand-up comedy routine, performs original songs on piano, saxophone, flute, and guitar and does various physical comedy and pantomime routines. Legendary comedian Jerry Lewis hails Stephen "the vaudevillian of the new Millennium." As far as meeting Elton back in 1979 when he was a Rocket crew member, he recalled: "Seeing him away from the

A man they call Fantastic: Stephen Sorrentino as Elton John.

lights and fans, I thought Elton had a very kind, loving side, very personable and witty." Sorrentino summed up, "He was more than just a musician. It was from him that I first realized what "star quality" truly was. It's something that you're born with, you can't learn or purchase something like that. I hope to someday be able to make even a fragment of the mark on the world that Elton John has, but in my own way."❖

The Other Eltons

In the mid-seventies, Elton John fans used to go wild for look-alike Ron Singer. "It's all a bit of a giggle," said Singer, who was 34 when this photo was snapped. Of course, he made it clear that he didn't go around posing as the real thing, even when he was offered the VIP treatment from hotels and restaurants.

Elton continued to tour throughout most of 2000, performing mostly solo shows. These one-man shows featured just Elton and his piano.

CHAPTER ELEVEN

Millennium Man

Broadway? Eminem? Who would have though the first year and a half of the new millennium would start off this way. Well, in the world of Elton John, one never knows what musical direction he is going to go in. The much-anticipated *Aida* was Broadway bound as Elton and Tim Rice continued weaving their magical for film and stage. *Aida* was a smash hit on Broadway and went on to win four Tony Awards including Best Original Score at the Fifty-fourth Annual Tony Awards ceremonies. Elton also teamed up again with Tim Rice for the Dreamworks inspired animated feature, *The Road to El Dorado*. But this time however, the hits weren't as forthcoming. The first and only single "Someday Out of the Blue" failed to crack the Top 40 and it was evident, that this was not

Elton with boyfriend, filmmaker, David Furnish, at the 1999 premiere of David's film, *Talking Dirty*.

to be a second *Lion King.* With a huge promotional campaign behind the release and Elton seemingly being everywhere to promote it during the middle of March 2000, including a record signing at Tower Records in Los Angeles, March 14. But the soundtrack had little effect on a fickle public.

Perhaps, more significant about this release is that Elton teamed up with Patrick Leonard (hot from Madonna's *Ray of Light* album) to produce the album. Patrick Leonard knew how to capture some of the old seventies style trademarks of Elton's best singles and album track.

This would set the stage for Elton and Bernie's return-to-form for the late 2001 release *Songs from The West Coast.* This would become an instant and immediate favorite from die-hard Elton fans. Taupin's picturesque lyrics and timely, topical subjects fit comfortably into Elton's country influenced melodies.

Elton continued to tour through much of 2000 doing mostly solo shows to get his edge back and play some obscure album tracks that long time fans have been waiting to hear for decades. The one-man shows were nearly

three hour musical feasts with just Elton and the piano.

Back in 1972 Elton and Bernie wrote a hit song that would be used in a critically acclaimed film nearly thirty years later. That song, "Tiny Dancer" plus two other Elton songs were featured in the Cameron Crowe epic *Almost Famous.* The movie about a groupie following a seventies rock band across the country hit a nerve with with movie goers over thirty-five who were teenagers during that decade. The highlight of the film as many Elton John fans would agree was the moving scene on the tour bus where the film's characters began singing along to "Tiny Dancer" on the radio. Another fact that Elton John's music remains timeless.

November 16, 2001 *Goldmine* cover featuring Elton John and Bernie Taupin.

After more than thirty years in the music business, some gratuitous and deserving awards were on hand as well. He picked up the predictable Grammy Legend Award, TV Guide Award for his *One Night Only* special, taken from the live album of the same name; and was named MusiCares person of the year by the National Academy of Recording Arts & Sciences. But no other award would trigger so much attention than the Gay & Lesbian Alliance Against Defamation (GLAAD) awarded Elton the organization's Vito Russo Entertainer Award, which is presented to an openly lesbian or gay individual who work to battle discrimination and encourage tolerance for their respective community.

This award would also come back to haunt Elton the following year when he performed with rapper Eminem at the 2001 Grammy Awards. Never one to shy away from controversial issue, Elton was invited to sing the chorus to Eminem's "Stan." Elton, who championed the rapper's album, *The Marshall Mathers LP* praised the singer's songwriting skills and energy. This was shocking to most of the public since Eminem was known for hardcore lyrics that some women and gays found intolerable. Elton, never undaunted, performed because he didn't believe Eminem was as hateful as everyone had made him out to be. Plus, he wanted to build bridges, not walls. Amid protests prior to the broadcast, it didn't matter. The duet went on and Elton was still standing.

Celebrating his fifty-fifth birthday on March 25, 2002, he continues to enjoy his career more than ever. Delving into music for film and theater seemed to be natural extensions on an exhaustive career that just keeps going. He as also been inspired by a reinvigorated relationship with Bernie Taupin; and a new album that has been hailed as easily their best work in some twenty-five years. He continues, to this day to lend his moral support behind the most noble of causes including a stellar two song solo performance at the *Concert for New York* on October 20, 2001. The concert was a benefit and tribute to the victims of the September 11, 2001 terrorist attacks in New York City. Elton sang "I Want Love" and the fitting "Monas Lisas and Mad Hatters" to a very emotional crowd at Madison Square Garden. Even old friend Billy Joel helped out on the duet of Elton's signature favorite "Your Song."

Elton John is a big fan of television and in November 2001, made an appearance on the Fox hit show, *Ally McBeal.* "I love the show," he said. "I'm a big *Ally McBeal* fan. I was asked to do the show and I said, 'absolutely, I will do it.' I did *The Nanny* once (1997) and I really

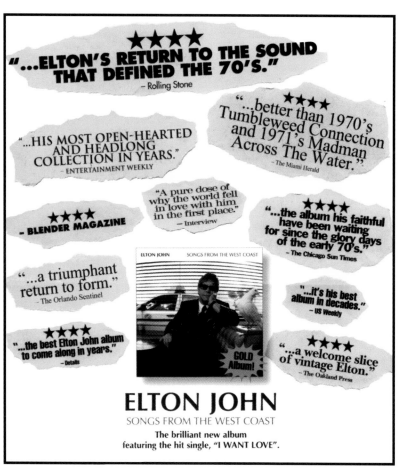

Universal Records' promotional flyer for the 2001 release of *Songs from the West Coast,* Elton's 40th album.

Signed publicity photo from Elton's 1998 album, *The Big Picture.*

liked that. Any chance I get to do something out of the ordinary, or to do something different, I will do it. You jump at the chance if it's a really good show."

Elton John is a multi-talented and diverse entertainer and songwriter. If the start of the new millennium is any indication, his fans will have a lot more songs and concerts to look forward to. And what more can anyone ask? "I live my life one day to the next," he has said. "Every day is a new challenge for me. Every day when I get up is like a new occasion for me.

I treasure it. I have a remarkable life—a really Incredible life. I am very grateful for it."❖

"I live my life one day to the next. Every day is a new challenge for me."

Elton teamed up again with Tim Rice for the DreamWorks animated feature film, *The Road to El Dorado*. During March 2000 Elton promoted the project, including a rare record signing at Tower Records in Los Angeles.

THE ROAD TO
EL DORADO

Chorus of Light Exhibit: Elton's Gift to Atlanta

At an April 11, 2000 press conference held in New York's lavish St. Regis, Sir Elton John spoke of his exclusive 20th Century photography collection. He was flanked by Jane Jackson, his Atlanta art dealer and Thomas Southall, the High Museum photography curator.

Throughout his hour-long discussion, Sir Elton presented several slides of noted photographs as well as some of his personal favorites. It was obvious by Elton's comments that he was quite well-versed about his collection and credited Jackson for being instrumental in locating many of the photographs he owns. Today, Sir Elton John is regarded as one of the leading private photography collectors in the world. He lives with his astonishing Twentieth century photography. His passion for acquiring photographs is endless. Surprisingly enough, he doesn't collect photographs for the obvious potential value aspect, but simply because he likes the way they look or what they will contribute aesthetically to his collection.

Dubbed *"Chorus of Light: Photographs from the Sir Elton John Collection"* the exhibit debuted exclusively at Atlanta's High Museum of Art. The two-venue exhibit organized by the High Museum and John featured over 390 works by more than 100 renowned photographers including Berenice Abbott, Diane Arbus,

Man Ray's famous "Noir et Blanche," 1926 "Black and White" is one of Elton's all-time favorite photographs.

Chorus of Light

PHOTOGRAPHS FROM
THE SIR ELTON JOHN COLLECTION

Henri Cartier-Bresson, Walker Evans, Andre Kertesz, Tina Modotti, Paul Outerbridge, Norman Parkinson, Irving Penn, and Man Ray.

During the past decade, Elton has built his remarkable collection of over two thousand works. He has called Atlanta his home for nearly as long and referred to "Chorus of Light" as his "gift" to the city of Atlanta. "I became clean and sober in Atlanta," he said at the press conference, "and that's where I first started collecting photographs." In 1996, he became a member of the High Museum and soon thereafter joined it's prestigious Director's Circle. Visitors to the High viewed John's works of art which are normally hung in his homes in Atlanta, England and France. The exhibition dates were from November 4, 2000 to January 28, 2001. A hardcover book accompanied the major exhibition. *Chorus of Light: Photographs from The Sir Elton John Collection* includes an introduction by the exhibition's curator, Ned Rifkin, and an appreciation of the collector by Jane Jackson, an adviser to the collection.

The following is an edited version of Elton's New York press conference.

Elton's opening speech to the press:

"I started collecting photography in 1990. I encountered collecting by accident. I live in a world where cameras are on me constantly. I never really thought about photography as an art. I don't know why. It never occurred to me till I went to a friend's house in France. There was this photographic exhibit on the walls. I thought some of the photographs were the most beautiful I had ever seen. It was at that moment I became passionate about photographs. Perhaps more passionate than I have ever been about collecting. I am a passionate collector. I collect a lot of things. I mean, I do collect a lot of things (laughs). It's something I love. Now I collect mostly 20th Century pieces. I taught myself about photograph collecting. I love to go to exhibits, I don't go to auctions anymore. It's too dangerous for me to go to auctions! (laughs). I am

able to lend these photographs to the High Museum. Unfortunately my apartment is going to be bare! I'll have to rent some furniture! (laughs).

"I love to be around people that love photography. I've been lucky enough to have my picture taken by some of the best photographers in the world. When I travel I am always looking for photographs to add to my collection. Wherever I go I try to find photographs that appeal to me. Of course, I'm always delighted to find something new, like when I'm in Australia. I found these (refers to images on the screen) by a brilliant Australian photographer named Bill Hanson. His work is very exciting. When I first met him, we just talked about photography. and the people he has photographed. He is just amazing. I have never been so excited about a visual art form before in my life. I am very proud of my collection. My collection is an ongoing thing. I'll have to buy another apartment soon. I started out by buying a two-thousand square foot duplex apartment in Atlanta in 1991. Then I started collecting photography. I now have eighteen thousand square feet with eight hundred to nine hundred photographs on the wall.

"I now have photography in my houses in Nice and Windsor as well. I'm getting rid of the gold records on the wall. I don't need them anymore. I am so delighted to participate in this event. I feel like a real Freshman at this. I'm so excited about photography."

How do you collect?

"I usually collect by my eye. If I don't like something, I'm not going to buy it even if it's a brilliant photograph and historically important. It's important that I like it. If I don't then I don't buy it. There aren't a lot of visual photographers works that I don't like. I don't collect everything. I have an eye for certain things. I collect what attracts me. If the photograph turns out to be famous or a collectible, then it's a bonus for me. You should always collect what you enjoy the most. The joy of collecting is to be able to collect what you enjoy the most."

Can you possibly look at all 900 images every day?

"Oh yes, every day (laughs). I walk around my entire apartment. By the time I finish it takes me forty-five minutes to look at everything. I mean look at them every day. It's a source of real enjoyment for me. I wander around my apartment thinking how lucky I am to be to afford to collect such beautiful things.

"In America, photographs are much more appreciated than in my home country of Britain. I have to stress I consider Atlanta my American home base right now. In England it is not taken so seriously as it is in other places in Europe."

Do you ever take any of your own photographs?

"I never carry a camera around with me. I just don't do it. I know I would leave it somewhere. I've had my photo taken so many times. I used to have a camera, but I gave it up. I prefer other people's photos to mine anyway."

What are some of your favorite rock and roll photographs?

"I really don't have that many rock and rollers in my collection. Actually, I have Richard Avedon's Beatles, which is so beautiful. I have some jazz pictures, too—Billie Holiday, Chet Baker, who I adore as a musician and is a beautiful human being, Miles Davis, Dinah Washington. I tend to collect really legendary musicians more than rock artists. Sting's in the exhibit, too. He's a friend of mine."

Who selected the photographs for the exhibit?

"They came to me. (The High Museum) They know what kind of photographs I like. I'm on the road most of the time—close to a year or so. The people at the museum have pretty good judgment about what I would want to buy."

Who are some of the young photographers you like to buy from and why?

"I collect all kinds of photography. I like the work of this one photographer named Paul Smith. I collect photographs from photographers you never heard of before. There's this one photographer that just photographs Tupperware. Sounds really boring, but actually the photographs are pretty tremendous. Jim Burton is another photographer I like."

You've been photographed by many of the photographers whose work you also collect. Do you find that you've become a bigger fan of their work after that?

"There are several photographs of me in the exhibition taken by these very same photographers. I can't remember all the names. There are photographs by Norman Parkinson, Irving Penn, Chuck Close, Andy Warhol. I can't remember there are so many people. The photographers I mentioned, I really love their work. Irving Penn took my photograph. I like his work. I was very nervous at first when he took my picture. I've had my photograph taken by many of these photographers. It's fascinating to be able to relate to their work."

You have collected over a thousand photographs. Where do you keep the ones that are not in the exhibit?

"The ones that are not in the exhibit are in my homes. The others are in storage which are not framed. I've got about seventy in the exhibition that are framed. Eventually I am in the process of getting them all framed. I'm very big on framing photographs. When you go see an exhibition, you just don't want to see black frames. It looks okay, but it always doesn't give the picture justice. These are beautiful works of art and they deserve beautiful representation. I have interior designers that do great work. Some frames that are used are very ornate, some are simple."

Since your photograph collection is split up between, England, France and America, do you eventually want to keep everything in one place?

"This is something that I have been thinking about for a long time. I eventually don't want to keep the photographs split up."

Your photograph collection is obviously very personal to you. How do you feel about being separated from them?

"I'll be sleeping at the museum every night (laughs). I live in Atlanta, and the reason why I wanted the High Museum to have these photographs for an exhibit is because I knew they would treat them very well. I love the museum, it's a great museum. My play, *Aida* started out in Atlanta. I have nothing against New York, Paris or where ever. I just thought it would be nice to do it in the town that has showed me so much love and that has welcomed me—opened its arms to me. This is something I have been wanting to do for ages."

Is there anything in the exhibition that may be found offensive?

"Maybe not in the exhibition there isn't, but in my apartment, there's a lot! (laughs). There's these little old ladies in my building who come to my apartment all the time. They thought some of the photographs were very colorful. They really don't know what they are, though."

What does this collection say about you?

"I don't know. I have no idea. You would have to ask someone else. I just love the art form. I love collecting beautiful images like this. For me, it's the one true art form of the twentieth century. I started collecting black and white and now I collect color. There's always something new to collect. A new gallery to go to. I collect paintings as well. I'm not as enthusiastic or as diligent about collecting paintings as I am collecting photographs. In an way I would go stark raving mad if I didn't collect."

Do you think you will reach a point where you won't want to collect photographs anymore?

"I would be very happy living with the collection I have now. But there's always another photograph waiting to be bought. Another new photographer to discover. Collecting is what makes me happy."

Do you know how much you've spent on your photo collection so far?

"I don't know. I have no idea (laughs). You would have to ask my accountants that question. I don't collect for value. The first time I bought a really expensive photograph was in London. I think it was the early nineties. I paid something like one-hundred thousand dollars or something like that. I thought, 'hmm, this is serious'. I bought it because I loved it so much. I have very expensive photographs and some that are not that so expensive. It doesn't have to be expensive for me to like it. As I've said before, I enjoy collecting. I have a great passion for collecting photographs. A lot of my friends are into collecting photographs now. They don't have the money I have, but they still collect. Anyone can start. You don't have to spend as much money as I do. You can start with a $500 photograph or less and go from there."

How do you view your collection?

"My collection is a work in progress. I expect to be collecting for the next few years or so. It's very difficult to judge one's collection. I hope that when people collect, they enjoy what they look at. I enjoy my collection. At one time I had no idea what a collection was. Collecting is very, very personal. It's like having a child. Having your photographs hang in a museum for three months is a very nice thing to do. These pieces are like part of my family in a way. These are pictures of real people. That's a part of me."

Sir Elton Speaks

Elton is outspoken on everything from his musical influences to his personal life and back again. But unlike rockers who seem to have rehearsed answers to interviewers' questions, Elton seems to always have a fresh take (even if it's a question he's answered one thousand times). Elton's sense of humor—mainly the ability to laugh at himself and music business as a whole—has always made him a darling of the media.

Elton's favorite topics for discussion include the Beatles, fashion (no surprise), his fans, how he struggled in the early days, the poignant moments of his childhood as a self-proclaimed "fat kid," and his love of soccer. But he is a well-rounded guy who can also chat about more serious subjects such as world politics, art, terrorism and health issues. Even though he is known privately as a deeply emotional person, Elton comes off as a level-headed, cordial, funny Englishman in interviews, and has never had a tiff with the press (that has been on the record, anyway). He genuinely seems happy for the attention he gets and that someone actually wants to print his words!

Perhaps when Elton is speaking of the love for his fans that he seems the most glowing. He is beyond grateful they followed him through over thirty years of ups-and-downs,

At the Smash Hits auction event in 2000,

including making the awkward transition from simple "rock star" to "video artist" with the advent of *MTV* in 1981. Elton's deep love for his fans is echoed the loudest not in his quotes though, but in the fact that he thanks each and every fan that asks for his autograph.

So read on for Elton's most interesting and revealing quotes. As time has gone on and his celebrity has grown, he has become even more comfortable with opening himself up to interviewers. Over the years, he has announced his

"My stage clothes put me in the right mood for a performance. The clothes thing is very me. Without them, I wouldn't feel like Elton John."

Elton at a *Planet Hollywood* event in Las Vegas.

retirement several times, and then taken it back. Could it be that he's finally comfortable both emotionally and physically in the spotlight?

You never know what's going to come out of EJ's mouth, just as you never know what's going to come out of his trademark piano. So let's raise our glasses to the piano man, and let him speak rather than tickle the ivories right now…

On the United States of America:

"I love this country. I love these people. I can't forget this is where it all started."

On leaving Bluesology:

"I was totally frustrated with Bluesology because nobody had any ambition. I wanted to go further than where we'd already came from. I wanted to write and sing. I began to feel held down. So I finally left. I had enough."

On his early musical influences:

"My parents collected records when I was a child. I grew up on artists like Guy Mitchell and Johnny Ray, and then later Elvis. I was always surrounded by good music when I was a kid. I still remember when my father bought me 'Songs For Swinging Lovers.' As a pianist, I was influenced by Little Richard and Jerry Lewis and then later on Ray Charles. I love the Beatles, but I don't think they influenced me as a songwriter. The Beach Boys' sound and their way of writing and their melodies were a much bigger influence on me."

On clothes:

"I'm not your rangy rock idol in skinny leather pants, I wear flamboyant clothes. My stage clothes put me in the right mood for a performance. The clothes thing is very me. Without them, I wouldn't feel like Elton John."

"I've been throwing clothes out and I think, 'Did I really wear that?' There's no limit to what I can wear onstage. Platform shoes—that had to be the worst era of fashion ever. I had some of the prime worst examples. I cornered the market in platform shoes. The higher they went, the higher I used to get them!"

"When I was a kid, my dad was real strict and I had to wear really dull clothes. When I got the chance, I went to the opposite extreme. I don't have the sexiest body in the world, so I like to have comedy in my act."

On extravagances:

"You can only take so much of this way of living. There comes a time when your inner self begins to hunger for more."

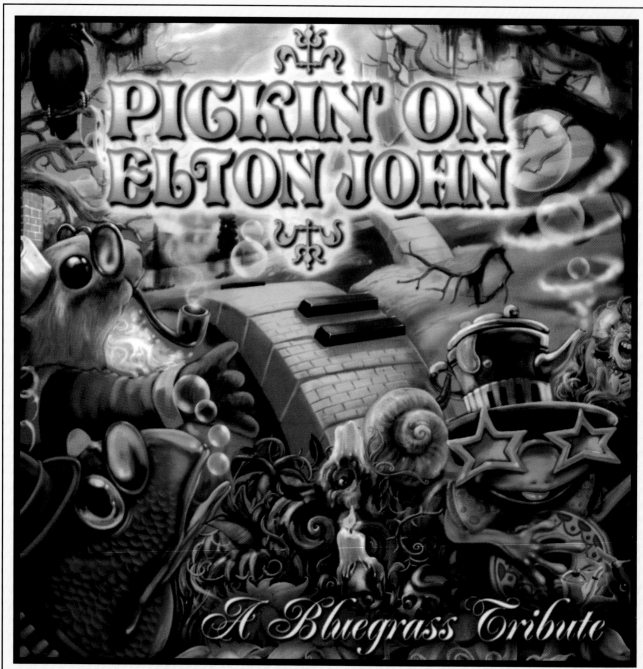

Pickin' On Elton John: **A Bluegrass Tribute.**

"I think I burnt myself out by touring and making too many albums and doing a lot of other things personally to myself which weren't conducive to making you feel particularly great. I still retained that wanting to listen and wanting to compete."

On worldwide acclaim:

"There's a whole damn exciting world out there to explore. There's a river of human drama every second. My kind of music is great for what it is, but there's the world of painting, literature, the dance. I could go on and on. There's so much I don't know about these things."

On Bernie Taupin:

"Thirty years writing with someone is pretty amazing. I'm very proud of that, Bernie and I are like brothers. I don't remember ever having a major argument with him. We done writing outside the relationship we have professionally. I think that's what keeps us together. We've never been jealous of each other's professional accomplishments. Bernie is a very pure person. He is the perfect writing partner. Today, we are closer than we ever were."

"I think the reason why our relationship has lasted so long is because we have both given each other permission to write with other people. We don't live in the same place anymore. He lives in Los Angeles—actually San Ynez. I live in England. Yet, because of our strong bond, the love that we have for each other has never ever waned. In fact, it's only gotten stronger over the years."

"Bernie always writes the words of a song first and then gives them to me and I write the tune. It always works perfectly and I think we gain from doing it that way. I can't write lyrics and I know what Bernie wants, so it always comes out right. We don't write a lot—generally it comes in spasms when we feel like it."

"Bernie and I are very close. I know what he's getting at. If I sang about myself all the time, it would be very doom-laden. I don't think Bernie gets enough credit for the older, more successful songs."

On Eric Clapton:

"I have played with Eric. Eric is obviously a musician that is admired by everyone...and as a person, I admire him too. We're friends. Okay, we're not close friends, but we are friends."

On Axl Rose:

"I really like him. I like his music and I like him as a person. I think he's really misunderstood by some of the comments that he makes."

On Freddie Mercury:

"He's gone and he was a friend, and a big influence as far as a musician. We did a lot of things together in our tours. We were successful in America at the same time. I was fortunate enough to see him in the last year of his life. He will always be in my heart."

On multiple addictions:

"I was so ill and so worn out and physically and mentally tired of abusing myself with alcohol and drugs and bulimia. I was tired of running. I had to ask for help. It was either that or I was going to be dead. I didn't really want to die, even though there were times when I thought, 'Oh God, I can't go on like this anymore.' I had everything to live for, but I was very lost."

"I was confronted by a friend about my drug and alcohol problems and also my eating. I used to purge myself. I was the fattest bulimic probably there has ever been. I just did it as a way to keep my weight down. I did not know how dangerous it was. Bulimia was quite interesting to learn about. I have a lot of sympathy for people who are bulimic."

"I was spiritually bankrupt before I got sober. I know I couldn't have done it on my own. I believe something helped me. I don't understand it, but I have faith in it."

On Renate Blauel:

"I met someone that I liked a lot and wanted to marry her. It happened at a moment when I was tired of my old style of living."

"I'm relieved that it is over and that everything has come out in the open. I'm happy I don't have to carry on living a lie. I got so fed up having to fib about our marriage and say everything was rosy, when it wasn't. But what could I do. The pressure was horrendous."

On his Atlanta residence:

"I love it. I fell in love with the people here (Atlanta), which makes a big difference. I felt, it's not Los Angeles, and it's not New York, and I don't have any business friends in Atlanta."

On the Watford Football Club:

"I've had a lot of abuse in my business from the press and other people who were jealous or whatever. But I never had that in football. I have had a lot of wonderful things and seen a lot of places. I've met a lot of wonderful people for whatever reason."

"I've been to Buckingham Palace, I've been to the White House. I've been to the House of Parliament. But in my life, one of the nicest things that ever happened to me was as a boy, going to watch the Watford Football game with my dad. I never thought I would someday become the chairman of the club that I loved so much."

On John Lennon:

"I met John through a mutual friend of ours. I think I met him at a video shoot in Los Angeles. We hit it off like a house on fire. He was so great. We hung out together. May Pang was there. We all had a ball together. When I think of John…it's like I expect to see

him walking down the street. It's so strange. I think John's death will always stay with me. His death has a lasting effect. I still haven't gotten over it. His death stays with me all the time. It's a personal thing."

On the Rolling Stones:

"I saw the Rolling Stones in 1989 on their 'Steel Wheels' Tour. I thought they were possibly the best rock and roll band I have ever seen. I was really pleased because people say, 'oh, they are so old.' There's nothing wrong with getting old as long as you maintain an interest in what's happening with younger musicians and keep up with them."

On the Dee Murray Tribute:

"It's a sad night, but it's a magical night because we're paying tribute to to someone who gave the world a lot of love and a lot of music. Dee affected me as a musician and as a person. I didn't realize how much until he was gone. When Dee passed away a couple of months ago (1992), he left a big hole in my life. I'm here tonight to say thanks to him. I feel truly blessed to have had Dee in my life and to have know him, to have known his courage. I just want to say, 'Dee, I love you. You're in my heart, always.'"

On Prince (The Artist Formerly Known As):

"I remember going up to Prince one day. I just wanted to say how great his *1999* album was. It took all this courage to go up to him because I am so shy. And I was speaking, 'I really like your stuff.' He just looked at me and walked away. I've hated that little bastard ever since."

On life:

"I've got a very good outlook on life. I'm very healthy, emotionally and physically. Music has always been my connection with life. Everything's fitting into place. I'm interested in personal happiness. Just the fact that I can be with the people I want to be with and I've had a lot of the same people around me for a very long time. That makes me happy."

"I'm rich enough to be able to do what I want to do in life. I should not throw away that privilege. I want to play and feel happy about doing it. I always believed, if you are given a gift, you should capitalize on it."

"Life is an achievement if you conquer it. If you manage to go through the neurotic tantrums I've thrown and other people have thrown and still end up being friends—that's an achievement."

On "Your Song":

"I think the favorite song of mine would have to be "Your Song," because of the wonderful lyrics. It's the one song I've never gone through the motions singing."

On Blue Moves:

"Blue Moves is one of the best albums we've made. It was done during a time when Bernie and I were going through quite a lot of personal traumas. Bernie was getting divorced and some of the lyrics he wrote were so heavy, I couldn't even record them."

On music:

"I play music every day, I've never been happier with my music. Whatever mood I'm in, I can change it, I can play whatever music I want to fit. It does nourish and it does cleanse.

Elton with LeAnn Rimes during the "Written in the Stars" photo session for the *Aida* collection.

If I can make someone's day happier, if I can make someone's day a little bit more light. I just don't get carried away with it, but I can say this; it blow me away."

On his generosity:

"It makes me happy to give away things as well as receive. I'm in a position to give a lot of things, and since I've got the money, I've always been like that. When I didn't have any money, I'd spend it or give it to someone. One thing I have always been able to do is share things with people."

On being competitive:

"Bernie listens to a lot of blues music and he's starting to listen to a lot of jazz. I've always had a wide taste in music. The only thing I don't listen to is rap music. I listen to most things. If I hear something that I really like, then it's really exciting, especially if it's by a newer artist. I'm in a competitive business. It keeps you sharp to be competitive."

On the human spirit:

"The thing about traveling around the world is that you realize every country has different problems and attitudes, but that basically people are the same wherever you go. There's that same human spirit, and I'm a great believer in the human spirit."

157

"I firmly believe the human spirit is basically a good one and that's why it's important to become involved in issues like Live Aid or the crisis with the rain forests. Performers can make more people aware by supporting these causes and talking about them. I know a lot of cynics accuse of jumping on the bandwagon, but what are they doing about these problems?"

On rock and roll:

"I had a very boring childhood. If it wasn't for the fact that I suddenly heard rock and roll for the first time—in England, we had nothing you have to remember. American music changed my life. God bless, America."

"I like to pay tribute to the people that were my biggest influences: Little Richard, Jerry Lee Lewis, Fats Domino, Ray Charles, George Shearing. Anybody who played piano and who played rock and roll. There are so many people on the bill that I used to go and see. Duane Eddy and the Animals. Alan Price of the Animals, who played a Vox Continental organ. Organs have been the downfall of my life somewhat. Or, I guess, they've been the upswing of my life, I don't know."

On being gay:

"The gay business hurt me a lot. I stopped touring after announcing that I was a homosexual and had nothing else to do. If it hadn't had Watford I might have become a very big causality. I had to learn to take defeat as well. If you take your seat at a football ground and 20,000 people are singing 'Elton John is a homosexual' you learn fairly quickly."

"I'd rather be honest, than live my life as a lie. I don't flaunt it, but if I can help other people like that. I support any suppressed movement, but I don't think gay people are supressed anymore."

On the 1979 Soviet tour:

"It was one of the memorable and happy tours I've been on. The country is not dark, gray, grim or drab. It's beautiful, and the people are very warm. Leningrad was a marvelous city and the hospitality, tremendous. This was the first time they had really experienced rock and roll at the level we gave them. We played 'Back in the USSR' every night without anyone objecting."

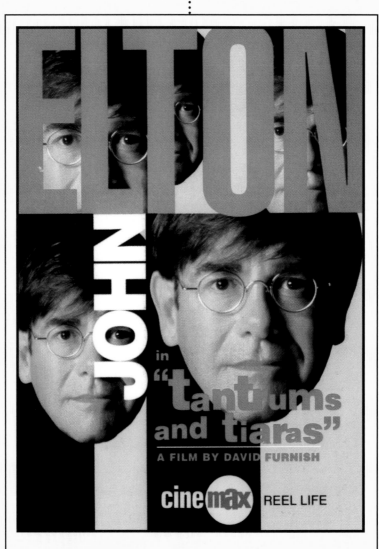

Tantrums and Tiaras, a film by David Furnish, first premiered on September 3, 1997, as a Cinemax Reel Life Exclusive before it was made into a home video.

On his favorite Elton album:

"It's difficult 'cause I don't listen to them very much. But having listened to the albums when they were remastered I'm very proud of the *Captain Fantastic* album because it tells a story and it's about me. So when I was writing the song I felt an allegiance to the lyrics straightaway because it was autobiographical. I think *Blue Moves* is a great musical album and *Yellow Brick Road* is a pretty good double album. I like *Don't Shoot Me* and I like *Tumbleweed*."

On his throat surgery:

"My voice is going to be fine. About two months after the operation, I was very frightened I wouldn't get any falsettos. I think that in timbre, my voice has gone down in pitch, but I got my falsettos back."

On performing:

"Performing is my forte. Hopefully, I will be remembered for being a good live actor. That's what has sustained my career. No matter how your records sell, if you are good onstage, people will come to see you, In the end, if people say you were a great performer, the records or the songs don't matter. All I ever wanted to do was to a great performer."

On fame:

"I always knew that I would be famous one day. I was always convinced, although I knew I would have to wait until I was fifty-three. The only thing that kept me going was my ambition. I'd like to become a legend, I'm hung up with legends. I'd like to be like a Mae West or something like that, but I don't think I will because they are so very, very special."

On playing the piano:

"I was an up-tempo piano player who wanted to use his piano like a guitar. But you can't kick a piano or you'll break your foot. So you jump on it, you do everything you can to make it interesting. Otherwise you're stuck behind a nine foot plank."

On the Tantrums and Tiaras video:

"I wanted to be as honest as possible. I wanted to show people what it really is like touring for a year. The pressure you go on, how impossible you can be, how funny situations can be. You read interviews and it's always how wonderful they are. And you see a documentary about someone and it never really examines the darker side of someone. And it was the first thing about me that I could watch all the way through without flinching, because it was accurate. I mean, when you do a talk show and you go on you kind of put on a different persona. A lot of people didn't like it. It was a very good experience for me, a very kind of cleansing experience as well. I was a monster in some of it, but I just sat there and laughed at all. I just thought 'God, this is so funny.'"❖

TAUPIN ~~CRITIC~~ RELEASES ALBUM

East End Lights

#23/Summer 1996 ● The Magazine for Elton John Fans

$5 per issue

Video reveals private Elton

Pavarotti and EJ duet on 'Horses'

"When I Think of Those East End Lights..."
The Gospel According to Elton

In the autumn of 1990, publisher and editor, Tom Stanton launched *East End Lights (EEL)*, the first national publication dedicated solely to Elton John. It had been the magazine fans of all ages had waited for and now, more than a decade later, still can't get enough of it. It's a fact from the 30-plus-years die-hard to the newbies of the last few years, Elton John fans are insatiable when it comes to getting the latest up to date news on him. Stanton knew this and thus set out to create *East End Lights* to fill the much-needed void.

"I had been an Elton John fan for many years," he explained. "So Like many of my Elton pals, I used to scan *Rolling Stone*, local dailies and *Billboard* for information of Elton. Most of the time I was disappointed, so that's why I started *East End Lights*. It was also an experiment in niche publishing. I wanted to see what kind of demand there would be for a high quality magazine focusing on a single entertainer.

Prior to the launch of *East End Lights*, Stanton had co-founded the first of five weekly newspapers in the Detroit, Michigan area. He stressed that *East End Lights* was never intended to compete with the fan clubs or the popular publications like *Rocket Fan* (now known as *Hercules)*, because their presence was important, although their purposes were very different.

"I like to think that *EEL* and the four international Elton Expos we organized over the years changed how Elton and his organization viewed his legion of fans. I think it brought us greater respect in their eyes and increased the level of our input related to his career and activities. Elton enjoys a devoted following of fans. Many of whom have followed him since their days in junior high in the early 1970s and who have

Mark Norris and Tom Stanton

matured with him. It's a special relationship and *East End Lights* is a special publication. It was a wonderful ten-year run and a glorious experience. It brought me into contact with other fans who appreciated the genius of Elton John and Bernie Taupin."

In addition to publishing *East End Lights*, Stanton co-authored *Rocket Man*, an encyclopedia on Elton John (Greenwood Publishing Group) in 1995. In 2001, Stanton decided it was time to hand over the reigns to new publisher and major Elton fan, Mark Norris so he could pursue his own artistic dreams in the literary world. His debut came

The U.K. based *Hercules* was never intended to compete with *East End Lights*.

in the way of hard cover book titled *The Final Season* published by St. Martin's Press in 2001.

Today, *East End Lights* is in its twelfth year of publishing and continues to be the world's most authoritative source for information on all things Elton John. The magazine is still published four times a year, and has increased its editorial from twenty-two pages to forty-four. *East End Lights* continues to feature news, photos and in-depth interviews with current and former band members as well as covers the latest information and a behind-the-scenes look at Elton John in a way no other music or fan related publication can.

Gus Dudgeon and Nigel Olsson sign autographs at one of the Elton Expos sponsored by *East End Lights*.

THE EARLY DAYS; A FRIEND REMEMBERS

East End Lights

#24/Fall 1996 ● The Magazine for Elton John Fans

$5 per issue

'MY LIFE AS A DOG'

Taupin says his new band fulfills a lifelong dream

INSIDE: RINGO WANTED TO BE IN ELTON'S BAND

0 74470 83792 3

42

East End Lights

#27/Summer 1997 ● The Magazine for Elton John Fans

$5 per issue

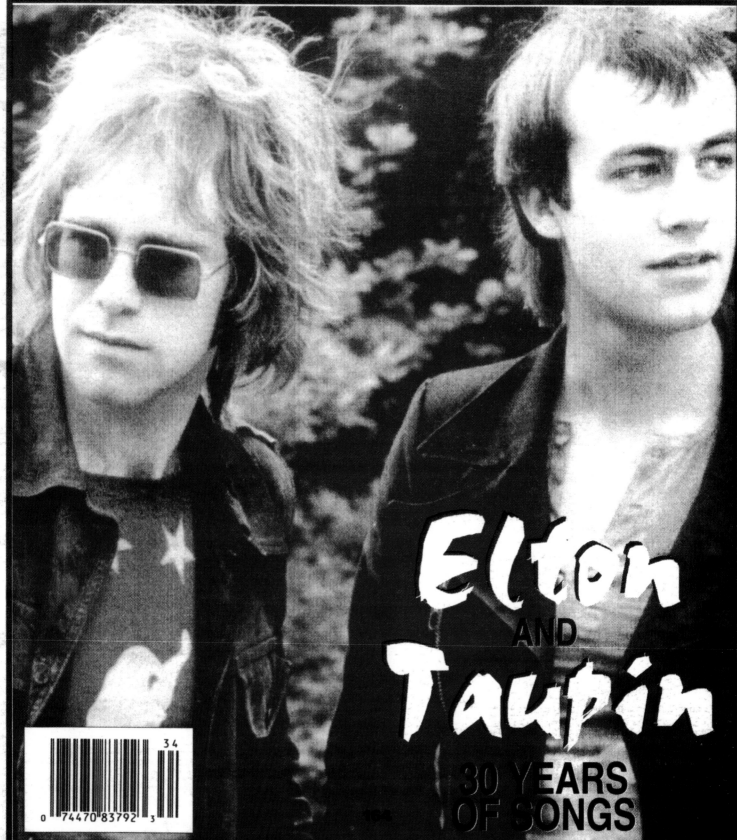

Elton AND Taupin

30 YEARS OF SONGS

0 74470 83792 3   34

"I am often surprised at the depth of knowledge the fans have about Elton," noted Norris. "It is sometime scary how much they know! The one thing I don't think many people understand is that *EEL* is not a big business. I am simply a fan who wanted to share my love of Elton with anyone who would listen or in this case, read. I had been involved with *EEL* for about six years and had been a regular subscriber myself before taking it over. *East End Lights* is a mission of love, and I am always trying to find ways to cut the expenses while maintaining the kind of quality fans have come to expect."

One of the aspects of running the revamped publication is offering space to Elton associates like Nigel Olsson and the Hercules fan club. Norris is proud of the fact that *East End Lights* has continued to offer what he views and many agree as "truly outstanding Elton coverage and objective writing."

"We don't go out of our way to sugarcoat anything," he added. "We tell it like it is. One thing that people who are not familiar with *EEL* are always saying is that it doesn't read like the usual fan magazine. It's not all fluff. In fact, I would say it's just the opposite. *EEL* is more of a reporting magazine."

Just as when Stanton founded the publication, *East End Lights* is not supported in any way except through subscriptions. It also contains a classified section so readers can buy, sell or trade their Elton memorabilia with other fans. A paid subscription will access readers to even more information via through the publication's popular website at *www.eastend lights.com*. Late breaking news and information such as tour dates that didn't make it into the printed magazine usually find it's way onto the virtual pages along with a few special promotions and one-of-a-kind items. *East End Lights* can be found at many retailers such as Books a Million, Tower Records, Borders, Nuggets and various specialty stores. ❖

Big supporters of *East End Lights:* Elton's longtime musical director/guitarist Davey Johnstone and original drummer Nigel Olsson.

East End Lights

#28/Fall 1997 ● The Magazine for Elton John Fans $5 per issue

THE
Big
Picture

The
New
Album

East End Lights

#30/Spring 1998 ● The Magazine for Elton John Fans $5 per issue

A Year on
the road
for Elton
BIG TOUR FOR BIG PICTURE

Nigel Olsson
remembers
Dee Murray

Taupin
runs with
The Dogs

The magic
touch of
Gus Dudgeon

Fans tell Elton
where to go
...musically

East End Lights

THE MAGAZINE FOR ELTON JOHN FANS • ISSUE #38 SPRING 2000 • $5 PER ISSUE

Elton's
El Dorado

New DreamWorks CD
promises gold

ALSO INSIDE

- Aida hits Broadway
- Industry piles honors on EJ
- Bob Birch reflects on eight
  years as Elton's bass player

East End Lights

THE MAGAZINE FOR ELTON JOHN FANS • ISSUE #39 SUMMER 2000 • $5 PER ISSUE

Elton, Taupin prepare
for September
studio date

With band, just
like the old days,
EJ pledges

ALSO INSIDE

- Nigel Olsson back at the drums?
- Final Elton Expo set for New York area
- Picture passion: EJ to share photo collection

eastendlights
the magazine for elton john fans

COVER PRICE

A WALK IN THE GARDEN

AN INSIDER'S PERSPECTIVE ON GREATEST HITS SHOW

41

UE FORTY-ONE

Past Elton Expos

ELTON

Elton is one of the top-selling solo artists of all time.

CHAPTER TWELVE

Fascinating Facts

lton's packed a lot of living into the last four decades: he's a rock pioneer and he's had things happen to him that only a pop star could experience. Fortunately, he's had a great sense of humor even during the tough times when, thanks to the prying eyes of the press, he thought he was yesterday's news.

However, he never became yesterday's news (but you already knew that!). He has grown in leaps and bounds as time has gone by, lovingly growing with musical trends, but starting most of them himself!

THE SEVENTIES

The seventies first brought Elton to these shores as what we initially perceived to be a mellow, hippie-style piano player with glasses and a turtleneck. But hey, with the advent of glitter rock in '72, EJ had to out-glitter them all. He had electric suits that could cause a blackout in the Empire State Building and a piano prowess pop fans had never encountered before. But he eventually made it into the world of AOR (adult-oriented rock) with "Philadelphia Freedom," his personal poem to the wondrous Billie Jean King, a close personal friend. He brought in the grown-ups, but never lost the young fans who had been with him in more outrageous times.

Did You Know...?

• Elton secretly practiced playing guitar?

• Elton was superstitious?

• Elton once tried to solve his weight problem by taking diet pills?

• The nearest and dearest to Elton's heart (besides music) was Rocket Records—the company he owned (and still owns today) and the Watford Football Team of England, of which he was the chairman?

• Elton preferred to wear striped socks over solid colors?

• Elton preferred to sleep on the right side of the bed?

• Elton had a leather mattress that was a reproduction of one that belonged to the Empress Josephine?

• Elton would drink only fresh-squeezed orange juice?

• Elton enjoyed playing practical jokes on his friends and entourage?

• Elton wore the zany eye wear to cover up his serious inferiority complex?

• Elton kept a private journal, mostly writing entries about his tour experiences?

• Because Elton had a weight problem, he spent time at an Arizona Tennis ranch to shed the pounds?

• Elton spent most of his money on art?

• Elton called himself "the human dustbin" because he liked to eat a lot of junk food?

• Elton was awarded a star on the Hollywood Walk of Fame on October 21, 1976?

• The American Optical Society gave Elton an award in 1975?

• Accordingly to *Billboard*, *Captain Fantastic and the Brown Dirt Cowboy* and *Rock of the Westies* debuted at the coveted Number-One position?

• Elton was the first white performer to ever appear on *Soul Train?*

• When Elton received a star on Hollywood's Walk of Fame Los Angeles officials declared it Elton John Day?

"Grandpop" Elton John as he looked for a comedy skit on Cher's TV Show in 1975. "It was laborious putting on all the make-up," said the 27-year-old rock legend at the time. "But it was great fun, too."

• In 1977, Elton was the first non-athlete to be honored in New York's Madison Square Garden Hall of Fame?

• The American Society of Composers, Authors, and Publishers awarded Elton the Golden Note Award in September, 1978. At the time, Elton was only one of three other performers to ever receive such a prestigious honor?

• As a bonus, in early 1971, new subscribers to *Rolling Stone* received a free copy of *Tumbleweed Connection?*

• In 1970, when Elton was just getting started in America, rock critics often described his singing voice to Jose Feliciano?

• In the mid-1970s rock pianist, Bruce Horsby, used to perform an Elton John parody

In a rare performance Elton has been known to play guitar.

complete with flamboyant costumes and over-sized eyewear?

THE EIGHTIES

The eighties were a trying time for Elton as his sound became more mature while New Wave and disco were raging around him. By the time those movements died, around 1984, Elton was doing some of his most intense material, including the politically messaged "Nikita."

He also changed his look, going more for the subtly sophisticated Versace suit rather than the beaded jumpsuit of gaudier days.

Did You Know...?

• "Nikita" was Elton's fortieth Top 40 single since 1970?

• Elton began to wear more wide-brimmed hats onstage in the early to mid-80s, which replaced the flat cap of the late 1970s?

• Elton was thirty-three years old when he released his 21st album in 1980—hence the title—*21 at 33?*

• "Kiss the Bride" was played at Elton's wedding to Renate Blauel?

• At the 1985 Live Aid concert performers were limited to four songs, but showman Elton managed to extend it to five? He actually shared the stage twice that night—once with Kiki Dee on "Don't Go Breaking My Heart" and then again with George Michael on "Don't Let The Sun Go Down on Me"?

• The undertaking of the Australian concerts were elaborate affairs? The second half of the performance saw Elton don an "Amadeus" outfit (his tribute to the Melbourne Symphony Orchestra). Onstage the total of musicians was a staggering 101?

• Elton performed a free concert in Central Park where over 450,000 people attended?

• Elton sued the British tabloid *The Sun* after it published allegations that he took drugs and had sex with "rent boys" (male prostitutes)?

• Film director Ken Russell, who worked with Elton in the hit movie, *Tommy*, directed him again a decade later in the 1985 video for "Nikita"?

• Despite Elton's throat problems in 1986, he still recorded a fine live album, who's big radio hit that year was a live version of "Candle in the Wind"?

• When Elton and Bernie wrote the song, "Act of War," they had hoped Tina Turner would record it? But when she rejected the song, Elton record it with feisty soul singer, Millie Jackson?

• In 1985 Elton and his bride Renate attended the wedding of the Duke and Duchess of York? Both bride and groom were big fans of Elton?

• Anti-apartheid demonstrators staged a protest outside of the Auckland hotel where Elton was staying because they were angry over his decision a year earlier to perform in Sun City, the South African resort?

• Elton filmed the video for "Passengers" at St. Tropez in the south of France?

• For a wedding present to Fergie, Elton re-recorded her favorite song, "Song for Guy"?

• The song "Princess" was dedicated by Elton to Princess Diana?

• Elton joined Gladys Knight, Stevie Wonder and Dionne Warwick on the single "That's What Friends Are For," which went to number one on the US charts?

• Elton confessed on the BBC that he considered suicide after revealing his gay love life?

• Elton poured a bottle of expensive champagne all over himself when England beat Australia in the third set of soccer?

Elton performed for his largest audience ever in Central Park in 1980.

• Elton appeared on Bob Dylan's *Under the Red Sky* album. He played piano on the track, "2 x 2"?

• Elton wrote songs with lyricist Gary Osborne and musician Tom Robinson?

• The album *Too Low for Zero* reunited Elton and Davey Johnstone with original bandmates, bassist, Dee Murray and drummer, Nigel Olsson?

• In 1988, seventy-five pairs of of Elton's elaborate eyeglasses were sold off at an auction?

• Country singer Kathy Mattea recorded a version of "Ball & Chain"?

• Elton was a big fan of the classic British television comedy, *The Goon Show*? In 1981 he bought a bunch of collector scripts from the show.

THE NINETIES AND THE NEW MILLENNIUM

As Elton moved into his forties, he questioned if he was "too old to rock'n'roll." Of course, his fans thought not, but he did have his periods of announcing his retirement and then not following through (a la Frank Sinatra). But the Big E loved what he did too much, and kept cranking out the hits despite personal addictions. (He eventually got help for his substance abuse and still raises money for the centers that helped him through this difficult period.) He purchased a lavish apartment in Atlanta and also played some private parties for charities in Atlanta, New York, London and Los Angeles

As the new millennium rolled around, Elton's greatest moments included dueting with Eminem on the 2001 *MTV Awards,* appearances on numerous *VH1* specials including *100 Greatest Moments In Rock 'n' Roll* and *From the Waist Down* (where he openly discussed the old days when he was hiding his sexuality), and tour with fellow piano man Billy Joel (the dynamic duo's 2001 appearance on the *Tonight Show* was one of late night's finest moments).

At the end of 2001, Elton is at the top of the charts with his *Songs from the West Coast* CD (Hollywood has always been near and dear to his heart even though he has been known to refer to it as "Hollyweird"). He's a performer who has come full circle and is still creating great music—and awesome trivia his fans will always have somewhere in the recesses of their minds! (And these days, he doesn't do anything stronger than Diet Coke). We'll have him around for decades to come—and we suspect he'll take over the movie world next!

Did You Know...?

• The album *Made in England* was co-produced by Elton and Greg Penny?

• Elton entered rehab in Chicago for multiple addictions?

• British newspapers reported that Elton was the second wealthiest rock star in England? Paul McCartney was the first?

• Elton filmed two television commercials for Diet Coke?

• In 1992, all profits from Elton's singles would be donated to various AIDS charities?

• Elton was nominated for five Grammys in 1994 and took home the Best Male Pop Vocal?

• The Elton John AIDS Foundation was formed in 1992?

• Elton was nominated for three Academy Awards in 1994 and won his first Oscar in 1995 for "Can You Feel the Love Tonight?"

• Elton performed the part of an angel in songwriter Randy Newman's musical, *Faust?*

• In 1990, Atlanta became Elton's part-time residence?

When Elton shops for new CDs, he usually buys four copies of each title, one for for each house he owns.

• Sir Elton was knighted in 1998?

• Elton was inducted into the *Rock and Roll Hall of Fame* in 1994? He gave his award to Bernie.

• Elton auctioned off his massive private record collection in 1993? His record collection was considered one of the world's premiere private holdings.

• British citizen, Elton confessed to a London paper that he has never voted?

• Elton hosts the annual post-Oscar parties? The first event was held in 1993.

• Though Elton has been a featured wax figure in various wax museums around the world, he prefers the latest addition of himself (dressed in red Versace suit) from Madam Tussaud's in New York City?

• *Songs from the West Coast Coast*, Elton's follow-up to *The Big Picture* was released in Fall 2001 and received critical acclaim from *Rolling Stone?*

• Elton and Billy Joel collaborated on a song called, "Red, White and Blues," which has yet to be officially released?

• "Don't Let The Sun Go Down on Me," by George Michael and Elton went to Number One in both America and Great Britain?

• "Candle in the Wind 1997" not only sold over 400,000 copies world wide, it also became the first John-Taupin song to be a hit in three different versions recorded by the same artist?

• Elton broke Elvis Presley's prestigious Top 40 Record with the release of the single "Simple Life"? This meant that for twenty-four consecutive years, Elton had a Top 40 hit on the American music charts.

• Elton wrote twenty-one songs in twenty-one days for the Broadway soundtrack to *Aida?*

• Elton autographed a photo for country music legend, Tammy Wynette? He inscribed: "To the queen of country music from the Queen of England."

• Elton was made an Officer of Arts and Letters in France and an honorary member of the Royal Academy of Music in London?

• Since 1992, all proceeds from Elton's U.K. and U.S. profits from his singles are donated to his AIDS foundation?

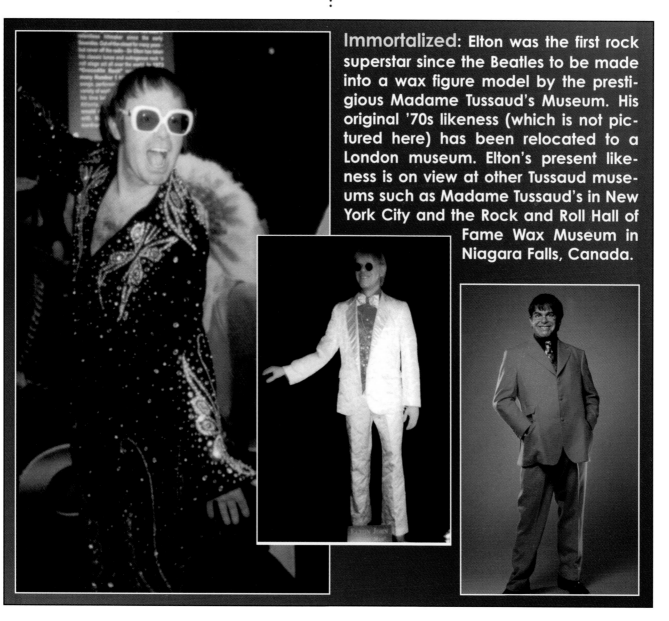

Immortalized: Elton was the first rock superstar since the Beatles to be made into a wax figure model by the prestigious Madame Tussaud's Museum. His original '70s likeness (which is not pictured here) has been relocated to a London museum. Elton's present likeness is on view at other Tussaud museums such as Madame Tussaud's in New York City and the Rock and Roll Hall of Fame Wax Museum in Niagara Falls, Canada.

Elton John Songs in Movies

In addition to cameo appearances in a few popular films, Elton has had many songs featured in movies and on soundtracks. Some he contributed directly and others were chosen at random by a movie's producer simply because the enhanced the mood of the scene.

Following is a list of selected Elton John songs featured in movies. (The items are listed in alphabetical order according to the film titles.)

"Your Song" (*Alex: The Life of a Child*)
"Daniel" (*Alice's Restaurant*)
"Tiny Dancer" and "Mona Lisas and Mad Hatters" (*Almost Famous*), Blues for Baby and Me" (*Aloha Bobby And Rose*)
"The Last Song" (*And the Band Played On*)
"Candle in the Wind" (*Candle in the Wind*)
"You Gotta Love Someone" (*Days of Thunder*)
"Amoreena" (*Dog Day Afternoon*)
"I'm Still Standing" (*Driving Me Crazy*)
"Saturday Night's Alright (for Fighting)" (*The Entity*)
"Saturday Night's Alright (for Fighting)" (*Fandango*)
"Some Other World" (*Ferngully*)
"But Not for Me," "Chapel Of Love," and "Crocodile Rock" (*Four Weddings and a Funeral*)
Several songs written and performed by Elton appeared in *Friends*: "Friends," "Honey Roll," "Variations on Friends," "Variations of Friends Theme (the First Kiss)," "Seasons," "Variations on Michelle's Song," "Can I Put You On?" "Michelle's Song," "I Meant to Do My Work Today," 'Four Moons,' "Seasons: Reprise."
"From Denver to L.A." (*The Games*)
"Love Is a Cannibal" (*Ghostbusters II*)
"Candle in the Wind" (*Goodbye Norma Jean*)
"We all Fall in Love Sometimes" (*Ice Castles*)
"Stone's Throw from Hurtin'," performed by Wynona Judd (*Leap of Faith*)
"Runaway Train" (*Lethal Weapon III*)
Musical score by Elton and Tim Rice (*The Lion King*)
"Don't Let the Sun Go Down on Me," performed by Roger Daltry (*The Lost Boys*)
"Goodbye Yellow Brick Road" (*Love on the Orient Express*)
"Your Song," performed by Ewan McGregor (*Moulin Rouge*)
Musical score (*The Muse*)
"Tiny Dancer," and "Bennie and the Jets" (*My Girl 2*)
"Blue Eyes" (*My Own Private Idaho*)
"Return to Paradise," and "Song for Guy" (*Oh, Heavenly Dog*)
"Rocket Man" (*Rocket Man*)
"The Measure of a Man" (*Rocky V*)
"Candle in the Wind" and "I'm Still Standing" (*The Ryan White Story*)
"Sorry Seems to Be the Hardest Word" (*Slapshot*)
"Daniel" (*Smokey and The Bandit*)
"Take Me Down to the Ocean" (*Summer Lovers*)
"True Love" (*To Die For*)
"Pinball Wizard" performed by Elton (*Tommy*)
"Your Song" (*Welcome Home*)

Elton's Top 25 Favorite Albums by Other Artists

Elton's passion for collecting records started in his teens and continues today. His three favorite stores to buy the latest CDs are HMV (in London) and Tower Records (in Los Angeles and Atlanta).

In the 1970s and 1980s, it was highly publicized that Elton was fast becoming one of the world's largest private record collectors. By 1993 he had amassed amazingly over 25,000 albums, and 23,000 singles, all of which were sold in two separate lots in a third Sotheby's auction and brought in over $270,000 for AIDS charities.

The following is list of twenty-five out of literally hundreds of Elton's personal favorite albums, (from old and new artists) some of which were sold in the Sotheby's auction. (The albums are not in any particular order.)

1. *Rubber Soul*, The Beatles
2. *Pet Sounds*, The Beach Boys
3. *Gasoline Alley*, Rod Stewart
4. *The Band*, The Band
5. *Highway 61 Revisited*, Bob Dylan
6. *Heartbreaker*, Ryan Adams
7. *Saturate Before Using*, Jackson Browne
8. *Nilsson Schmillsson*, Harry Nilsson
9. *Leon Russell*, Leon Russell
10. *Sgt. Pepper and the Lonely Hearts Club*, Beatles
11. *Songs of Leonard Cohen*, Leonard Cohen
12. *Loudon Wainwright III*, Loudon Wainwright III with *Love and Theft*, Bob Dylan
13. *Private Dancer*, Tina Turner
14. *Anthology*, The Temptations
15. *Yes, I Am*, Melissa Etheridge
16. *Electric Warrior*, T. Rex
17. *Marshall Mathers LP*, Eminem
18. *Marianne Faithful's Greatest Hits*, Marianne Faithfull)
19. *Tapestry*, Carole King
20. *Rockin' the Suburbs*, Ben Folds
21. *Let It Bleed*, The Rolling Stones
22. *Court and Spark*, Joni Mitchell
23. *No More Drama*, Mary J. Blige
24. *Shaved Fish*, John Lennon
25. *Who's Next*, The Who

Do you know how old Elton was when he first decided it was time to tone down his flamboyant image?

CHAPTER THIRTEEN

Ultimate Elton John Pop Trivia Quiz

So, you claim you're such a huge Elton fan that you even know the name of the hospital he got throat surgery in back in 1987? And you swear you know the name of every star he's dueted with, both on vinyl and on stage?

That's impressive, but our staff of Elton experts think we can stump you! If you get eighty percent of the questions answered correctly, you will win our Private Fantastic Award (sorry, but the name Captain Fantastic is already taken).

Questions

1. What was the name of the Los Angeles club where Elton performed his first shows in the United States?

2. Who was first approached to produce the Elton John album, which was ultimately produced by Gus Dudgeon?

3. Who sang the duet "Flames of Paradise" with Elton?

4. On November 24, 1974, Elton John played a Thanksgiving concert at New York's Madison Square Garden with special guest John Lennon making what would be his last concert appearance. What songs did Lennon perform with Elton and his band?

5. Who inspired the title for the 1973 album, *Don't Shoot Me, I'm Only the Piano Player*?

6. What hospital in 1987 did Elton Have throat surgery?

7. What is the name of Elton's favorite venue of all time to perform in?

8. How many albums did Elton release on the Geffen label?

9. Which Elton album was the first to go straight to number one on the U.S. charts?

10. What was the title of the 1969 song that Elton and Bernie wrote for popular British singer, Lulu?

11. Who struck back at Elton John in 1988?

12. In 1973, Elton formed his own record company named Rocket Records. Who was the first musical act signed to the label?

13. In what city did Elton and Tim Rice's *Aida* play first open?

14. What was the title of Bernie Taupin's book that included all his lyrics to Elton John's songs from 1968 to 1976?

Elton portrayed the Pinball Wizard in the 1975 hit movie, *Tommy*.

15. What year in the 1980s did Elton and his then-manager John Reid sue MCA Records for breach of contract?

16. What was the date that Elton received a star on the Hollywood Walk of Fame?

17. What early Glam rocker influenced Bernie Taupin to write the song "I'm Gonna Be a Teenage Idol?"

18. What was the name of the woman Elton was once engaged to as referenced on "Someone Saved My Life Tonight"?

19. Reginald Kenneth Dwight was Elton's birth given name. Who was he named after?

20. Elton appeared on the 1975 cover of *Time* magazine, what was the big headline on the cover?

21. Name the artist that illustrated the imaginative cover for the *Captain Fantastic and the Brown Dirt Cowboy* album?

22. Where did Elton first meet his ex-wife Renate Blauel?

23. What's the name of the former famous porn star that introduced Elton at his landmark 1973 Hollywood Bowl concert?

24. What Beach Boy appeared on the *Caribou* album?

25. What famous teen star portrayed Elton in the video for "This Train Don't Stop There Anymore?"

26. What is the name of the pricey auction house that Elton sold all his personal possessions to in the late 1980s?

27. Who was the house producer at Liberty Music who gave Reg Dwight a set of lyrics from a seventeen-year-old aspiring lyricist named Bernie Taupin?

28. On what album is the song "Elderberry Wine" featured?

29. What is the name of the popular London newspaper from which Elton sought a public apology?

30. What famous designer created many of Elton's most flamboyant costumes and also designed for Cher?

Pickwick International released *Chartbusters Go Pop,* in 1994 featuring 20 cover songs from 1969 to 1970 as sung by Elton John.

31. Where did Elton write the songs for *Captain Fantastic and the Brown Dirt Cowboy*?

32. What is the name of the popular black female vocalist, Bluesology backed in London during the late sixties?

33. What is Elton's legal middle name?

34. What country did Elton record *Sleeping with the Past*?

35. What was the name of the first rock group, Reg Dwight formed when he was in his teens?

36. Elton wrote a song called "Snookeroo." Who recorded a version of it?

37. What is the name of the duet Elton sang with Neil Sedaka?

38. What was Elton's first number-one single in the United States?

Elton clowning with the audience.

39. What was the date of Elton's big free record-breaking concert in Central Park that brought in over 450,000 people?

40. In which year did Elton become the first Western pop star to tour USSR?

41. What was the name of the record company that first signed a twenty-one-year-old Elton John in the United Kingdom?

42. Elton made some TV commercials in the USA to promote Diet Coke. Which female singer co-starred in the first series?

43. What legendary folk artist visited Elton and Bernie backstage at the New York Filmore East in 1970?

44. Who wrote "Love Song," the only non-John-Taupin composition on *Tumbleweed Connection?*

45. In 1985 Elton and Millie Jackson had a hit with "Act of War," but what hot female singer originally turned it down?

46. Who sang the duet "Honey Man" with Elton?

47. What are the names of the two characters Elton invented that he sometimes uses as aliases?

48. Which song contains the lyrics, "And it hurts me most to cheat and that's no lie."

49. In 1972 Elton made a guest appearance in which movie?

50. In what country did Elton marry Renate Blauel in 1984?

51. What was the title of the first album Elton recorded for Geffen Records?

52. How old was Elton when he publicly decided to tone down his flamboyant image?

53. Elton rarely has opening acts at his performances. But in 1982 he did. Name that band.

54. Who produced *Jump Up!*?

55. Which song contains the lyrics, "I'd like to find a compromise and place it in your hands."

56. John Lennon also is credited with playing guitar on Elton's number-one cover rendition of "Lucy in the Sky with Diamonds." What alias did Lennon use for those sessions?

57. On which album is the big hit, "I'm Still Standing" featured?

58. What did Elton name the first house he purchased in England?

59. On *The Fox*, Elton collaborated with three different lyricists. How many songs did Bernie write for the album?

60. What is the title of the debut Elton John single released in the United Kingdom?

61. What was the name of the church in Australia that Elton and Renate Blauel were married in?

62. Elton was the chairman of what famous football team in London?

63. Name the first Elton album that did not contain all Bernie Taupin lyrics.

64. In what popular music video did Elton make his animation debut?

65. What was the date that Reg Dwight legally changed his name to Elton Hercules John?

Answers

1. The Troubadour
2. Steve Brown
3. Jennifer Rush
4. "Whatever Gets You Through the Night," "Lucy in the Sky with Diamonds," "I Saw Her Standing There," "Bitch Is Back"
5. Groucho Marx
6. St. Vincent's Hospital in Sydney, Australia
7. Madison Square Garden
8. Six
9. *Captain Fantastic and the Brown Dirt Cowboy*
10. "I Can't Go on Living Without You"
11. Reg, on the *Reg Strikes Back* album
12. Neil Sedaka
13. Atlanta
14. *The One Who Writes the Words for Elton John*
15. 1981
16. November 21, 1975
17. Marc Bolan of T-Rex
18. Linda Woodrow
19. His mother's brother
20. Rock's Captain Fantastic
21. Alan Alridge
22. In Monserrat during the recording of his *Too Low for Zero* album
23. Linda Lovelace
24. Brian Wilson
25. Justin Timberlake
26. Sotheby's
27. Ray Williams
28. *Don't Shoot Me, I'm Only the Piano Player*
29. *The Sun*
30. Bob Mackie
31. In Colorado at the Caribou Ranch
32. Patti LaBelle
33. Hercules
34. Denmark
35. The Corvettes
36. Ringo Starr
37. "Bad Blood"
38. "Crocodile Rock"
39. September 13, 1980
40. 1979
41. Dick James Music (DJM)
42. Paula Abdul
43. Bob Dylan
44. Cindy Bullens
45. Tina Turner
46. Cat Stevens
47. Lord Choc Ice and Lady Choc Ice
48. "Crystal"
49. *Born to Boogie*
50. Australia
51. *The Fox*
52. Forty years old
53. Quarterflash
54. Chris Thomas
55. "Tonight"
56. Boogie O'Winston
57. *Too Low for Zero*
58. Hercules
59. "Just Like Belgium," "Fascists Faces," "Heels of the Wind," and "The Fox"
60. "I've Been Loving You"
61. St. Marks
62. Watford
63. *A Single Man*
64. "Club at the End of the Street"
65. January 7, 1972

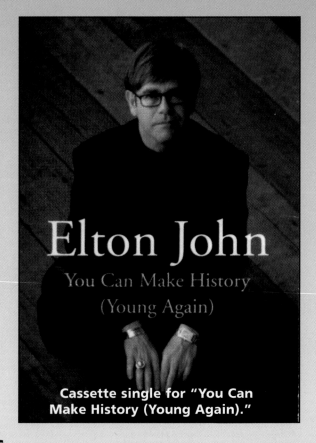

Elton John
You Can Make History
(Young Again)

Cassette single for "You Can Make History (Young Again)."

186

Astrologically Speaking

General Astrological Profile

The Sun in Aries makes Elton energetic and direct, with a strong sense of individuality; he enjoys a challenge and initiating action; he hates giving up, and needs to learn patience and moderation. Elton is adventurous and enthusiastic. He needs to achieve, to succeed in all of his aims—whether in the music business or socially, and can sometimes be selfish in attaining them. Lack of success affects him more than most people, and he is likely to become irritable and self-obsessed as a result.

Elton tends to fall in love at first sight and can win hearts easily. His potential partners must be lively and quick to react to him both intellectually and sexually.

The Mercury-Mars conjunction in Pisces in Elton's chart indicates that he is hardworking, assertive and competitive with a quick-thinking mind, who keeps well ahead of rivals in business or sport. Elton has a lively mentality and knows where he is heading; at best this makes him cut to the quick of an issue and always look to turn words into deeds. As a child he was extremely competitive and thrived best in a flexible, stimulating environment.

Elton has a bright and breezy approach to relationships, but needs a great deal of mental stimulation—preferably sparring partners for lively debate; he is fearless about speaking the truth. Elton has a vigorous practical mind that learns quickly, and he initiates ideas to get things done. His forthright views are upheld by his willingness to act on his convictions.

Elton lives up to his Aries sign of being a natural leader who possesses the ability to inspire love and respect from the masses.

Elton John was born on March 25, 1947, in Pinner, Middlesex, England, making him an Aries. General Aries traits are the following: Passionate, Dynamic, Courageous, Driven, Uses Initiative, Impulsive, Aggressive, Dominating.

Elton is hardly impulsive, buoyant, communicative and sociable. He tends to crave excitement and is therefore inclined to direct his energies outward into the world around him.

Elton is very much his own person and has problems adapting to the demands of others. Typically, he holds on to his views tenaciously and give little ground to people who disagree with him. Often motivated by a strong need for freedom, he is likely to be extremely self-sufficient. However, a dislike of discipline and routine can prove to be a particular stumbling block.

Romantic Astrological Profile

Aries like Elton have a cool, romantic glamour that others find highly attractive. He enjoys romance but often he is not prepared for a relationship with all the compromises and obligations that ensue. He is a kind and thoughtful friend and is financially astute. He shares his wealth with his lover of the moment and lavishes them with fine gifts. Typical Aries traits when it comes to romance are: relaxed and approachable; puts emphasis on friendship in close relationships; often finds deep emotions hard to handle; and may be too rational and naïve.

The intensity of Elton's emotions and passions is high and consequently he may be jealous and demanding in a relationship. However, overall as a lover, he is kind and considerate. An imaginative and rewarding sex life has always been his for the taking. In a nutshell, Captain Fantastic has his own very original idea of love, emotions and relationships. He marches to a different drummer when it comes to pursuing a lover.

Financial Astrological Profile

Elton may profit from an inheritance and in addition he has a well-developed business sense and a flair for investment. Typical Aries financial traits: seeks to share at the deepest level; often gets friends involved with his various business dealings, and has great flair for business but may find desires for starting unusual new businesses constantly thwarted.

Positive Personality Traits

Elton is energetic and direct, with a strong sense of individuality. He enjoys a challenge and initiating action; he hates giving up. He is adventurous and enthusiastic. He is a natural leader with the ability to inspire love and respect in large groups of people. He is understanding and sympathetic, with a longing to put the world right and promote international peace—an ideal disposition if he was ever interested in politics.

Elton is a hard and tireless worker with absolute determination—and with the ability to carry great projects through to completion. Always the protector to those he comes to know, he tends to have long and secure relationships. Since Elton (despite outward appearances), is a natural conservative, those older than himself (authority figures) tend to benefit him.

The positive Sun-Saturn aspect in Elton's chart signifies common sense and a practical restrained outlook. On occasion, enthusiasm is restricted, especially when he is faced with challenging situations, although this is not really a big problem.

Elton knows how to make lemonade out of lemons, as the expression goes. He is a cautious and circumspect person who takes risks only after careful deliberation. Saturn gives the Sun the power of endurance, and thus the ability to conserve anything that is felt to be of value; at best, this aspect can build lasting achievements based on hard experience.

Elton needs to build lasting relationships on strong and stable foundations and has the ability to hold things together in the face of adversity. Capable of being immensely thoughtful and trustworthy in his relationships, he has a surefooted approach to life based on a profound awareness of his limitations yet has the ability to overcome his feelings of inadequacy. He desires to build a "true" sense of identity.

Typical strengths of Aries: any activity in which hard work, long-term planning and responsibility are prerequisites; achievements through steady application and working in seclusion.

Elton has an uncanny sense of justice coupled with an innate ability to interpret the law, whether man-made or natural. This may manifest through his showing others the way through, or beyond, the problems in their lives. He has a practical sense of how to manipulate the opportunities that appear in life (or is it just plain luck?). He has a natural love for those with more experience or authority. A teacher, or benefactor, is likely to play a big role in his life, even if it's someone he met when he was just a tike.

The positive Sun-Jupiter aspect in Elton's chart brings a certain amount of good fortune, perhaps because he is so optimistic. He also has the impulse to broaden his mind and expand his intellect.

Elton communicates very well both on vinyl and off, and it is easy for him to give others a feeling for whatever he's thinking. He tends to believe that there is almost no problem that cannot be handled with words, by talking it out. He is a fine public speaker. His natural sensitivity for the feelings and thoughts of those around him make Elton a valued member of both the celebrity and charity communities.

Future Challenges In Elton's Chart

Elton is last of the big spenders! He is by no means conservative, and overindulgence of all kinds is sort of second nature. He tends to ignore the realities of life in favor of the perks. This may bring him hard up against natural or human law, again and again. No one can accuse him of lacking ambition. The straight and narrow is unappealing to our hero; Elton would rather range along the fringe. He is a nonconformist. Both Venus and Jupiter are traditionally held to be "beneficial" planets, so negative aspects between them cause little trouble—although restlessness and discontentment can sometimes appear.

Recklessness in investment can also show itself, as may overindulgence in food and drink, leading to weight gain. Jupiter can inflate the pleasure principle in Venus, producing an extravagant, self-indulgent nature; at worst this combination can lead to his squandering resources and opportunities.

—"Madam" Anne M. Raso

Breaking down the barriers:
Elton on stage, where he brings people together—and where he feels the
most at home.

CHAPTER FOURTEEN

"Making friends for all the world to see..." The Elton John Fan Survey

An informal survey of Elton John fans conducted for this book via *East End Lights*, the quarterly magazine for Elton John fans, and the internet reveals that Elton's appeal is not only unique, but extraordinary. Perhaps what fans admire about him the most, besides making music are his frank honesty and his wicked sense of humor. For more than three decades now, Elton has had a wide circle of fans ranging from as young as age five to as old as eighty-five. With each new project, whether it's an album, the score for a Broadway-bound play, or a tour, Elton wins converts of all ages. Meanwhile, longtime legion of faithful fans still remains connected to him, just as strongly as ever.

If you were to create a formula for success, Elton John's career would be an outstanding model. From the songs he composes to his concert performances, and from his television appearances to his tireless AIDS charity work, this multi-faceted artist has been and always be one of the few people in the small elite group of artists called timeless. His many-splendored songs will be referenced and called to mind forever, even as songs from others fade away. His amazing and unselfish desire to see the end of AIDS as we know it on this planet will always be an example. One can truly see that this gifted man deserves every single fan he has in this world.

There's no doubt fans stick with Elton through every facet of his fascinating and enduring career. They seem to feel that they can identify with him and easily relate to the songs he sings, particularly, those penned by longtime lyricist, Bernie Taupin. *Baltimore Sun* newspaper journalist and longtime fan, Lori Sears explained: "Elton is a brilliant songwriter and a terrific pianist. I'm thankful to his grandmum for sitting him down at the piano as a tot. Look at the joy we've all been fortunate to share in. I can only hope that he never stops writing music—chords and melodies."

"I think it was a miracle of God to put these two musical geniuses together to drive us wild!," added Pam Quier from Brentwood, California. "The music they have written together will be with us all our lives, and I believe it will of course, go down in musical history and will be remembered by generations to come!"

"There's no doubt that Elton's fans love him for life and they love Bernie, too." noted Robert Johnson, 40, from Dallas, Texas. "Without Bernie, there certainly would be no Elton John." David Sigler, former publisher of *Taupin,* a quarterly newsletter on Bernie Taupin published in the eighties concurred: "I've been a fan of Elton as well as Bernie since 1974 when I heard "Bennie and the Jets" for the first time. Elton's sound has so many different styles from rock to ballads, his music is always there for the right time. I've only met Elton once and that in 1995 on his *Made in England* Tour. I will never forget that day. He was so cordial and nice. Just what you'd expect."

What about true love? Can a pop rock music legend like Elton John be a catalyst? Or are some of those romantic ballads like "Tiny Dancer" and "Your Song" that Bernie Taupin so passionately pens be the cause? "I have been an EJ fan since 1970," recalls Teresa Johns from Wales. "I have loads of memorabilia dating back to the seventies. I once liked a man who had ginger hair and wore sunglasses, and EJ reminded me of him, and so I bought Elton's album and haven't stopped since. That ginger-haired man has now been my husband of twenty-seven years! "Don't Let the Sun Go Down on Me" was "our song" in the first year of our marriage. I even wrote about "Skyline Pigeon" in my school exams.

"EJ's music has helped me through good times and bad times," Teresa continued. "I listen to his music every day. I log on to all the fan sites every day. I read books and buy magazines. I long for concert dates to be announced. I play his music at work. When my dear Mum passed away, it was Elton's music that helped me through that tough time, and still helps me today."

It's not just the old faithful who admire Elton John and the music he makes, but the under twenty crowd as well. Ceri, age fourteen is a second generation fan who accompanies her mom to Elton's concerts. "My daughter attended her first Elton concert when she was about nine years old," continued Teresa. "We had second-row seats and I said to her 'if I move quickly stick with me!' She looked puzzled but soon realized what I meant when Elton came onstage, and everyone moved forward.

**"Brown Dirt Cowboy,"
Bernie Taupin, circa 1978.**

We got to the front, and Elton held my daughter's hand for a few minutes, in between signing autographs, and although she knew the music, that was her first experience of a concert, and [she] was hooked from then on. Elton's music has grown on her over the years, and although she likes new singers and bands, she also likes Elton's music. Her favorite song is Philadelphia Freedom. At first her friends laughed at her for going to Elton concerts, especially with her mum! But when she said that she had met Elton they were impressed, and her friends know what a big fan I am, so there is not a problem anymore!"

As the new century progresses, there is no doubt that Elton John remains one of the most beloved pop-rock music stars and will continue to be for years to follow. The fan survey embodied many significant aspects of the musician's lure beginning with a question on how one became a fan in the first place.

The number one response was the inevitable—his music—and the number-two response was a tie between his concert performances and his humanitarian efforts. First and foremost, Elton himself will tell you he is musician and that it is his life's work. "I am a musician, that's what I do," he has said. "As a musician I really can't change the world. All I can do is help break down the barriers and bring people together. It may sound cliché, but music really is the universal language."

As a performer, Elton is no less than the consummate showman, giving his all to his fans. Back in the seventies, when he was at the height of his superstardom he told a cheering throng of twenty-thousand fans at a Los Angeles concert, "I would play for you even if I had just one finger left!" (His right hand bruised and bleeding from pounding the piano keys). And you can bet he meant it too.

It's no surprise that many Elton John fans have seen him live in concert more than once. In fact, some even dozens of times comparing and sharing musical memories from the 1973 tour at the Hollywood Bowl, where Elton wore several wild outfits and his 1985 world jaunt, for which he pulled out some of his most glitzy stage outfits in years. Fans hold fond memories of Elton John concerts in high regard. Whether it's Elton simply at the piano minus the band, or onstage with the Melbourne Symphony Orchestra, fans connect in a very personal way.

"Elton fans are some the best people in the world!," said Marie Casselli from Hoboken, New Jersey. "Many of us are willing to share our memorabilia, personal experiences, and photos with other Elton fans. The average Elton John fan is like me—someone that collects lots of memorabilia and goes to several shows a year. The fans I've met a long the way that I now consider friends make sure you are lacking zero when it comes to Elton John material. It's true and I confess, I'm over thirty and a day doesn't go by that I don't speak of him in some way to another human being, whether it's online, or lunching with my co-workers on the job. Elton is a very necessary part of my life and will be for years to come."

When asked to explain what makes Elton John incomparable in the eyes of over three generations of followers, a variety of responses were generated. The biggest reasons given were that he is a true rock and roll legend who just doesn't appeal to one group of people and that he is a crusader fighting for AIDS causes. Second to this, fans revere Elton's natural musical ability, claiming that perhaps, no one even comes close to his stature, except, maybe Paul McCartney. One respondent wrote: "There is nobody better than Elton John when it comes to crafting the perfect Top 40 pop song. He has been a constant presence on the international music charts since 1970. Nearly everything he has ever released has been a hit. Nearly every classic rock, contemporary pop, or oldie radio station in America plays nearly as many Elton John songs as they do Beatles songs."

Elton John fans also sense that he possesses qualities that they look for in a special friend: honesty, loyalty, generosity and genuine concern for their fellow man. "Elton is very giving. He has a big heart," noted Robert Hanson from London, England. "I have met him several times and asked for an autograph or a picture and Elton also obliges. He can be very shy, too when he first meets you, but he's always very polite. Fans who know will tell you that Elton always tries to sign as many autographs as possible when he can. Even when he's on stage, there's a point in his show where he stops to shake hands and sign autographs for the few lucky fans up front."

When describing what makes Elton so unique to so many, respondents stressed how he has changed them on a deeply personal level. "I used to play *Goodbye Yellow Brick Road* to put me at ease in my teens," acknowledged Gary Gerhardt of Three Oaks, Michigan. "I couldn't afford the double album and we didn't have a record player, so I recorded it on a cassette and played it over and over till the tape would go bad. Seems like so many of his songs made my life make sense and carried me thru good and bad times. Of the times when I was ready to give up, I could always turn on Elton and feel renewed again. Elton and Bernie are two gifted souls who instill hope and faith in us all through their music. The first time I heard "The One" I was searching my heart as if a special someone would ever exist for me. A song like that makes you wonder about your life."

"Elton's music has kept me alive," offered

Marie Casselli. "I was thirteen when my grandmother died and the only thing that got me through was my *Tumbleweed Connection* album. I was so devastated…I felt so alone, but I had Elton's music and Bernie's words to comfort me."

One young survey respondent who only referred to himself as a "Reghead" (affectionate term for a die-hard Elton fan) was able to recall thek exact moment he became a true fan: "I attended one of Elton's mid nineties concerts and he sang: 'Skyline Pigeon.' I actually never heard that song before. It touched me so deeply. I soon learned that it is a firm fan favorite. I can see why. I don't know, but it brought tears to my eyes. I became a devoted fan from that moment on."

Caryl Simpson from Mattoon, Illinois, explained: "I had always loved 'Daniel' from the first time I heard it on the radio. I've been a fan since that point on. I mean I even named my son Daniel, who is almost nineteen, after that song. In a sense that song became prophetic. After a bitter divorce, my son Daniel spent years 'traveling tonight on a plane' visiting either his dad or returning home. Never once did the line 'I can see the red tail lights' not pop into my head as I watched him leave. And since he was always going to Pueblo, Colorado, which is a very Spanish town, even the phrase 'heading for Spain' seemed appropriate enough. I cried the first time I heard Elton sing it live. Elton and Bernie's music has been with me for thirty years and I hope they will be with us for another thirty years."

Interestingly enough, the survey was conducted one month before Elton was to release his forty-second Amercian album release, *Songs from the West Coast*, the highly anticipated studio follow up to *The Big Picture*. Introductory tracks "I Want Love" and "The Ballad of the Boy in the Red Shoes," as well as the harder edged "Birds," were being played on FM contemporary and rock radio stations across the country. At various Elton John internet newsgroups, fans were favoring "Ballad of the Boy" over "I Want Love" which was slated to be the first single, because of its perfect blend of melodic melody and touching lyrics. "Ballad," a song with incredible depth, harks back to the early seventies, something which fans had been waiting for such a long time. "It's the kind of Elton John song you expect to hear blaring out of car windows," offered Rose Delaney, from Buffalo, New York. "This is simply one his very best and ranks up there with 'Goodbye Yellow Brick Road', 'Candle in the Wind' and 'Sweet Painted Lady.'" A.J. Canton from Las Vegas, Nevada, reiterated: "'The Ballad' is like a mix of my two favorite Elton songs, 'Tiny Dancer' and 'The Last Song.' This song is definitely a keeper and will be a significant song for Elton to sing years from now."

The survey asked fans what their favorite Elton John song is of all time and as you can imagine brought on more agonizing over the answer. The top three included "Skyline Pigeon," "Candle in the Wind" and and "The One"—all of course with lyrics written by Taupin. Other favorites that came in a close second included "Funeral For a Friend," "Sacrifice" and surprisingly, "The Greatest Discovery." Despite the fact that such hit songs as the ballad "Daniel," the hard rocking "Saturday Night's Alright (for Fighting)" and even "Bennie and the Jets" are Elton John classics, they were not mentioned in the favorite song category.

The survey also asked respondents to name their three favorite Elton albums. The best-selling *Goodbye Yellow Brick Road* came in first place followed by *Captain Fantastic and The Brown Dirt Cowboy*, and *Sleeping with the Past*. Clearly, these three albums reached the faithful then and without a doubt, still do today. *Madman Across the Water* and *Tumbleweed Connection* earned several mentions as did *The One* and *Made in England*.

The survey also asked some of these most adamant Elton John fans around the world to name their favorite line or lines from a Bernie Taupin-written lyric. Yes, again, even more

agonizing choices to make. Though there were too many different lines to determine which one is the favorite, it would be safe to say that the original "Your candle burned out long before your legend ever did" from the original version of "Candle in the Wind," "It's four o'clock in the morning, damn it, listen to me good" and "I'm strangled by your haunted social scene, just a pawn outplayed by a dominating queen" from "Someone Saved My Life Tonight" surfaced more than a few times. Also mentioned often were "You danced in death like a marionette on the vengeance of the law" from "Ticking" and "There's treasure children always seek to find" from "Curtains"; and "It's two hearts living in two separate worlds, but it's no sacrifice" from "Sacrifice" with an honorable mention going to "And sees his future in the water, a long lost heart within his reach" from the "The One."

Of course, this survey wouldn't be complete without asking fans what their least favorite Elton John album and song are.

These choices were unanimous straight across the board: "the dreadful 1979 disco offering, *Victim of Love*, which had no songs written by Taupin, and the least favorite song was anything from *Victim of Love*. The 1978 *A Single Man,* again, an album with no songs by Taupin and the Geffen album *Leather Jackets* came in a close seconds.

When asked to cite any other big stars they regard as highly as Elton John, this discriminating group of fans claimed there was no one else who could possibly rate any higher than Elton. Elton is obviously in a league of his own!

Finally, fans were asked what they say to Sir Elton if they were ever fortunate enough to meet him face-to-face. The leading response would be to thank Elton for enriching their lives. "It has been a lifelong dream of mine to meet Elton," says Charlene Anderson from Tulsa, Oklahoma. "I would like to thank him for making some of the best music in the world. Elton is a true treasure in the music world. I can't imagine what life would be like without Elton John." Lisa Womack from Rowlett, Texas wrote: "Elton has made me a better person. Through his humanitarian efforts, I have learned how to be more giving. I want to thank him for giving me so much through his music."

Interestingly enough, respondents also stated that they would like talk to Elton and tell him how they feel about him and why they admire and care about him so much. "A big music superstar like Elton John would never understand what a friend he has been to me over the years," said Lisa Winger from Ridgefield Park, New Jersey. "He has really transformed my life for the better. I would do anything for him. I could never repay him for all the enjoyment and comfort his music has given me over these past thirty-five years. I only hope that Elton continues making music and pleasing his fans."

For those fortunate to meet the man himself, it was a once-in-a-lifetime experience to be cherished always. U.S. Hercules International Elton John Fan Club coordinator, Sharon Kalinoski has met Elton several times, but of course, it's never enough. "I've had only very brief encounters like when I went to London in 1994 and waited outside of Watford Stadium," she sid. "I watched Elton come out and when I saw the chance I told him I had come from America to see him. I asked for a photo and he said, 'All right, but we have to make it quick.' I was in heaven! Then two years later I saw him in Atlanta at his big Out of the Closet sale at Neiman Marcus. Again, he was gracious, and said 'Hello, darling' as I walked up to him. I couldn't believe it! Then he kissed me on the cheek. I was absolutely speechless! I will never forget it. Never!"

"I have met Elton twice," explained Gina Herring, from Scottsdale, Arizona, of her encounter. "The first was in Los Angeles when Elton did a record signing for the release of *The Road to El Dorado*. When it was my turn to get my CD signed, of course, I froze and didn't say the things I had planned to say. It was

so awesome, though because he seemed so genuine with the fans. I was thrilled to have those few precious seconds. The second was in Birmingham, Alabama. *Eltonjohn.com* had made available fifty backstage hospitality passes for Rocket Members. I was lucky enough to get one, and during that meeting I got the courage up to ask for a picture with him. He was so great about it, and even joked with me to stop shaking and calm down! Can you imagine? I tried so hard not to act that way, but you just never know when your time comes to meet Elton face-to-face and how you will respond."

Overall, to his fans, Elton John is much more than living rock legend, and a tireless humanitarian, but someone who has survived personal tragedy. Throughout his remarkable life and career, Elton John has accomplished plenty, as well has done a lot of outrageous things along the way. He has certainly blazed a path for many to follow, but none dare to be his equal. Marion Joy Friedman from Ocean City, New Jersey attests: "Throughout Elton's career, he has suffered but kept fighting his own demons and life's evils and did not give up on life or humanity. He defied the odds of stardom and is doing more now than ever for himself and for others. Elton is such an inspiration and a role model for us all."❖

For over three decades Elton had acquired a wide range of admirers, like little Kyle Hilliard of Oak Forest, Illinois.

Through his career's highs and lows, there's no doubt that Elton's fans truly love him for life.

Collecting Elton John
"Money Talks, See What It Catches"

Elton's career has spanned over four decades and on keeps getting better as it is introduced to a new generation of fans. Collecting Elton John in the new millennium has never been so intoxicating and fulfilling— not to mention profitable— for fans of all ages as it is in this new millennium.

There's thousands of Elton John collectibles ranging from vinyl records to official concert merchandise. Collectibles cover a vast range including basic tour books, shirts, poster, 45 picture sleeves to the pricey Bally Captain Fantastic pinball machines. If you are fortunate enough to own a certified gold or platinum award or even a pair of Elton's designer eyewear and stage outfits, it could cost you your life's savings.

At first glance collecting Elton can be overwhelming. Considering that together with Bernie Taupin, he has incredible mass market appeal on nearly every continent in the world. Each passing decade brings an abundant of new collectibles to be had. Fresh listeners won over for a new album are most likely to seek out the early years. For most faithful fans, collecting Elton is a lifelong enjoyable obsession—and at times, expensive.

Some collectors seek a specialty to their collection like maybe paper collectibles like color photos, magazines and posters, while others can't get enough of bootleg recordings—of which there are literally hundreds of these live recordings available. In fact, many that were once only sought-after on vinyl are now available on CD in good quality and easy to find on the internet.

Then there are others prefer to run the gamut and collect everything within reach and financially possible. How many fans out there own a vinyl, eight-track and cassette copy of every early Elton recording? One is opened and played repeatedly and the other two are sealed for life.

What does the typical Elton John collector search for in memorabilia? The face of collecting has changed drastically over the last few years. The vinyl single is no longer even a format in the United States and most countries are barely holding onto the CD single. The twelve-inch and seven-inch vinyl record are essentially dead everywhere but in a few countries around the world. The CD-ROM has allowed people to trade concerts and television appearances around the world with no noticeable loss in clarity, (remember those fourth-generation cassette tapes?). Because of this, most bootlegging—that is, of silver-pressed CDs with full inserts and such—has ceased. It is not worth the time and money anymore to make pressings by those holding the masters. There are plenty of legitimate sources now for collectors.

With every new publishing renegotiation, there have come a slew of reissue CDS from the "Classic Years." Of course there's promotional CDs and samplers, too. If you are a beginning collector, there's no need to fill pressured to have everything from the seventies. Start simply. Collect what interests you, without the concern of future trends or market values. If you like that $2 sealed *Caribou* eight-track tape, buy it. It's value may always remain at $2, or it may rise to $6 or even $8. There are so many directions to follow that the sky is the limit. Be sure to start with a budget. There is so much product out there, (official and otherwise), that it could be mind-boggling to attempt to collect it all.

So, what does the most serious of Elton collectors look for? "Absolutely anything that they don't already have," says noted Elton John collector, Alan McCormic, who probably has one of the largest collections in the world. He lives in England over in the Lincolnshire region where Bernie Taupin hails from. "Elton fans are just fantastic," he says. "I have made some really good friends over the years." McCormic has been buying and selling his much in-demand Elton wares since 1994. In the past few years, he has attended several Elton John-only fan conventions where he has sold mostly vinyl records, CDs and small laminated promotional posters. His business started easily enough as a hobby in 1980 as a means to support his own growing collection. Today his catalog and website, appropriately titled, Wrap It Up sells everything from vinyl (including picture discs and box sets), CDs, cassettes, tour programs, books, videos and posters. A recent search on his website for higher-end vinyl and CD items found:

• The rare seven-inch vinyl single from Bluesology, "Since I Found You Baby" backed with "Just a Little Bit" in very good condition for $350.

• A near-mint seven-inch vinyl of "I've Been Loving You" back with "Here's to the Next Time" for $299.

• The Songs of Elton John and Bernie Taupin: 1974-1993, a very rare U.S.A. promo double CD released by Warner Chappell. Includes 30 tracks for $125.

• A twelve-inch vinyl Leather Jackets that is a U.K. white-label test pressing with a unique (promotional) gatefold sleeve detailing the marketing plans for the release, for $125.

• A seven-inch vinyl single from the Bread and Beer Band of the Dick Barton Theme "Back with Breakdown Blues." This is a stock version of the first issue in February 1969 for $125.

• A twelve-inch vinyl promotional copy of "Bite Your Lip (Get Up and Dance)" (long/short) with a letter from Rocket Records confirming that only five hundred copies of this rare item were pressed for $110.

• An ultra-rare seven-inch vinyl single of "Lady Samantha" backed with "Across the Havens" that is an original issue on the Philips label for $99.

• A twelve-inch vinyl picture disc of *Captain Fantastic and the Brown Dirt Cowboy* with card insert, for $99.

• A Canadian promotional CD, excerpts from *To Be Continued…* that includes sixteen songs and six radio announcement tracks with the original green-and-white front liner, (it was not issued with a back liner), for $99.

Some mid to lower priced collectibles and winning fan favorites include:

• A U.K. twelve-inch vinyl record of *Don't*

A rare Rocket Records 1974 publicity photo of Bernie Taupin.

Shoot Me, I'm Only the Piano Player that is a re-issue in good condition, for $2.

• A German seven-inch vinyl single of "Mr. Bloe, Curried Soul" backed with "Mighty Mouse" for $2.

• An American seven-inch vinyl single of "Goodbye Yellow Brick Road" backed with "Young Man's Blues' on the MCA Rainbow label, for $3.

• An American cassette of "Don't Go Breaking My Heart" that is a single mix and edited twelve-inch remix, for $5.

Is there a significance of the color vinyl used for Elton John albums in the seventies? It depends on the album. If you are fortunate, you will find a few albums on color vinyl. For example *Goodbye Yellow Brick Road* was pressed on yellow vinyl was available in Britain and Australia. *Blue Moves* was printed on blue vinyl in France, and a special promotional version of *Captain Fantastic and the Brown Dirt Cowboy* was pressed on brown vinyl. In the mid-to-late seventies, a complete set of Elton's early recordings was issued in Japan on red vinyl, and these are now highly collectible and extremely rare.

Popular Los Angeles collector Peter Dobbins, who buys and sells similar Elton items, offers his take on the various levels of Elton John fandom: "Elton fans range from the casual listener to the fan who follows him around the world. There are those who attempt to collect every live show he has done (he did over two hundred plus just in 2001),

and the ones who are happy to have the last-row obstructed-view seat in a huge coliseum. Like any artist, there are the solid family and stable job fans—all the way to the off the center 'I want to have your love child' fan, and everyone in between. All come together for one main purpose—the love of the music, the man, and the memories."

Then there are those obsessive collecting fans but they are usually within their certain areas of expertise, which can be clothing, photos, backstage passes or anything imaginable, (and in a few cases unimaginable). What do average fans look to buy the most? Usually import CDs of songs not released in their own country. A good example is a CD single for "I Want Love" released in England in 2001 that featured tracks that were not released anywhere else in the world. McCormic reported more than forty requests in one week for this elusive import CD.

There is no better way to experience Elton, than in a live capacity. Of course, unofficial "live" recordings—and their are hundreds available from the early seventies to present—are on top of the list for the most die-hard of collectors. Then there are the countless unreleased. Then there's the countless unreleased songs, cover versions, demos, outtakes, session tracks and songs written by or recorded by "John-Taupin." Also in demand are videos, laser discs, and DVD of Elton's hundreds of television appearances from around the world on shows ranging from England's *Top of the Pops* (1970s to the present) to older popular American talk shows such as *Mike Douglas* and *Tomorrow with Tom Synder* to the

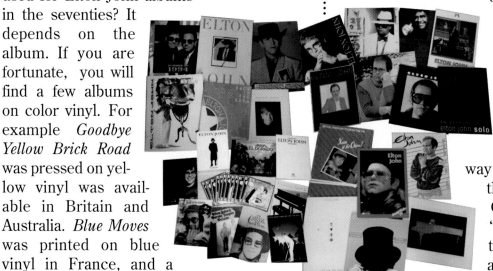

Tour programs and music books from the '70s to the present.

Various Elton memorabilia, including: Boy London watches, song sheets, Rocket Man ties, buttons, official Elton candles, promotional items, crystal Elton angel, vinyl albums, CDs, signature eyeglasses from the Oliver Peoples line, Elton's personal clothing, autographed photos and a Fender guitar signed by both Elton and Bernie.

The original Bally, Captain Fantastic pinball machine.

A selection of backstage passes.

The Elton John Singing Doll from the Yaboom Toy Company, 2000.

Rock 'n' Roll Comics tribute to Elton John, 1993.

Two pairs of vintage Elton eyeglasses, depending on the size and style, can fetch up to $10,000 a piece.

currently popular *Oprah*, *Late Show with David Letterman* and the *Tonight Show with Jay Leno*.

However, continue to heed caution about "unofficial" live shows; watch what you buy. Some recordings are third- or fourth-generation copies and questionable in quality and sound. Since the prices can be steep, ranging from $25 to $65, don't be in a big rush to purchase them. It's always good to research the background on an item. You can ask another collector for advice.

What about pre-Elton John (Reg Dwight or Bluesology) singles? These are equally hard to come by. A fair price could range from the $500-to-$850 depending on its condition. It's been documented that Reg Dwight back in the mid-sixties released three singles with Bluesology: "Come Back Baby" backed with "Times Getting Tougher Than Tough," on the Fontana label; "Mr. Frantic" backed with "Every Day (I Have the Blues)" on Fontana and "Since I Found You Baby" backed with "Just a Little Bit," on Polydor. Another extremely rare item on vinyl is a charity single Elton recorded in 1977 for a Watford benefit. It is rumored that only five hundred copies were printed and some even autographed by Elton himself for the football club's major investors. "The Goaldiggers Song" was featured as side A, while the flipside included a conversation of less than five minutes with Elton and a few choice soccer players.

Whether you are a novice or a thirty-year-plus Elton collector, never put a financial strain on your budget. Collecting Elton should be a jovial journey. If you can't buy something you want the first time around, you will most likely have a second chance thanks to the wonders of eBay. Enjoy the experience and meet some new friends along the way. "Many people have told me that you shouldn't turn a hobby into a business," McCormic remarked. "I disagree, but don't expect to make a fortune. Have fun with it."❖

15 (Selective) Elton John Collectibles

1. The 1965 premiere single by Bluesology titled "Come Back Baby" written and performed by Reg Dwight on the Fontana label.
2. The 1968 "I've Been Loving You" single on the Philips label.
3. A deck of playing cards that promoted Elton's 1980 *21 at 33* album.
4. An autographed limited-editon brown vinyl promotional copy of *Captain Fantastic and the Brown Dirt Cowboy*.

A rare Fillmore East program from November 20 to 21, 1970.

5. A 1970 Fillmore East show program with Leon Russell.
6. Any of Elton's personalized tour luggage tags. Most had his name printed on the front with the title of the concert tour. The back featured his management office information and the number 1 indicating Elton as the first one in the entourage.
7. A promotional *A Single Man* address book.
8. A brass belt buckle palm tree design from Elton's 1974 *Caribou* tour.
9. Any RIAA-certified gold or platinum record awards presented to Elton.
10. Any pair of Elton's elaborate eyeglasses from the seventies.
11. A full-size standup of Elton from the cover of *A Single Man* album.
12. A promotional jigsaw puzzle of the cover of the *Captain Fantastic and the Brown Dirt Cowboy* album.
13. Elton's self-titled American debut album on the Uni label, which was an affiliate of MCA Records.
14. A promotional *Breaking Hearts* bandana.
15. A promotional *Reg Strikes Back* wooden pen shaped like a baseball bat.

Navigating Elton on the Web

Hundreds of Elton John websites and newsgroups exist on the internet. Listed here are some of the more highly rated ones preferred by Elton's fans from around the world.

Official Elton John Websites

Official Elton John Website:
http://www.eltonjohn.com

Official Elton John Merchandise Page:
http://www.eltonjohnstore.com

Official Elton John Chat Page:
http://www.eltonjohnchat.com

Official Aida Site
http://disney.go.com/disneyonbroadway/aida/

Elton John AIDS Foundation Website

Elton John AIDS Foundation
http://www.ejaf.org
This is the information website for The Elton John AIDS Foundation. There are also two mailing address for the EJAF in the United States. For information on the foundation and on AIDS-related issues, write to:

Elton John AIDS Foundation
P.O. Box 17139
Beverly Hills, CA
90209-3139
To send in donations, write to:
Elton John AIDS Foundation
P.O. Box 2066
San Francisco, CA
94126-2066
Please do not send fan letters to Elton at either addresses.

Fan Club and Fan Publications Websites

East End Lights Magazine
http://www.eastendlights.com
email: *eel@accessthemusic.com*
The information website for the Elton John fan magazine. It includes a photo album, links, classified ads, news, tour and information pages. It is updated daily. Subscription are $26 a year in America, $36 in Canada, and $50 elsewhere, payable by check, money order (U.S. Funds), or credit card (MasterCard, Visa, American Express, and Discover). To contact the magazine by mail, write to:

East End Lights
P.O. Box 621
Joplin, MO 64802-0621

Hercules
http://www.eltonfan.net
email: *Hercules USA@eltonfan.net*
(in United States and United Kingdom), or stephan@eltonfan. net (in Germany).
This is the website of the German and British-based *Hercules* fan club. It is the most comprehensive Elton fan site on the Internet, offering links, news, tidbits, photos and fan events. Originally called *Rocket Fan*, the *Hercules Fan Club* was founded in 1988, with the website launched in 1997. Membership in the club includes a quality quarterly fanzine in English and German, as well as a French supplement based on which which language you choose.

To contact the fan club by mail, write to:
Hercules USA/Canada
Sharon Kalinoski
P.O. Box 398
La Grange, IL 60525
U.S.A.

Hercules Worldwide
Stephan Heimbecher
Orleansstr. 59
D-81667 Müenchen, Germany
For subscription info see
http://www.eltonfan.net

Bernie Taupin Website
Official Farm Dogs Website
http://www.farmdogs.com

Band Member Websites
Official Davey Johnstone Website
http://www.daveyjohnstone.com

Official Nigel Olsson Fan Club
http://www.angelfire.com/ca/nigelfanclub

Nigel Olsson Merchandise Page
http://www.nigelolsson.com

John Jorgenson and Hellecasters Website
http://www.hellecasters.com

Charlie Morgan Website
http://www.charliemorgan.co.uk

Elton John-Related Websites
Official Kiki Dee Site
http://www.kikidee.co.uk

David Furnish Fan and Film Club
http://www.davidfurnish.com
(fan club: Film club)
http://clubs.yahoo.com/clubs/davidfurnishfilm-club (film club)
This website is devoted to David Furnish, Elton's current and longtime boyfriend. The fan club and film club are two websites in one for fans to gather and get the latest news, pictures, do puzzles, and shop on Elton John and David Furnish. Says the site owner: "No one ever pays any attention to David because he is Elton's partner. This site acknowledges what a truly wonderful person and filmmaker he is."

Elton John Impersonator Website
http://www.eltonjohnson.com
Ray "Elton John" Son, Elton John Look-alike

Favorite Elton John Fan Websites
The Illustrated Elton John Discography
http://www.eltonography.com
email: *dave@eltonography.com*
This website is devoted to Elton's music. The Illustrated Elton John Discography originated as an online guide for collectors who were interested to know all the various American and British releases, as well as bootleg CDs and books on Elton. The most popular feature of the website is the searchable listing of the complete Elton John song lyrics. Both *Rolling Stone* and Yahoo! have hailed this site as one of the best.

Crazy Water
http://members.aol.com/crazywater/CrazyMain.htm
This is an Elton fan website boasting news, links, U.S. chart history, Top 40 Streak, forum (the best on the net) Water Reflections webcast, discussion list and more.

The Elton John Fan Survey
http://www.geocities.com/michtahoe
email: *Michtahoe1@home.com*
This website is used to conduct extensive research on Elton John's career to assess the impact of his music in the eyes of his true fans. The site was used as a high-tech vehicle to assess fan interest and involvement. Fan surveys were then developed and became a critical database element. In addition, this site provides countless fans with the opportunity read news articles from around the world and openly share their views of Elton John.

The Elton John Fan Network
http://www.elton-fan.com
email: *jackhandy@elton-fan.net*

Elton John Fanatic
http://www.eltonjohnfanatic.com
email: *litlgina@eltonjohnfanatic.com*
Not the typical fan site. As the owner explains: "I feel my site stands out because I have several different types of information on it. All of my Elton 'adventures' are featured, along with pictures. There is also information about not only Elton, but also Bernie and Elton's past and present band members. There are interactive things to do like a message board, a quiz, and a survey."

The One Site
http://www.eltonjohnchords.com
Email: *marcel1234567@hotmail.com*
This website's main purpose is to help fans learn to play Elton's songs. The website owner says: "If the song you want to learn is not on my site, e-mail me and I will transcribe it for you. I have also collected many MIDIs and have lyrics available. You can even buy sheet music if you need it to learn a song."

EJ's #1 Fan
http://www.msnusers.com/ej1fan
email: *ej1fan@earthlink.net*
As the title implies, this is a website that's a trip down the Yellow Brick Road of one fan's many Elton Adventures. There's backstage and concert photos, lots of 1970s memorabilia and much more.

Elton John Discussion Groups
The 22nd Row
http://www.the22ndrow.com
email: *the22ndrow@mac.com*
The was the first internet resource about Elton and Bernie Taupin and their fans. Started in 1992, this is a free-of-charge electronic newsletter that arrives in your email account's mail box. The subscribers are the writers/contributors. The focus is on all things Elton and Bernie Taupin with a special emphasis on discussing the music and stories behind the songs. Currently, The 22nd Row reaches approximately 100 fans and is free. Besides being the first Internet resource about Elton and Bernie, it is also noted for it's quality of discussion and writing and lack of "noise" and "spam."

The alt.fan.elton-john Usenet Discussion
This is a world-wide public domain Internet discussion group. The discussion is unmoderated, so anything goes, which results in a lot of spontaneity and relaxed discourse (the upside), but also lot of "noise," "spam" and non-Elton-related discussion and ads (the downside). Because it is an open forum, Elton

bashers occasionally show up as well. Producer Clive Franks has been known to make an appearance to clarify certain discussion topics.

All Experts
http://www.allexperts.com
Got a question on Elton that you don't know the answer to? No doubt one of the dozens of Elton John purists at the All Experts site will have the answer. Type Elton's name in the search box and choose from one of the many experts listed on the page who are waiting for your email.

Elton John on Internet Radio
The Elton Mohito Radio Show
http//www.eltonmohito.net
email: *listeners@eltonmohito.net*
The Elton Mohito Radio Show is a constantly running Internet radio show playing nothing but Elton John tunes. There's enough Elton hits, album cuts, b-sides and obscure tunes to keep the old faithful content for hours. The Elton Mohito Radio Show is totally non-profit and does not accept any donations or payments. If you are wondering where the Mohito part derives from, it's kind of tongue in cheek—hence the name "Elton Mohito Radio." The deejays drink lots of Mohitos—what else, but their favorite drink.

Collecting Elton
Wrap It Up
http://homepage.ntlworld.com/eltonjohn
email: *eltonjohn@ntlworld.com*
This is the largest selection of Elton John collectibles for sale that you could ever find, and all being sold by someone who has been a fan and collector for more than thirty-one years, Alan McCormic. For a free catalog, write to:

Wrap It Up
PO Box 220
Lincoln LN2 1XB United Kingdom

ebay

http://www.ebay.com

The best and largest selection of Elton collectibles of any online auction site. You can't beat it anywhere! Averages 400 to 600 listings a day.

Elton John on Television

Rock on TV

http://www.RockOnTV.com

The complete guide to music on television.

Elton on Tour

Pollstar

http://www.Pollstar.com

Home to the world's largest database of international concert tour information.

Ticketmaster

http://ticketmaster.com

The world's largest online ticketing resource. Ticketmaster.com is the online extension of Ticketmaster Corporation, the global leader in live event ticket sales.

Tickets.com

http://www.tickets.com

Second only to Ticketmaster.com for purchasing concert tickets online.

Biographies, News and Miscellaneous Information

MTV Online

http://www.mtv.com

All Music/Artist Direct

http://www.allmusic.com

Rock On the Net

http://www.www.rockonthenet.com

Wall Of Sound

http://www.wallofsound.com

Rolling Stone Magazine

http://www.rollingstone.com

VH1

http://www.vh1.com

Special autographed postcard from Elton to *Hercules*, the international Elton John Fan Club. It reads: "To all the fans around the world. Thanks for your kindness, generosity and loyalty. Love, Elton."

Appendix One

Selected American Television Appearances

When Elton appears on television, it's usually to promote whatever his new single or album may be. Since he's shy and sometimes dislikes answering show host's questions, he may grant only a few choice on-camera interviews a year. He prefers to perform his songs instead, letting the music as it is said, "speak for itself."

The Seventies

Henry Mancini Special (November 15, 1970)
Guest at composer Henry Mancini's Santa Monica Civic Center concert.

Andy Williams Show (1971)
Performed "Your Song" and "Georgia on My Mind" with Ray Charles and "Heaven Help Us All" with Cass Elliot.

David Frost Show (1971)
Performed "Your Song" and "Take Me to the Pilot."

Grammys March 14, 1972)
Nominated for Original Music Score for the film, *Friends.*

Elton John and Bernie Taupin Say Goodbye to Norma Jean and Other Things (May 17, 1974)
ABC television special.

American Music Awards (January 1975)
Nominated for Male Pop Vocalist.

Cher and Other Fantasies (February 12, 1975)
Performed "Bennie and the Jets" with Cher and "Lucy in the Sky with Diamonds" solo, plus appeared in a comedy skit.

Grammys (March 1, 1975)
Nominated Male Pop Vocalist for single "Don't Let the Sun Go Down on Me" and album *Caribou.*

Wide World Special (March 26, 1975)
The West Coast Premiere of the movie *Tommy.* In the film, Elton portrayed the Pinball Wizard.

Soul Train (May 17, 1975)
Performed "Philadelphia Freedom" and "Bennie and the Jets."

Rock Music Awards (August 9, 1975)
Co-hosted with Diana Ross. The Elton John Band nominated for Best Group and Gus Dudgeon was nominated for Best Producer. Elton won Best Pop Male Vocalist in a Rock Movie (*Tommy*); Best Rock Single for "Philadelphia Freedom"; and Rock Personality of the Year.

Midnite Special (October 31, 1975)
Performed "Your Song" as part of an Elton tribute.

Midnite Special (July 16, 1976)
Performed "Don't Go Breaking My Heart" with Kiki Dee.

American Bandstand (January 1976)
Performed "Don't Go Breaking My Heart" with Kiki Dee.

Don Kirshner's Rock Concert (October 8, 1976)
Performs "Don't Go Breaking My Heart" with Kiki Dee.

Tomorrow with Tom Synder (November 10, 1976)
Interviewed.

American Music Awards (January 1977)
Won for Male Pop Vocalist and "Don't Go Breaking My Heart" with Kiki Dee.

The Today Show (October 11, 1977)
Interviewed.

The Mike Douglas Show (November 7 and 8, 1977)
Interviewed.

The Muppet Show (January 5, 1978)
Performed "Don't Go Breaking My Heart" with Miss Piggy and "Crocodile Rock" and "Bennie and the Jets" solo. Also appeared in comedy skits.

David Frost's Headliners (June 7, 1978)
Interviewed.

Elton John's Farewell Concert (November 1978)
Concert at Wembly Stadium in England on November 11, 1977.

The Eighties

American Music Awards (January 18, 1980)
Hosted and performed "Sorry Seems to Be the Hardest Word" and "Elton's Song."

Olivia Newton-John Special (April 14, 1980)
Performed "Candle in the Wind" with Olivia Newton-John and "Little Jeannie" solo.

America's Top Ten (July 4, 1980)
Performed "Little Jeannie."

Tomorrow with Tom Synder (September 17, 1980) Performed "Little Jeannie" and "Sartorial Eloquence."

The Phil Donahue Show (October 15, 1980)
Interviewed by Phil Donahue and studio audience and performed "Your Song."

The Tonight Show Starring Johnny Carson (November 5, 1980)
Interviewed, and performed "Sorry Seems to Be the Hardest Word."

Elton John Plays Central Park (February 1981)
HBO special concert in New York City on September 13, 1980.

Tomorrow with Tom Synder (June 11, 1981)
Interviewed and performed "Nobody Wins," "Just Like Belgium," and "Breaking Down Barriers."

To Russia…with Elton (September 22, 1981)
Documentary of historic Soviet concert in 1979.

Saturday Night Live (April 5, 1982)
Performed "Empty Garden" and "Ball & Chain."

Solid Gold (June 11, 1982)
Premiere of the "Blue Eyes" video.

Grammys (February 23, 1983)
Nominated for Male Pop Vocal for "Blue Eyes."

The Today Show (June 1 and 2, 1983)
Interviewed.

Entertainment Tonight
Various appearances and mentions in news reports throughout 1983.

MTV
Various appearances and mentions in news reports throughout 1984.

Live Aid (July 13, 1985)
Performed "Don't Let the Sun Go Down on Me" with Wham; "Don't Go Breaking My Heart" With Kiki Dee; and "I'm Still Standing," "Bennie and the Jets," and "Rocket Man" solo.

The Joan Rivers Show (1986)
Performed "Your Song," "The Bitch Is Back" and "Twist and Shout."

Prince's Trust Concert (HBO, October 18, 1986)
Performed "I'm Still Standing, and "Your Song."

Entertainment Tonight
Various appearances and mentions in news reports throughout 1987.

MTV
Various appearances and mentions in news reports throughout 1987.

VH1
Various appearances and mentions in news reports throughout 1987.

American Music Awards (January 26, 1987)
Nominated in Group or Duo for "That's What Friends Are For."

The Return of Bruno (February 7, 1987)
Cameo appearance.

Showtime Presents Elton John Live In Australia (July 11, 1987)
Concert in Australia in 1986.

The CBS Morning Show (August 18 -21, 1987)
Four-part interview with Elton from Britain.

MTV Stand By Me Concert (August 23, 1987)
Performed "Will You Still Love Me Tomor-

row?" and "I Guess That's Why They Call It the Blues."

MTV Video Music Awards (September 11, 1987)
Elton and Bernie Taupin received the Lifetime Achievement Award.

Prince's Trust All-Star Concert (September 13, 1987)
Concert at Wembley Stadium in England, June 6, 1987.

MTV
Various appearances and mentions in news reports throughout 1988.

Entertainment Tonight
Various appearances and mentions in news reports throughout 1988

American Music Awards (January 25, 1988)
Segment on Elton's past appearances on the show.

Totally Minnie: Minnie Mouse Special (NBC, March 25, 1988)
Performed "Don't Go Breaking My Heart" with Minnie Mouse.

ABC's A Royal Gala (May 25, 1988)
Performed "Saturday Night's Alright (for Fighting)" and "Candle in the Wind."

Dionne & Friends (1988)
Performed "That's What Friends Are For" with Dionne Warwick, Gladys Knight and Stevie Wonder.

The Nineties
Ryan White Funeral (April 1990)
Performed "Skyline Pigeon" and "Candle in the Wind" at funeral service in Indiana.

The Arsenio Hall Show (1990)
Interviewed and performed "Sad Songs (Say So Much)" and "Sacrifice."

MTV Unplugged (August 5, 1990)
Performed "Sad Songs (Say So Much)", "Sacrifice," "Tiny Dancer," "Daniel," "Don't Let

The Sun Go Down on Me," "Bennie and the Jets," "Candle in the Wind" and many other hits.

International Rock Awards (1990)
Presented an award to Eric Clapton and publically called comedian Sam Kinison a pig.

MTV Rockumentary (1990)
Historical overview that included Elton's career.

David Frost Special (November 1991)
Interviewed.

Good Morning America (1992)
Interviewed.

The Whoopie Goldberg Show (1992)
Interviewed.

The Arsenio Hall Show (1992)
Elton and Bernie Taupin interviewed, and appeared in brief comedy skit.

MTV Music Awards (September 9, 1992)
Performed "The One" and played piano on "November Rain" by Guns N' Roses.

The Aretha Franklin Special (April 1993)
Performed "Border Song" with Aretha.

The Tonight Show Starring Jay Leno (April 1993)
Interviewed, and performed.

The Barbara Walters Special (March 21, 1994)
Interviewed.

Late Show with David Letterman (March 1995)
Interviewed, and performed "Made in England."

Academy Awards (March 27, 1995)
Performed "Can You Feel the Love Tonight?" and received Oscar award.

VH1 Fashion And Music Awards (December 3, 1995) Performed "The Bitch Is Back" with Tina Turner and "Blessed" solo.

The Rosie O'Donnell Show (November 15, 1996) Interviewed, and performed "You Can Make History (Young Again)" and "Levon."

Late Night with Conan O'Brien (November 18, 1996)
Interviewed, and performed "You Can Make History (Young Again)" and "Border Song."

20/20 (September 5, 1997)
Interviewed by Barbara Walters during the days following the death of Diana, Princess of Wales.

Funeral of Diana, Princess of Wales (September 6, 1997)
Performed "Candle in the Wind 1997" at funeral service in Westminster Abbey.

VH1's Storytellers (September 19, 1997)
Live broadcast from The House of Blues, New Orleans, Louisiana. Solo piano performance with commentary. Performed "Your Song," "Talking Old Soldiers," "I Don't Wanna Go on With You Like That." "I Guess That's Why They Call It the Blues," "Daniel," "Levon," "Something About the Way You Look Tonight," "Long Way from Happiness," "Bennie and the Jets," "Sorry Seems to be the Hardest Word," "Take Me to the Pilot," and "Don't Let the Sun Go Down on Me."

The Tonight Show Starring Jay Leno (September 22, 1997)
Interviewed, and performed "Something About the Way You Look Tonight."

The Oprah Winfrey Show (September 24,1997)
Interviewed, and performed "Your Song," "Something About the Way You Look Tonight," "Bennie and the Jets."

Late Night With Conan O'Brien (September 25, 1997)
Interviewed, and performed "Something About the Way You Look Tonight," and "Saturday Night's Alright (for Fighting)."

The Rosie O'Donnell Show (October 1, 1997)
Interviewed and performed "Something About the Way You Look Tonight, and "Tiny Dancer."

The Nanny (October 8, 1997)
Guest appearance on sitcom starring Fran Dressler.

South Park (October 7, 1998)
Supplied voice for animated Elton John on "Chef Aid" episode of this animated series, and performed "Wake Up Wendy."

25th Annual People's Choice Awards (January 10, 1999)
Performed "Written in the Stars" from Aida with LeAnn Rimes. Received award for Special All-Time Favorite Musical Performer.

Shania Twain In Miami (January 17, 1999)
Performed "You're Still the One" and "Something About the Way You Look Tonight" with Shania Twain. Played piano on "Amneris' Letter" sung by Shania.

The Simpsons (February 14, 1999)
Supplied voice for animated Elton John in "Apoo" episode of this animated series and performed "Your Song" with revised lyrics.

The Rosie O'Donnell Show (March 19, 1999)
Performed "Your Song," and "Written in the Stars" and sang "Happy Birthday," to Rosie.

The Tonight Show Starring Jay Leno (March 22, 1999)
Interviewed, and performed "Written in the Stars" with LeAnn Rimes.

The Today Show (March 25, and 26, 1999)
Interviewed, and performed "Written in the Stars" with LeAnn Rimes.

Late Show with David Letterman (March 27, 1999)
Performed "Written in the Stars" with LeAnn Rimes.

60 Minutes II (April 7, 1999)
Interviewed.

VH1's Divas Live '99 (April 13, 1999)
Performed "The Bitch Is Back" with Tina Turner and "Proud Mary, with Tina Turner and Cher, and "Written in the Stars" with LeAnn Rimes as well as "Like Father, Like Son" and "I'm Still Standing" solo.

CNN's World Beat (May 23, 1999)
Discussed the *Aida* project.

One-On-One with David Frost: Elton John: My Gift Is My Song (August 15, 1999)
Interviewed.

The New Millennium

Good Morning America (March 13 thru 17, 2000)
Interviewed.

The Tonight Show Starring Jay Leno (March 13, 2000)
Appeared with Billy Joel. Interviewed and performed "Goodbye Yellow Brick Road" with Billy.

VH1 Behind the Music (March 19, 2000)
Documentary of Elton's music and career.

The Road to El Dorado Concert (March 19, 2000)
Interviewed and performed several songs from the Disney animated film.

HBO: The Making of El Dorado (March 21, 2000)
Brief clip about the music to the animated movie.

The Rosie O'Donnell Show (March 22, 2000)
Interview and peformed "Someday Out of the Blue" and "I Know the Truth."

The El Dorado Concert (March 25, 2000)
Interviewed briefly by kids in the audience of this Nickelodeon special. Performed "El Dorado," "Can You Feel the Love Tonight?," Crocodile Rock," and "Someday Out of the Blue."

The Today Show (March 31, 2000)
Part of the "Friday Outdoor" concert series. Performed "El Dorado," "Someday Out of the Blue," "Without Question," "Circle of Life," and "Crocodile Rock."

The View (March 31, 2000)
Interviewed.

Late Show with David Letterman (October 1, 2001)
Interviewed and performed "I Want Love."

The Today Show (October 2, 2001)
Interviewed.

Regis and Kelly (October 3, 2001)
Interviewed and performed "I Want Love" and part of the "Star-Spangled Banner."

MTV Total Request Live (October 3, 2001)
Appeared as mystery guest. Interviewed and showed video for "I Want Love."

The Concert for New York (October 20, 2001)
Performed "I Want Love," "Mona Lisas and Mad Hatters" and "Your Song" with Billy Joel.

Ally McBeal (November 26, 2001)
Guest appearance on comedy series starring Calista Flockhart.

Appendix Two

Selected American Video Appearances

This list does not include editions on laser disc, DVD, or other visual formats. However, many of these titles have been or are now available on such formats.

To Russia with Elton (1979)
Visions (1981)
Breaking Hearts Tour (1984)
Live in Central Park (1986)
To Russia with Elton (1986)
Night Time Concert (1986)
Live in Australia (1987)
Two Rooms: Celebrating the Songs of Elton John & Bernie Taupin (1991)
One-On-One with David Frost (1991)
The Last Song (1992)
Live in Barcelona (1992)
Tantrums and Tiaras (1995)
One Night Only (The Greatest Hits Live at Madison Square Garden) (2001)
Classic Albums—Elton John: Goodbye Yellow Brick Road (2001)

Selected American Promotional Videos

"Your Song" (1971)
"Goodbye Yellow Brick Road" (1973)
"Don't Go Breaking My Heart" with Kiki Dee (1976)
"Sorry Seems to Be the Hardest Word" (1976)
"Rocket Man" (1977)
"Little Jeanne" (1980)
"Chloe" (1981)
"Nobody Wins" (1981)
"Empty Garden" (1982)
"Blue Eyes" (1982)
"Ball & Chain" (1982)
"I Guess That's Why They Call It the Blues" (1983)
"I'm Still Standing" (1983)
"Kiss the Bride" (1983)
"Sad Songs (Say So Much)" 1984
"Passengers" (1984)
"In Neon" (1984)
"Act of War" (1985)
"Cry to Heaven" (1985)
"That's What Friends Are For," with Dionne Warwick, Gladys Knight and Stevie Wonder (1985)
"Nikita" (1985)
"Wrap Her Up" (1985)
"Candle in the Wind" live (1987)
"Take Me to the Pilot" (1987)
"Flames of Paradise," with Jennifer Rush (1987)

"I Don't Wanna Go on With You Like That"
"A Word in Spanish" (1988)
"Sacrifice" (1989)
"Healing Hands" (1989)
"You Gotta Love Someone" (1990)
"Club at the End of the Street" (1990)
"Don't Let The Sun Go Down on Me" with G
"Michael" (1991)
"The One" (1992)
"Runaway Train" (1992)
"The Last Song" (1992)
"True Love" with Kiki Dee (1993)
"Don't Go Breaking My Heart" with RuPaul
"Can You Feel the Love Tonight?" (1994)
"Circle of Life" (1994)
"Believe" (1995)
"Made in England" (1995)
"Blessed" (1995)
"You Can Make History (Young Again)" (19
"Something About the Way You Look To (1997)
"Recover Your Soul" (1997)
"Written in the Stars" with LeAnn Rimes (19
"Someday Out of the Blue" (2000)
"I Want Love" (2001)
"This Train Don't Stop There Anymore" (200

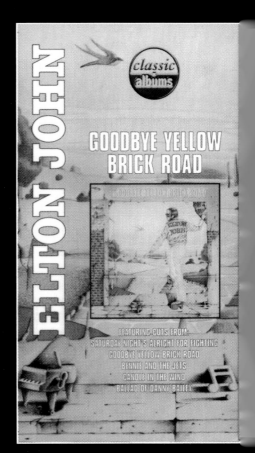

Goodbye Yellow Brick Road

Appendix Three

Discography

This brief discography is not intended to be extensive, but to merely acknowledge the Elton John studio and live albums and singles officially released in the United States from 1970 to the present. (The items are listed in order of release.) Promotional releases, foreign recordings, and miscellaneous projects have been omitted.

Incredibly, if we included the British offerings on this list, it would contain more that two thousand entries. Hard to believe, but true.

Albums

Empty Sky (1969)
Elton John (1970)
Tumbleweed Connection (1970)
11-17-70 (1971)
Friends (soundtrack) (1971)
Madman Across the Water (1971)
Honky Chateau 1972)
Don't Shoot Me, I'm Only the Piano Player (1973)
Goodbye Yellow Brick Road (1973)
Caribou (1974)
Greatest Hits (1974)
Captain Fantastic and the Brown Dirt Cowboy (1975)
Rock of the Westies (1975)
Here and There (1976)
Blue Moves (1976)
Greatest Hits, Volume II (1977)
A Single Man (1978)
Victim of Love (1979)
21 at 33 (1980)
The Fox (1981)
The Best of Elton John, Vol. I (1981)
The Best Of Elton John, Vol. II (1981)
Jump Up! (1982)
Too Low For Zero (1983)
Breaking Hearts (1984)

Ice on Fire (1985)
Leather Jackets (1986)
Your Songs (1986)
Decade: Greatest Hits, Volume III 1979-1987 (1987)
Live in Australia with the Melbourne Symphony Orchestra (1987)
Reg Strikes Back (1988)
The Complete Tom Bell Sessions 1989)
Sleeping with the Past (1989)
To Be Continued… (1990)
The One (1992)
Rare Masters (1992)
Greatest Hits 1976-1986 (1992)
Duets (1993)
The Lion King (soundtrack) (1994)
Made in England (1995)
Love Songs (1996)
The Big Picture (1997)
Elton John and Tim Rice's Aida (1999)
The Muse (soundtrack) (1999)
The Road to El Dorado (2000)
One Night Only (2000)

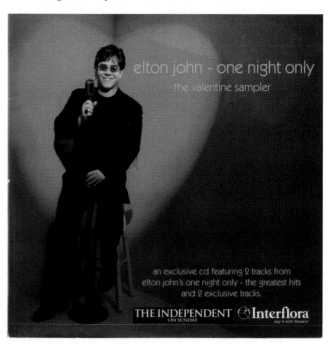

Songs from the West Coast (2001)

U.S. Singles

"Lady Samantha" (1969)
"From Denver to L.A." (1970)
"Border Song" (1970)

"Your Song" (1970)
"Friends" (1971)
"Levon" (1971)
"Tiny Dancer" (1972)
"Rocket Man" (1972)
"Honky Cat" (1972)
"Crocodile Rock" (1972)
"Daniel" (1973)
"Saturday Night's Alright (for Fighting)" (1973)
"Goodbye Yellow Brick Road" (1973)
"Step into Christmas" (1973)
"Bennie and the Jets" (1974)
"Don't Let the Sun Go Down on Me" (1974)
"Bitch Is Back" (1974)
"Lucy in the Sky with Diamonds" (1974)
"Philadelphia Freedom" (1975)

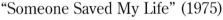

"Someone Saved My Life" (1975)
"Island Girl" (1975)
"Grow Some Funk of Your Own"/"I Feel Like a Bullet (in the Gun of Robert Ford)" (1976)
"Don't Go Breaking My Heart" (1976)
"Sorry Seems to Be the Hardest Word" (1976)
"Bite Your Lip (Get Up and Dance)" (1977)

"Part-Time Love" (1978)
"Song for Guy" (1979)
"Mama Can't Buy You Love" (1979)
"Little Jeannie" (1980)
"Don't You Wanna Play This Game No More" (1980)
"Nobody Wins" (1981)
"Chloe" (1981)
"Empty Garden" (1982)

"Blue Eyes" (1982)
"Ball & Chain" (1982)

"I'm Still Standing" (1983)
"Kiss the Bride" (1983)

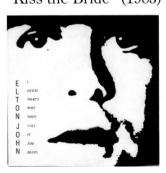

"I Guess That's Why They Call It the Blues" (1983)
"Sad Songs (Say so Much)" (1984)

"Ego" (1978)

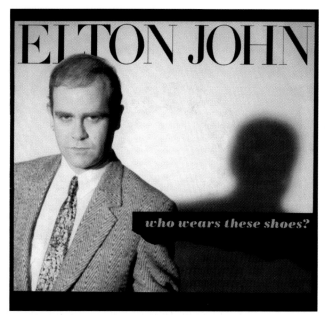

"Who Wears These Shoes?" (1984)
"In Neon" (1984)
"That's What Friends Are For" (1985)

ACT OF WAR

ELTON JOHN   MILLIE JACKSON

"Act of War" (1985)
"Wrap Her Up" (1985)
"Nikita" (1986)
"Heartache All Over the World" (1986)
"Flames of Paradise" (1987)
"Candle in the Wind" (live) 1987
"Take Me to the Pilot" (1988)
"I Don't Wanna Go on with You Like That" (1988)
"A Word in Spanish" (1988)
"Through the Storm" (1989)

"Healing Hands" (1989)
"Sacrifice" (1989)
"Club at the End of the Street" (1990)
"You Gotta Love Someone" (1990)
"Don't Let the Sun Go Down on Me" (live) (1991)
"The One" (1992)
"Runaway Train" (1992)
"The Last Song" (1992)
"Simple Life" (1993)
"True Love" (1993)
"Don't Go Breaking My Heart" (1994)
"Can You Feel the Love Tonight?" (1994)
"Circle of Life" (1994)

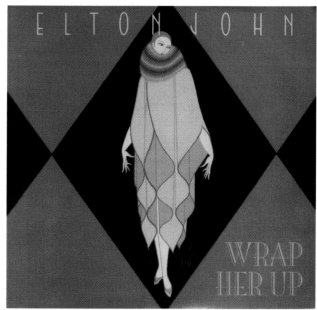

"Believe" (1995)

"Made in England" (1995)

"Blessed" (1995)

"You Can Make History (Young Again)" (1996)

"Candle in the Wind 1997" (1997)

"Something About the Way You Look Tonight" (1997)

"Recover Your Soul" (1998)

"Written in the Stars" (1999)

"A Step Too Far" (1999)

"Someday Out of the Blue (2000)

"Friends Never Say Goodbye" (2000)

"I Want Love" (2001)

"This Train Don't Stop There Anymore" (2002)

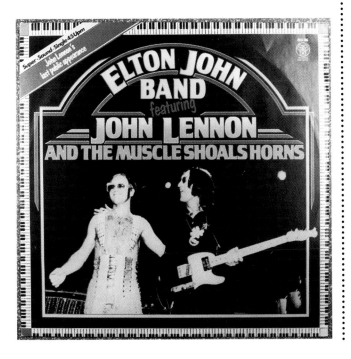

Japanese 45 Picture Sleeves.

Appendix Four

Selected American, Canadian and United Kingdom published books on Elton John (minus song publishing texts)

Over the years, more than forty books have been published on Elton John. Some are hardcovers, many softcovers, and a few are quickie mass-market paperbacks. Several of these books are now long out-of-print, but still obtainable through the internet and used book stores.

The following are selected titles.

The Seventies

Five Years of Fun, by Robert Hilburn (Bouthwell Enterprises, Inc., 1975)

Elton John, by Cathi Stein (Futura Publications Limited, 1975)

A Conversation With Elton John and Bernie Taupin, by Paul Gambaccini (Proteus Books, 1975)

The One Who Writes the Words for Elton John: Lyrics from 1968 Through Goodbye Yellow Brick Road, by Bernie Taupin (Knopf Publishers, 1976)

Elton John, Dick Tatham and Tony Jasper (Octobus Books, 1976)

Elton John, by Gerald Newman and Joe Bivona (Pocket Books, 1976)

Elton John: A Biography in Words and Pictures, by Greg Shaw (Chappell and Co., Ltd, 1976)

Elton John: Reginald Dwight & Co. (Men Behind the Bright Lights Series, by Linda Jacobs, EMC Corporation, 1976)

Elton: It's a Little Bit Funny by David Nutter and Bernie Taupin (Penguin, 1977)

The Eighties

The Elton John Tapes, by Andy Peeples (St. Martins Press, 1981)

Elton John: The Illustrated Discography, by Alan Finch (Omnibus Press, 1982)

Elton John, by Paul Roland (Proteus Books, 1984)

Elton John: Only the Piano Player, by Alan Finch and Chris Charlesworth (Omnibus Press, 1984),

Elton John, by Chris Charlesworth (Bobcat Books, 1986)

The Nineties

Elton John, by Phillip Norman (Harmony Books, 1991)

Two Rooms, by Lorna Dickinson and Claudia Rosencrantz (Boxtree Limited, 1991)

The Many Lives of Elton John, by Susan Crimp and Patricia Burnstein (Birch Lane Publishing, 1992)

Elton John: A Visual Documentary by Nigel Goodall (Omnibus Press, 1993)

The Complete Elton John Discography, by John DiStefano and Peter Dobbins (East End Lights, 1993)

Elton John: In His Own Words, by Susan Black (Omnibus Press, 1993)

Elton John, by Mick St. Michael (Smithmark Publishers, 1994)

Elton John and Bernie Taupin: The Complete

Lyrics, by Bernie Taupin (Hyperion Books, 1994)

Rocket Man: The Encyclopedia of Elton John, by Bernardin/Stanton (Greenwood Press, 1995)

Rocket Man: Elton John From A-Z, by Claude Bernardin and Tom Stanton (Praeger Publishers, 1996)

Elton John's Flower Fantasies: An Intimate Tour of His Houses and Gardens, by Caroline Cass (Bullfinch Press, 1997)

Elton John: The Life And Music of a Legendary Performer, by Michael Heatley (CLB International Publishers, 1998)

Elton John: A Little Bit Funny by Patrick Humphries (Smithmark Publishers, Inc., 1998)

Elton John and Tim Rices Aida: Bringing the Broadway Musical to Life, by Michael Lassell (Hyperion, 2000)

Chorus of Light: Photographs from the Sir Elton John Collection, by Ned Rifkin (Rizzoli, 2001)

Books Mentioning Elton John

Tomorrow I'll Be Different: The Effective Way to Stop Drinking, by Baeuchamp Colclough (Overlook Press, 1994)

Disney's The Lion King by Tim Rice (Hyperion Books, 1994)

What Everyone Can Do to fight AIDS, by Anne Garwood (Jossey-Bass Publishers, 1995)

Rock and Royalty, by Gianni Versace (Abbeville Press, 1997)

The Lion King: Pride Rock on Broadway, by Julie Taymor (Hyperion Books, 1998)

Sources

Billboard
East End Lights
Hercules
Current Biography
Goldmine
16 Magazine
People Magazine
Creem
American Songwriter
Vanity Fair
Musican
The Music Paper
Song Hits
Hit Parader
Circus
Los Angeles Times
New York Times
Keyboard Player
New York Post
Talking with David Frost transcript
Rock Line
New Musical Express
Q Magazine
London Times
Contemporary Keyboard Player
Raves
Teen
After Dark
Big Picture Tour program
One Night Only Tour program
Various MCA, Geffen, PolyGram, Rocket Records, Disney, Discovery, Sire Records, Universal Records, EJAF, Dream Works, Lalique, Slatkin & Co. Rogers and Cowan, McMullen and Company, Boneau/Bryan-Brown, Cinemax, Atlanta's High Museum of Art promotional press kits ranging from 1971 to 2001.

Website Sources:
eltonjohn.com, farmdogs.com. eltonography.com, mtv.com and www.ejaf.org., wall of sound, E! Online and MTV.com, Rollingstone.com, RIAA.com

(previous) interviews with Elton John, Bernie Taupin, Davey Johnstone, Nigel Olsson, Gus Dudgeon, Billy Joel and Tim Rice by the author.

Selected Bibliography:
Bernardin & Stanton. *Rocket Man:* Elton John From A-Z, Praeger Publishers, 1996.

Black, Susan. *Elton In His Own Words,* Omnibus Press, 1991

Bright, Spencer. *Elton John: Essential Elton,* London: Chameleon Books, 1998

DiStefano, John. *The Complete Elton John Discography,* East End Lights, 1993

Elton John and Bernie Taupin: *The Complete Lyrics,* Hyperion, 1994

Goodall, Nigel. *Elton John: the Visual Documentary,* Omnibus Press, 1993

Heatley, Michael. *Elton John the Life and Music of a Legendary Performer,* CBL International, 1998

Humphries, Patrick. *Elton John: A Little Bit Funny,* Smithmark Publishers, Inc., 1998

Taupin, Bernie. *A Cradle of Halos: Sketches of a Childhood,* London: Aurum Press, 1988

Tobler, John. *Elton John 25 Years In The Charts,* Hamlyn 1995

Two Rooms: *Elton John and Bernie Taupin in Their Own Words,* London: Boxtree, 1991

Acknowledgments

This book would not have been possible without the invaluable assistance of entertainment journalists, Anne Raso, Carrie Fascia, David Sigler and Lori Sears, who more than helped when circumstances changed at the last second. Very special thanks to Jim Turano for his timeless Elton album reviews and other noteworthy contributions and Michelle Hilliard for various research duties.

For their considerable efforts, special thanks to Mark Norris, Tom Stanton, Alan McCormic, Peter Dobbins, Stephen Sorrentino, Sharon Kalinosky, Jim Mckay, David Bodoh, Nanette Bac, Stephan Heimbecher, George Matlock, Richard Fenkel, Greg Loescher, Cathy Bernardy, Kathleen Tempinski, David Furnish, Noreen Romano, Nigel Olsson, Marian Joy Friedman, Steven Miller, Robert Cargill, Gina Herring, Teresa John, Bruce Redfield, Lynn Baxter, Bob Arbasetti, Fred Zott, Liza Leeds, Marcel Gelinas, Austin Scott, Steve Betts, Johanna Chiarelli, Eva DuBuisson, Lisa McDonald, Caryl Simpson, Jodi Holley, Pam Quier, Sharon Leuschner, Silje Willumsen, Rita Ann Foreman, Rebecca Nichols, Gary Gerhardt, Janet Banschbach, Scottie Davis, Janice Tuffo, and Renee Daigle who openly shared their Elton memories, collections, and personal photographs.

For all the new friends I've met through the writing of the *Elton John Scrapbook,* thank you all for your generosity, encouragement and unfailing spirit. You reflect the very best of Elton, the man himself.

A gracious nod goes to *East End Lights* and *Hercules,* two of the very best Elton publications in print. I salute you!

Also a deep bow to my ever amazing agent, Jim Fitzgerald, who never stops believing in me. I would also like to gratefully acknowledge my extremely patient publisher, Bruce Bender and equally understanding editor, Elaine Sparber.

And I can't forget my longtime friend, Lisa Wagner, who kept me fueled with endless cups of gourmet coffee and much needed moral support. Also special thanks to book designer, Edward Alves, who's creative approach is always fresh and innovative.

I couldn't write this book without acknowledging my friend and publicist, Sarah Mc-Mullen. Without her assistance over the past two decades, I would have never been able to cover Elton or Elton-related projects as consistently or as professionally as I did. It was a privilege, indeed! Also thanks to Joe Dera, who in the early '80s always honored my requests for Elton press coverage.

Finally, I wish to acknowledge Sir Elton John (and Bernie Taupin, too), who over the years have provided the world with great songs and wonderful memories, which hopefully will never end.

Photo Credits:

Unless noted, many photos and other reproductions in this book are courtesy of MCA Records, Geffen Records, RCA Records, McMullen and Co., Rogers and Cowan, Disney, PolyGram Records, Universal Records, John Reid Enterprises, Michael Lippman Entertainment, Discovery Records, Warner Bros. Records, Rocket Records, DreamWorks Pictures, Atlanta's High Museum, HBO, PolyGram Video, Eagle Eye Media, Sotheby's, Cinemax, and the author's personal archive.

Other credits include:

Time-Life Magazines, *Circus, Creem,* Rock and Roll Comics, Leeds Music Corporation, BMG Music, Hal Leonard Music, PolyGram Music Publishing, Playbill Incorporated, *Stage Bill,* Home Theater, Oliver Peoples', Slatkin & Co., Prime Media Magazines, the (former) Elton John Fan Club and Hercules the International Elton John Fan Club.

All other images and print memorabilia provided by Celebrity Photos, PhotoFest, Bob Arbasetti, Fred Zott, Liza Leeds, Lori Sears, Scott Harrison/Caught in the Act, Nanette Bac, Sharon Kalinoski, M.Snawder/Wispersezine, David Sigler/Taupin Quarerly and The Fox Quarterly, and Artists Rights Society.

Permissions:

In additon, the author graciously acknowledges photographs and other reproductions with kind "permission to reprint granted by": American Songwriter Magazine, Atlanta Magazine/Leslie Harris/Greg Gorman, East End Lights Magazine, Hercules the Elton John International Fan Club, Hit Parader Publications, Rizzoli Books, Hal Leonard Music Publishing, Universal Music, Billboard Publications, High Museum of Art/Charlie McCullers, ManRay Trust/Artist Rights Society, Tussauds Group Limited, and Eagle Eye Media.

Every effort has been made to identify the copyright owners of the pictures used in this publication. The author and publisher apologize for any omissions and will make proper corrections in future editions.

ABOUT THE AUTHOR

Mary Anne Cassata is fascinated with pop culture and has had a celebrated career as an entertainment journalist and editor. She regularly contributes feature stories to various national publications, including *Goldmine, Discoveries, American Songwriter,* and *Hit Parader.*
Among the books she has authored are biographies of the Monkees, Cher, Michael J. Fox, Jonathan Taylor Thomas, Alicia Silverstone, and 'N Sync. Currently, Ms. Cassata is the editor-in-chief of two popular entertainment/teen publications, *Teen Dream* and *Faces in Rock.*